OpenGL™: A Primer

OpenGL™: A Primer

Edward Angel

Addison-Wesley

Boston • San Francisco • New York • Toronto • Montreal
London • Munich • Paris • Madrid
Capetown • Sydney • Tokyo • Singapore • Mexico City

Senior Acquisitions Editor:	Maite Suarez-Rivas
Assistant Editor:	Lisa Hogue
Executive Marketing Manager:	Michael Hirsch
Copyeditor:	Evelyn Pyle
Proofreader:	Pat Menard
Composition and Art:	Kim Arney Mulcahy
Design Manager:	Gina Hagen
Text Design:	Kim Arney Mulcahy
Cover Design:	Dick Hannus
Prepress and Manufacturing:	Caroline Fell

Access the latest information about Addison-Wesley books from our World Wide Web site:
http://www.aw.com/cs

Many of the designations used by manufacturers and sellers to distinguish their products are claimed as trademarks. Where those designations appear in this book, and Addison-Wesley was aware of a trademark claim, the designations have been printed in initial caps letters or all caps.

The programs and applications presented in this book have been included for their instructional value. They have been tested with care, but are not guaranteed for any particular purpose. The publisher does not offer any warranties or representations, nor does it accept any liabilities with respect to the programs or applications.

Library of Congress Cataloging-in-Publication Data

Angel, Edward.
    OpenGL™: a primer / Edward Angel.
        p. cm.
    ISBN 0-201-74186-5
    1. Computer graphics.   2. OpenGL.   I. Title.
    T385.A5135 2002
    006.6'869—dc21   2001033396

1 2 3 4 5 6 7 8 9 10—CRS—04030201

Contents

Preface

This small volume is intended to be both a companion to my graphics textbook—*Interactive Computer Graphics: A Top-Down Approach with OpenGL* 2d ed., Addison-Wesley, 2000—and a stand-alone beginner's guide to OpenGL for programmers who already know some computer graphics and wish to get started with OpenGL. Both of these objectives require some justification.

Interactive Computer Graphics takes a top-down approach to teaching computer graphics for seniors in computer science and engineering. The book is based on the premise that students learn modern computer graphics best if they can start programming significant applications as soon as possible. The OpenGL application programmer's interface (API) is used both for the programming examples and as an illustration of the graphics concepts in the book. This approach has been extremely successful, as evidenced by the large number of adoptions in universities and colleges around the world. Although it makes heavy use of OpenGL, *Interactive Computer Graphics* does not claim to be an OpenGL programming guide or a user's manual. Consequently, the information on OpenGL in the text is incomplete. Not all OpenGL functions are covered, and no detailed listing of the functions and their parameters is provided. For students, the former usually does not present problems; the latter, however, does. The missing information is found in the *OpenGL Programming Guide*—Addison-Wesley 2000—and the *OpenGL Reference Manual*—Addison-Wesley 2000—known as the Red Book and the Blue Book, respectively. Although the information in the reference manual can be obtained online, it is usually necessary to have physical access to the Red Book. For instructors and students, this situation poses a dilemma, since the cost of buying two or three books for a single course is significant, and these reference texts go beyond the scope of what is needed for someone to understand the basics of OpenGL.

Thus, my first motivation is to provide a low-cost supplement that will fill in the gaps in OpenGL in my textbook. This primer covers the OpenGL necessary to do the exercises and projects that come from the textbook and also includes additional OpenGL functions that are not in the text The primer's layout makes it easy for the student to find functions, their most important options, and their descriptions. It also includes supplemental examples and covers some programming topics that I could not fit into the textbook.

However, many people already know some computer graphics and want to learn something about OpenGL. At my SIGGRAPH tutorials over the past few years, I have worked with hundreds of such people, and they leave wanting some references to pursue OpenGL further. Often, even though they may know something about graphics, they do not want to pursue the more mathematical issues; rather, they are interested only in the programming aspects of the API. Such people are the ones who purchase professional books rather than textbooks. The obvious references are the Red Book and the Blue Book. However, again, these books can represent a large investment for someone who just wants to get started. The other books in the Addison-Wesley OpenGL series are aimed at specific areas, as are books targeted specifically for the Windows market. I believe that a small, self-contained volume, such as this primer, will appeal to many of these people.

Consequently, this primer is not intended to replace either the *Programming Guide to OpenGL* or the *OpenGL Reference Guide* but instead lies somewhere between a beginner's guide and these comprehensive resources. This primer has complete coverage of a subset of the OpenGL API and should allow you to get started without reference to these other worthy volumes.

The coverage is done almost entirely without the mathematics used in my textbook. So, for example, the chapter on curves and surfaces deals with the details of how to program applications using Bézier curves and surfaces but never derives them. The chapter on transformations shows how to use rotation, translation, and scaling but does not derive the underlying matrices. The order of topics roughly follows that of the textbook but also is a natural progression in learning OpenGL. We start with two-dimensional problems in Chapter 2, move on to interactivity in Chapter 3 and to basic three-dimensional programs in Chapters 4 and 5. Chapter 6 covers lights and materials. Chapters 7 and 8 cover using OpenGL to display discrete entities, first through pixels and bitmaps and then through texture mapping. Chapter 9 introduces curves and surfaces. Chapter 10 presents a longer example than in previous chapters; the example includes most of the topics covered in previous chapters and touches on some advanced OpenGL features.

This primer includes both complete programs and partial code. As you will discover, once you write your first few OpenGL applications, much of the code is repeated in subsequent programs. Consequently, after the first few examples, I have left out much of the repeated code. Readers can find the complete examples either through my Web site, www.cs.unm.edu/~angel, or at the FTP site ftp.cs.unm.edu under pub/angel.

Obviously, this primer cannot cover all OpenGL topics. Nor did I want to. Decisions on what to leave out were based on which topics would require more mathematics, such as NURBS curves and surfaces, and such topics as tessellation, which would require a lot of detailed OpenGL functions whose applicability is not very general.

Many people provided significant help in various aspects of this primer. In particular, I want to thank a group of people who are or were at Silicon Graphics for helping me learn and appreciate OpenGL. In particular, Mark Kilgard and Mason Woo helped me when I first started using OpenGL with my classes at the University of New Mexico. Mason, Kathleen Danielson, Dave Shreiner, and Vicki Shreiner invited me to teach OpenGL tutorials with them at SIGGRAPH over the past five years, an enterprise that forced me to learn much more about the API and formed many of my ideas about how to teach with OpenGL. Mark, Nate Robins, and Brian Paul have made great contributions to all of us who use and teach OpenGL, through the creation of the GLUT library, the Mesa implementation, and many OpenGL example programs. Tom Abbott was a great help in checking the examples in the text. William Shoaff of the Florida Institute of Technology and Parris Egbert of Brigham Young University provided early encouraging reviews that were helpful in developing this project.

Having done four books with Addison-Wesley, I still marvel at the competence and professionalism of the entire production crew there. My editors at Addison-Wesley, Maite Suarez-Rivas and Peter Gordon, are as good friends and dinner companions as they are editors. Rose May Molnar, my wife and partner in all things, has survived yet another book production cycle with me, something for which she deserves more credit than I can ever express.

Chapter 1

Getting Started

OpenGL is an application programmer's interface (API) that allows programmers to write programs that access graphics hardware. OpenGL has two important benefits for application programmers. OpenGL is close enough to the hardware so that programs written with OpenGL run efficiently, and it is easy to learn and to use. This chapter gives an overview of OpenGL: what it can and cannot do, how it is organized, and how we present it in this book.

1.1 The OpenGL API

Computer graphics is an important part of almost everything we do with modern computers. Whether we are accessing a Web page, playing an interactive game, or designing a house by using a computer-aided design (CAD) package, we are using computer graphics. As hardware and software have become faster and more sophisticated, so too have the graphical applications we use. Developers of these applications rely on standard software interfaces to build their applications. Such interfaces prevent the developer from having to write the code for standard functions that are common to many applications and shield the application from details of the hardware. Thus, programs can be developed more quickly and become more portable. The application programmer sees the graphics system through a set of functions with a well-defined interface that we call the **application programmer's interface (API)**.

Over the years, many graphics APIs have been used. Some, such as GKS and PHIGS, have risen to the level of international standards. Other graphics APIs have been widely used for specific applications. Most of these APIs have had short lifetimes. OpenGL came from an interface called GL developed for Silicon Graphics Incorporated (SGI) hardware. GL proved to be a simple but powerful interface and formed the basis for OpenGL, which could then be used with a variety of graphics hardware. OpenGL contains more than 200 functions for building application programs. Programs written using OpenGL are portable to any computer that supports the interface. Implementations are available for most hardware and operating systems. These implementations range from pure software implementations to implementations that use the most sophisticated hardware available. A typical OpenGL application program should run on any implementation after recompilation with the OpenGL libraries for that system.

The OpenGL API is concerned primarily with **rendering**, that is, taking the specification of geometric objects and their properties and forming a picture of them with a virtual camera and lights. OpenGL programs are meant to be platform independent. Thus, the OpenGL API does not have input and windowing functions, which tend to be platform specific. However, graphics programs must interact with an operating system and the local windowing system, be it Windows, UNIX, or the Macintosh. Rather than write platform-dependent code, we use a simple toolkit, the OpenGL Utility Toolkit (GLUT), which has been implemented for the standard programming environments. Its API includes the standard operations that are common to most windowing systems and allows us to use the mouse and keyboard in our applications.

1.2 Three Views of OpenGL

Although at one level, OpenGL is a library of functions that access the graphics capabilities of computers, OpenGL can be looked at in at least three ways. Understanding these views should help you better understand how OpenGL and graphics systems function and enable you to write better code.

1.2.1 The Programmer's View

Generally, most graphics application programs consist of three major elements:

- Specifying geometric objects
- Describing properties of these objects
- Defining how these objects viewed should be viewed

If the program is interactive, it will also have some input functions. Finally, all programs will have some initialization and termination functions that interact with the local operating system and window environment.

The programmer's view gives a way of categorizing the OpenGL functions. But it does not tell us anything about how OpenGL works.

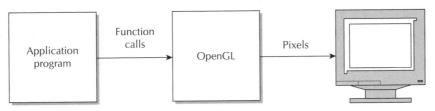

Figure 1.1 OpenGL as a state machine

1.2.2 The OpenGL State Machine

If we take a slightly different perspective, we can think of OpenGL as a **state machine** with inputs and outputs, as shown in Figure 1.1. The inputs are descriptions of geometric objects, such as line segments and polygons, and discrete objects, such as bitmaps, that are specified through OpenGL function calls. The output is an image that we see on our display. Between the inputs and the output is a machine that takes the objects and converts them to an image. How the machine processes its inputs depends on its state.

The state of the OpenGL machine is set by OpenGL functions that specify colors, viewing conditions, texture parameters, and many other variables. The state determines how the inputs are processed. From this perspective, OpenGL functions either change the state of the OpenGL machine or send inputs to the machine.

1.2.3 The OpenGL Pipeline

From an implementation perspective, we can view OpenGL program behavior in a different manner. OpenGL is based on what is called a **pipeline model**. A simple pipeline is shown in Figure 1.2. Primitives are generated in the application program and flow through the pipeline. Within the pipeline, each sequence of modules performs some functions on the primitives. Some modules do transformations that rotate, translate, and scale the object. Another module is responsible for positioning the objects relative to OpenGL's camera. Another module determines whether an object is visible. At the end of the pipeline, those primitives that are visible are converted into colored picture elements or *pixels* on the display.

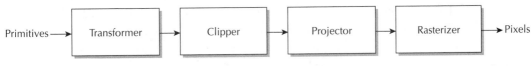

Figure 1.2 Pipeline model for OpenGL

We can look at the pipeline as an implementation of the OpenGL state machine. More important, the pipeline model is close to the way that most graphics hardware systems are built. The pipeline model also emphasizes that primitives are processed independently; that is, each primitive has its color and visibility determined independently of all other primitives.

1.3 OpenGL Functions

OpenGL contains over 200 functions. It is helpful to group them by their functionality.

- **Primitive functions** define the elements that can produce images on the screen. These functions are of two types: geometric primitives, such as polygons, that can be defined in two, three, or four dimensions; and discrete entities, such as bitmaps.
- **Attribute functions** control the appearance of primitives. These functions define colors, line types, material properties, light sources, and textures.
- **Viewing functions** determine the properties of the camera. OpenGL provides a camera that we can position and orient relative to the objects defined by the primitive functions. We can also control the lens of the camera to produce wide-angle and telephoto views.
- **Input functions** are not part of the core of OpenGL but because of their importance for interactive applications are contained in a library called GLUT. These functions allow us to control the windows on the screen and to use the mouse and the keyboard.
- **Control functions** allow us to start and to terminate OpenGL programs and to turn on various OpenGL features. These functions also allow us to find out the capabilities of a particular implementation.

1.4 OpenGL Versions and Extensions

OpenGL is controlled by the OpenGL Architectural Review Board (ARB), which has members from such companies as SGI, IBM, and Microsoft. The present version of OpenGL is 1.2. OpenGL is very stable, and most programs using the OpenGL 1.0 and 1.1 specifications have no problem running on version 1.2. The capabilities in OpenGL reflect what is available on most graphics systems. Even if a particular platform lacks the hardware to implement certain features, they are implemented in software.

Many high-end users have access to equipment with special capabilities or have need for particular functionality that is not very general. However, these application programmers still prefer to program with OpenGL. Implementers handle these situations through **OpenGL extensions**, which pass through the ARB but are not yet part of the official OpenGL specification. One popular extension is for image processing. The image-processing extensions are extensions of the pixel operations (discussed in Chapter 7) but often make use of special hardware features available in high-end graphics workstations.

1.5 Languages

We use the C binding, which is the most popular, for OpenGL. An official FORTRAN version also exists. Unfortunately, no official language binding exists for other popular languages, such as Java. You can find some unofficial Java bindings from the Web sites given later.

1.6 Programming Conventions

The OpenGL functions are contained in two libraries usually called gl and glu or GL and GLU. The first library, the core OpenGL library, contains all the required OpenGL functions, whereas the second, the OpenGL Utility Library, contains functions that are written using functions in the core library but are helpful to users to have available. Functions in the core library have names that begin with gl, such as glVertex3f(), whereas functions in the utility library have names beginning with glu, such as gluOrtho2D().

OpenGL is not object oriented, and we shall be using its C language binding. Thus, the API does not make use of features, such as overloading, that are available in object-oriented languages, such as C++. To support the variety of data types that C programmers use, many OpenGL functions have multiple forms. For example, the function glVertex3f() takes floats as arguments, whereas the function glVertex3i() takes integers as arguments. We use the notation glVertex*() to refer to all the forms of the vertex function.

Many OpenGL functions have arguments whose values are chosen from a small, discrete set of integers. To avoid the use of "magic numbers," OpenGL defines macros for these values; those macros are defined in the include files gl.h and glu.h. The prefixes GL_ and GLU_ define the include file from which the macro comes, such as GL_LINES or GL_LIGHT0.

OpenGL uses the basic C data types: floats, doubles, ints, and chars. However, to allow an implementation to redefine its basic types, the include file gl.h defines the basic types GLint, GLfloat, GLdouble, and GLchar. Although these types are generally what you would expect, they are used to define the OpenGL functions. For example, the following function defines a vertex in three-dimensional space, using three GLfloats:

```
void glVertex3f(GLfloat x, GLfloat y, GLfloat z)
```

In practice, gl.h has a line in for each type, of the form

```
#define GLfloat float
```

Occasionally, you will also see less familiar types, such as GLclampf for floats in the range from 0.0 to 1.0 and GLsizei for as large nonnegative integers as are available on the implementation.

OpenGL also provides an alternative function to many functions that require parameters to allow specification through pointers to vertices. These functions have a v before the argument list. Hence, we might use the function glVertex3fv() as

```
GLfloat point[3];
glVertex3fv(point);
```

In our description of functions, we use braces and the word TYPE to allow us to specify the many forms of a function. For example, we can list all the forms of glVertex*() as

```
glVertex{234}{sifd}(TYPE coords, ... .) ;
glVertex{234}{sifd}v{TYPE *coords);
```

We have to select a dimension—2, 3, or 4—and a data type—short (s), integer (i), float (f) or double (d). TYPE matches the data type. For the direct form, the number of parameters must be the same as the number of dimensions. For the pointer form, we need give only a pointer of the correct type. Thus, the following are all invocations of vertex functions:

```
GLint ix, iy;
GLfloat x, y, z, point[3];
glVertex2i(ix, iy);
glVertex2f(x, y);
glVertex3f(x, y, z);
glVertex3fv(point);
```

In the final form, point is assumed to be an array of the form

```
float point[3];
```

The details of each function will be in a description box of the form

> ```
> void glFunctionName(GLint param)
> ```
>
> This function does not exist, but the value of param can be GL_TRUE or
> GL_FALSE.

This box appears near where the function is first introduced. In addition, some
alerts or warnings are given and are preceded by a special icon.

 Read this important information!

1.7   Compiling

Generally, compiling an OpenGL program should not be a problem. For UNIX
systems, a typical compile line looks like

```
cc myapp.c -o myapp -lgl -lglu -lglut -lm -lX11
```

For Linux, you can use almost the same line, but the X libraries are usually in a
different place. Adding the following flag usually works:

```
-L/usr/X11R6/lib
```

You can make a simple make file that usually works for UNIX and Linux,
based on the four lines

```
CC = cc
LDLIBS = -lglut -lGL -lGLU  -lX11 -lm -L/usr/X11R6/lib
.c:
    $(CC)  $@.c $(LDLIBS) -o $@
```

A make file with these lines will allow you to compile a single file via the command line

```
make progname
```

This command will start with progname.c and result in the binary progname.
Occasionally, you may need to add -lXmu to the loader line.

You may have to add in the flag -L if your X libraries are in a nonstandard place or the flag -I if your OpenGL include files are in a nonstandard place.

Under Windows with Visual C++, you want to build a console application. The OpenGL32.dll and glu32.dll files should already be in the system folders. The corresponding lib files should be ..\VC\lib. The include files should be in ..\VC\include\GL. If these files are not already there, you can get them from the Microsoft site. You will have to get the GLUT files from the Web. You can get the files in a precompiled form or you can build them yourself from Nate Robins's GLUT site for Windows.[1] These files—glut.h, glut32.lib, and glut32.dll—go in the same places as the other OpenGL files. A version of OpenGL for Windows that originated with SGI is still around. Its files, named OpenGL.dll, OpenGL.lib, GLU.dll, and GLU.lib, require the GLUT files glut.lib and glut.dll. However, the latest version of GLUT for Windows uses a single version of GLUT that works for both distributions of OpenGL.

1.8　Sources

A wide variety of OpenGL information is available. First are the books on OpenGL. The most important ones, known by the colors of their covers as the "Red Book" and the "Blue Book" respectively, are

- OpenGL Architecture Review Board, *OpenGL Programming Guide,* 3rd ed. (Reading, MA: Addison-Wesley, 2000).
- OpenGL Architecture Review Board, *OpenGL Reference Manual,* 3rd ed. (Reading, MA: Addison-Wesley, 2000).

The Red Book uses GLUT for its examples.

If you want to develop code for the X Windows system, see

- M. Kilgard, *OpenGL Programming for the X Windows System* (Reading, MA: Addison-Wesley, 1996).

If you are developing applications exclusively for Windows, see

- R. Fosner, *OpenGL Programming for Windows 95 and Windows NT* (Reading, MA: Addison-Wesley, 1997).
- R. Wright, and M. Sweet, *OpenGL SuperBible* (Corte Madera, CA: Waite Group Press, 1997).

---

1. www.cs.utah.edu/~narobins.

This primer assumes that you already know some computer graphics. If you need an introduction to computer graphics using OpenGL, see

- E. Angel, *Interactive Computer Graphics, A Top-Down Approach with OpenGL*, 2nd ed. (Reading, MA: Addison-Wesley, 2000).

The standard reference in computer graphics is

- J. Foley, A. van Dam, S. Feiner, and J. Hughes, *Computer Graphics, Principles and Practice*, 2nd ed. (Reading, MA: Addison-Wesley, 1990).

Many Web resources are available. The best place to start is with the OpenGL org site (www.opengl.org), which is filled with pointers to books, code, articles, and documentation. Support for this book can be found from the Addison-Wesley site (www.awl.com) or from the author's site (www.cs.unm.edu/~angel or ftp.cs.unm.edu under pub/angel).

If your system lacks OpenGL, you can use an open source version, called Mesa, that is distributed as both source and as libraries with most Linux distributions. Mesa is available at www.mesa3d.org. You can obtain the GLUT library in a variety of places. Pointers are on the OpenGL Web site. The GLUT library is often included with the Mesa distribution.

SGI has its own OpenGL Web site at www.sgi.com/software/opengl, including pointers to a variety of resources and products.

Some very helpful OpenGL tutorial programs from Nate Robins illustrate viewing, transformations, texture mapping, and a few other topics. These tutorials are interactive and will give you the opportunity to experiment with a variety of OpenGL functions and parameters. The tutorials are available at www.cs.utah.edu/~narobins.

Many good demo programs are available. All the programs in the "Red Book" are available and are included with Mesa. Additional demos and test programs are included with Mesa and GLUT.

1.9 Who Should Use This Primer

Ideally, you read the preface before you bought this book. But in case you jumped right in, here is a reminder about who should and should not be using this primer. This primer is an introduction to the OpenGL API and is not intended to be complete. If you need complete coverage and documentation, see the "Red Book" and the "Blue Book." If you want to get started with OpenGL, this primer should be right for you.

It is assumed that you know some computer graphics. This primer pretty much avoids all mathematics, which is part of learning computer graphics. Some excellent graphics texts are around, including the two mentioned earlier. If you are a student taking a computer graphics class that is using OpenGL, this primer should help.

1.10 Outline

We start in Chapter 2 with two-dimensional problems. Although in OpenGL, two-dimensional graphics is a special case of three-dimensional graphics, it is easier to get started with two-dimensional problems. We introduce all the basic OpenGL primitives and their attributes.

Chapter 3 is concerned with interactivity. Although input functions are not part of the core of OpenGL, we use OpenGL for interactive applications. We use the GLUT library to develop simple, portable interactive applications.

Chapters 4 and 5 present three-dimensional graphics with OpenGL. Chapter 4 introduces three-dimensional objects that can be built from the basic OpenGL primitives, as well as some additional objects provided by the GLU and GLUT libraries. The chapter discusses how to produce an image of these objects by speci-fying the parameters for OpenGL's camera and positioning the objects relative to the camera. Chapter 5 introduces OpenGL's powerful transformation capabilities, showing how transformations can be used to create instances of basic objects at any desired size, orientation, and location. The chapter also discusses how transfor-mations can be used to model the relationships between parts of objects.

Chapter 6 introduces light-material interactions through the Phong lighting model that is implemented in OpenGL. The chapter also discusses how to work with translucent surfaces in OpenGL.

Chapters 7 and 8 are concerned with OpenGL's capabilities for manipulating bits and pixels. Chapter 7 discusses displaying patterns of bits directly and how to move bits between various buffers in OpenGL. Chapter 8 introduces texture map-ping, which allows us to combine the geometric and bit-manipulation capabilities of OpenGL.

Chapter 9 leaves the world of flat polygons. This chapter explains how to use OpenGL's curves and surfaces.

Finally, Chaper 10 surveys a few advanced features of OpenGL. The chapter also presents a final, nontrivial example that illustrates most of OpenGL's features.

This primer contains a mixture of code snippets and complete illustrative OpenGL programs. The complete programs are available on the author's Web and ftp, sites given earlier.

Finally, graphics programming is fun. Try to enjoy learning how to do it.

Two-Dimensional
Programming in OpenGL

OpenGL is a three-dimensional system. From an application programmer's perspective, OpenGL primitives describe three-dimensional objects that exist in a three-dimensional world. But some objects reside in a plane, and these two-dimensional problems are a special case of three-dimensional problems. This special case is important because many applications are two dimensional. For these applications, it is easier to work directly in two dimensions, something that OpenGL allows. We start with these simpler problems as a straightforward way of getting started with OpenGL.

In this chapter, we start by dissecting a very simple program to understand the basics of an OpenGL program. Then we enhance the program, introducing additional OpenGL functions. Finally, we introduce the full set of basic OpenGL primitives.

2.1 A Simple Program

Program 2.1 draws a white rectangle on a black background. Although it makes heavy use of default values for many parameters, the program nonetheless illustrates the structure of most OpenGL programs.

The program consists of two functions: `main()` and `display()`. The `main()` function initializes OpenGL, and `display()` defines the graphical entity to be drawn. First, we examine `main()`. Although OpenGL contains no input or window commands, any user program must interact with the window system, and interactive programs have input from such devices as the mouse and the keyboard. However, the user interface to window systems is system dependent. A program for Windows 98/NT differs from one with the same functionality written

```
/*simple.c */

#include <GL/glut.h>

void display()

{

    glClear(GL_COLOR_BUFFER_BIT);

    glBegin(GL_POLYGON);
        glVertex2f(-0.5, -0.5);
        glVertex2f(-0.5, 0.5);
        glVertex2f(0.5, 0.5);
        glVertex2f(0.5, -0.5);
    glEnd();

    glFlush();

}


int main(int argc, char** argv)
{

    glutInit(&argc,argv);
    glutCreateWindow("simple");
    glutDisplayFunc(display);
    glutMainLoop();

}
```

Program 2.1 simple.c

for the X Window System under Linux. We can interface with these systems by using a minimum amount of "glue" contained in system-specific libraries: GLX for X Windows, wgl for Windows, agl for the Macintosh. There is an alternative path through the GLUT library.

2.2 GLUT

The OpenGL Utility Toolkit (GLUT) is a library of functions that are common to virtually all modern windowing systems. GLUT has been implemented on all the popular systems, so programs written using the GLUT API for windowing and input can be compiled with the source code unchanged on all these systems. We use GLUT throughout this book.

```
void glutInit(int argc, char **argv)
```

Initializes GLUT and should be called before any OpenGL functions: `glutInit()` takes the arguments from `main()` and can use them in an implementation-dependent manner.

Starting with the first function in `main()`, `glutInit()`, we see that the name for all GLUT functions begins with the letters `glut`. Although we can pass in command line arguments from `main()`, their interpretation within GLUT is implementation dependent. We shall not use implementation-dependent arguments in our examples. The function `glutCreateWindow()` puts a window on the screen in a default position—at the upper-left corner—and at a default size— 300×300 pixels. The argument allows us to put a title on the top border of the window.

```
int glutCreateWindow(*char title)
```

Creates a window on the screen with the title given by the argument. The function returns an integer that can be used to refer to the window in multiwindow situations.

Altering the defaults in GLUT is discussed later.

2.3 Event Loops and Callback Functions

Most interactive programs are based on the program's reacting to a variety of discrete **events**. Events include mouse events, such as moving the mouse or clicking a mouse button; keyboard events, such as pressing a key; and window events, such as the user resizing a window or the covering up of a window by another window. The programming paradigm used to work with them is to have events handled by the operating systems and placed in an **event queue**. Events are processed sequentially from the event queue. The application programmer writes a set of **callback functions** that define how the program should react to specific events. In GLUT, the most common events are recognized. The application program can define its own callback functions, rely on default callbacks for a few events, or do nothing, in which case events without callbacks are ignored.

Program 2.1 contains only a single callback, the **display callback**, which is invoked whenever OpenGL determines that the display has to be redrawn. One such time is when the window is first opened. Consequently, if we put our graphics in the display callback, we can be assured that they will be drawn at least once. Note that the form of the display function, a function with no arguments, is fixed by GLUT.

```
void glutDisplayFunc(void (*func) (void))
```

The function func() is called each time there is a display callback.

If we wish to pass values to the display callback function, we must use globals in our programs. After the callbacks have been defined, the program enters the event loop by executing the function glutMainLoop(). Once we have entered the loop, we cannot escape except through a callback or an outside intervention, such as pressing a "kill" key. Any code after this call will never be executed.

 The form of GLUT callback functions is fixed. Consequently, global variables may be necessary to pass values between functions.

```
void glutMainLoop()
```

Causes the program to enter an event-processing loop. This statement should be the last one in the main() function.

2.4 Drawing a Rectangle

Now we have to define our display callback, which we have chosen to name display. First, note that we include the file glut.h, which is usually stored in a directory named GL wherever the standard include files are stored. This file contains the prototypes for the GLUT functions and the #defines for a variety of constants that are used in OpenGL programs. This file also contains the following lines to include similar definitions for the OpenGL and GLU functions and constants.

```
#include <GL/gl.h>
#include <GL/glu.h>
```

The fundamental entity for specifying geometric objects is the **vertex**, a location in space. Simple geometric objects, such as lines and polygons, can be specified through a collection of vertices. OpenGL allows us to work in two, three, or four dimensions through variants of the function `glVertex*()`.

```
void glVertex{234}{sifd}(TYPE xcoordinate, TYPE
    ycoordinate,....)
void glVertex{234}{sifd}v(TYPE *coordinates)
```

Specifies the location of a vertex in two, three, or four dimensions with the types short (`s`), int (`i`), float (`f`), or double (`d`). If `v` is present, `coordinates` is a pointer to an array of the type specified.

We shall use the notation `glVertex*()` to refer to all these variants. Thus, for example, `glVertex2f(x, y)` defines a vertex in two dimensions at the point (x, y), where x and y are floats, whereas `glVertex2fv(p)` specifies a vertex at the first two locations of an array of floats, that is, (p[0], p[1]).

Because vertices can define a variety of objects, we must tell OpenGL what object a list of vertices defines and where the beginning and the end of the list occur. We make this specification through the functions `glBegin()` and `glEnd()`.

```
void glBegin(GLenum mode)
```

Specifies the beginning of an object of type mode. Modes include GL_POINTS, GL_LINES, and GL_POLYGON.

```
void glEnd()
```

Specifies the end of a list of vertices.

 Don't forget to include the `glEnd()` after a list of vertices.

Using these three functions, we can define our rectangle as follows:

```
glBegin(GL_POLYGON);
    glVertex2f(-0.5, -0.5);
    glVertex2f(-0.5, 0.5);
    glVertex2f(0.5, 0.5);
    glVertex2f(0.5, -0.5);
glEnd();
```

Note that before we draw the rectangle, we clear the **color buffer**, where OpenGL puts the rendered image through the function glClear().

> void glClear(GLbitfield mask)
>
> Clears all buffers whose bits are set in mask. The mask is formed by the logical OR of values defined in gl.h. GL_COLOR_BUFFER_BIT refers to the color buffer.

After we finish specifying our one object, we force the renderer to output the results by issuing a glFlush(), in case the implementation is buffering commands for efficiency.

> void glFlush()
>
> Forces OpenGL commands to execute.

Figure 2.1 shows the output from our program. Although the program obviously produces an image, we need to address a variety of questions.

- What do we do if we want the image to be a different size?
- What do we do if we want the image to appear in a different place on the screen?
- Why does the white rectangle occupy half the area in the window?

Figure 2.1 Output from simple.c

- Why is the background black and the rectangle white? How can we use other colors?
- Can we end the program other than by using the kill box provided by the window system?
- How do we define more complex objects?

2.5   Changing the GLUT Defaults

First, let's add a few GLUT functions that will give us a little finer control over the image that appears on our screen. The functions `glutInitDisplayMode()`, `glutInitWindowSize()`, and `glutInitWindowPosition()` allow us to define what type of window we want, its size, and its position. Generally, an implementation will support a variety of properties that can be associated with a window on the screen. An application program, through the function `glutInitDisplayMode()`, requests the type of window that it requires. The most common window properties to specify are what type of color we wish to use and whether we need double buffering. The defaults in GLUT are RGB color and single buffering, which can be specified explicitly by the function call

```
glutInitDisplayMode(GLUT_RGB | GLUT_SINGLE);
```

> ### void glutInitDisplayMode(unsigned int mode)
>
> Requests a display with the properties in mode. The values of mode are combined by using the logical OR of options, such as color model (GLUT_RGB, GLUT_INDEX) and buffering of color buffers (GLUT_SINGLE, GLUT_DOUBLE).

The function `glutInitWindowSize()` specifies the size of the window on the screen, and `glutInitWindowPosition()` gives its initial position.

> ### void glutInitWindowSize(int width, int height)
>
> Specifies the initial height and width, in pixels, of the window on the screen.
>
> ### void glutInitWindowPosition(int x, int y)
>
> Specifies the top-left corner of the window, measured in pixels, from the top-left corner of the screen.

2.6 Color in OpenGL

OpenGL supports two colors models: **RGB, or RGBA, mode** and **color-index mode**. In RGB mode, each color is a triplet of red, green, and blue values. The eye blends these primary colors, forming the color that we see. If we use real numbers to specify colors, 0.0 is none of a primary, and 1.0 is the maximum amount of that primary. Thus, the RGB triplet (1.0, 0.0, 0.0) is a bright red, (0.5, 0.5, 0.0) is a dark yellow, (1.0, 1.0, 1.0) is white, and (0.0, 0.0, 0.0) is black. In RGBA mode, we use a fourth color component, A, or **alpha**, which is an **opacity**. An opacity of 1.0 means that the color is opaque and cannot be "seen through," whereas a value of 0.0 means that a color is transparent. We will not need opacity until much later. If we use an integer type to specify a color, the range is from 0 to the maximum value of the type. If, for example, we use unsigned bytes, the color values are from 0 to 255.

In color-index mode, colors are specified as indices into a table of red, green, and blue values. In this mode, we form a table of the allowed colors, usually with 256 possible colors. This mode is not the common one used at present and also requires more detailed interaction with the windowing system than does RGB color. Hence, we shall always use RGB or RGBA color.

2.6.1 Setting Colors

In Program 2.1, we used the default values for our colors. The default color for clearing the screen was black and the default drawing color—the color that was used to fill the polygon—was white. These definitions can be changed by the functions glColor*() and glClearColor().

```
void glColor3{b i f d ub us ui}(TYPE r, TYPE g, Type b)
void glColor3{b i f d ub us ui}v(TYPE *color)
void glColor4{b i f d ub us ui}(TYPE r, TYPE g, Type b,
    TYPE a)
void glColor4{b i f d ub us ui}(TYPE *color)
```

Specifies RGB and RGBA colors, using the standard types. If the v is present, the color is in an array pointed to by color.

```
void glClearColor(GLclampf r, GLclampf g, GLclampf b,
    GLclampf a)
```

Specifies the clear color (RGBA) used when clearing the color buffer.

2.6.2 Color and State

In OpenGL, our colors become part of the state. We can think of there being a *present drawing color*, which we set by `glColor*()`, and a *present clear color*, set by `glClearColor()`. These colors remain the same until we change them in the application program. Thus, colors are not attached to objects but rather to the internal state of OpenGL. The color used to render an object is the present color. In the code, it may appear that colors are associated with objects and their vertices. But in fact, OpenGL uses the present state to find the color at the time the program defines a vertex. Application programmers must be very careful about where in the code colors are changed. Later, we shall learn how to bind colors more closely to our objects.

With `glColor*()`, we can set either RGB or RGBA colors, using the standard C data types. OpenGL has only one internal form for the present color, which is in RGBA form. Using `glColor3*()` is the same as using RGBA color with the alpha value set to 1.0. The clear color specified by `glClearColor()` must be specified as an RGBA color, using floats in the range (0.0, 1.0) and values of type `GLclampf`.

 Don't lose track of state changes, such as changing colors.

2.7 **Coordinate System Differences between GLUT and OpenGL**

OpenGL uses a variety of coordinates systems. Generally, users describe their geometry in world coordinates. For two-dimensional applications, this coordinate system has the positive *x* values increasing to the right and the positive *y* values increasing as we go up. Thus, if we put the origin on at the bottom-left corner of this page, all the locations the page would have positive *x* and *y* values.

Most windowing systems use a system in which the values of *y* increase as we go down. In such a system, if we want all *x* and *y* values to be positive, we put the origin in the top-left corner. In most windowing systems, the screen is displayed from top to bottom, and the counting of rows and columns starts from the top-left corner. Because it interacts with the window system, GLUT uses the second form, and we should think of the origin of the screen as being in its top-left corner and the locations of the pixels as numbered from (0, 0) going down and to the right. For such functions as `glutInitWindowPosition()`, there should be little difficulty. Later, when we use input from the mouse, we will have to work with values in both systems, which can cause some confusion.

 For two-dimensional problems, the directions of positive increments in *x* and *y* in OpenGL are to the right and up. For input functions used in GLUT and windowing systems, positive increments usually are down and to the right.

2.8 Two-Dimensional Viewing

In Program 2.1, we used the default viewing conditions. In OpenGL, programs in two dimensions are a special case of three-dimensional programs. Two-dimensional objects have spatial coordinates of the form (x, y), but from an OpenGL perspective, these are three-dimensional (x, y, z) values, with z set to 0.[1] Consequently, two-dimensional viewing issues, such as which objects appear on the screen and at what size, are special cases of the same issues in three-dimensional viewing. However, because we are interested in getting started through two-dimensional programs, we can develop simple two-dimensional viewing independently.

The fundamental model we use in viewing is called the **synthetic-camera model**. It makes an analogy between a viewer—observer, photographer—forming a picture of a set of objects and what we do in the computer to produce an image. In two dimensions, we can define our objects by specifying or calculating a set of vertices, using some combination of glVertex*(), glBegin(), and glEnd() in our program. We can think of our code as describing objects on an infinite sheet of paper. The viewing step is specifying what part of that virtual sheet of paper is seen by our synthetic camera and thus appears on the screen. If we assume that the camera is aligned with the x and y axes, we need only specify a rectangular region through maximum and minimum values of x and y. We make this specification through the function gluOrtho2D().

```
void gluOrtho2D(GLdouble left, GLdouble right, GLdouble
    bottom, GLdouble top)
```

Specifies a two-dimensional rectangular clipping region whose lower-left corner is at (left, bottom) and whose upper-right corner is at (right, top)

The prefix glu indicates that the function is the GLU library—because it is a special case of the three-dimensional function glOrtho(). The rectangle defined by gluOrtho() is called the **clipping window**. Objects that lie within this window are visible, whereas objects outside are not and are said to be clipped out.

---

1. In reality, OpenGL uses four dimensions. Three-dimensional space is a special case of four-dimensional space, but we do not have to worry about that yet.

2.9 **Coordinate Systems and Transformations**

So far, we have seen two coordinate systems in our functions. The first, called **object coordinates**, or **world coordinates**, is the application coordinate system that users use to write their programs. Each application program can decide what units it prefers and then specify values in these units in OpenGL functions such as glVertex*(). Thus, we can use microns for problems in very large-scale integration (VLSI) design or light years for astronomical problems. The second coordinate system, called **window coordinates**, or **screen coordinates**, uses units measured in pixels. The allowable range of window coordinates is determined by properties of the physical display and what part of that display is selected by the application program.

OpenGL automatically makes a coordinate transformation from object to window coordinates as part of the rendering process. The only information required is the size of the display window on the screen and how much of the object world the user wishes to display. The former is determined by glutInitWindowSize()—and possibly modified by later interactions—whereas the latter is set by gluOrtho2D().

The required coordinate system transformations in OpenGL are determined by two matrices—the **model-view matrix** and the **projection matrix**—that are part of OpenGL's state. (We study these matrices in detail in Chapter 5.) However, we need to use a simple projection matrix in even the most basic programs. The function gluOrtho2D() is used to specify a projection matrix for two-dimensional applications. The typical sequence to set either of the matrices requires that we perform three steps.

1. Identify which matrix we wish to alter.
2. Set the matrix to an identity matrix.
3. Alter the identity matrix.

The second step is not required if we want to alter an existing matrix incrementally. Thus, if we want to set up a two-dimensional clipping window whose lower-left corner is at (−1.0, −1.0) and whose upper-right corner is at (1.0, 1.0), which are the default values we used in OpenGL, we execute the functions

```
glMatrixMode(GL_PROJECTION):
glLoadIdentity();
gluOrtho2D(-1.0, 1.0, -1.0, 1.0);
```

```
void glMatrixMode(GLenum mode)
```

Specifies which matrix will be affected by subsequent transformation functions. The mode is usually GL_MODELVIEW or GL_PROJECTION.

```
void glLoadIdentity()
```

Initializes the current matrix to an identity matrix.

Since these matrices are part of the OpenGL state, OpenGL will use their current values whenever a primitive is defined. These matrices can be changed virtually anywhere in an application program. For our simple example, without user interaction, we can set the matrices once as part of the initialization phase of the program. In Chapter 3, we will change the transformations in response to user events, such as the resizing of the screen window.

2.10 Second Version of a Simple Program

We can now incorporate all these changes into our program. The resulting program, Program 2.2, will behave the same as Program 2.1, but the structure of Program 2.2 is more general and characterizes more complex two-dimensional applications.

Program 2.2 illustrates the organization we use for almost all our programs in this book. Our programs consist of four major parts:

1. A main() function that initializes GLUT, puts a window on the screen, identifies the callback functions, and enters the main loop
2. An init() function that sets state variables to their initial values
3. A display callback, display(), that contains the code describing our objects
4. Other callbacks that deal with input and window events

Although other structures are possible, this organization has some advantages. The main() function is almost the same from program to program. Differences are usually related to which callbacks and menus are used in a particular application. Using init() allows us to place a lot of detailed state information and desired parameters in one place, separate from the geometry—which is in the display callback—and from the dynamics of animated and interactive programs, which usually are in the callbacks.

```
/* simple.c second version */
/* This program draws a white rectangle on a black background.*/


#include <GL/glut.h>          /* glut.h includes gl.h and glu.h*/


void display()

{
/* clear window */

    glClear(GL_COLOR_BUFFER_BIT);


/* draw unit square polygon */

    glBegin(GL_POLYGON);
        glVertex2f(-0.5, -0.5);
        glVertex2f(-0.5, 0.5);
        glVertex2f(0.5, 0.5)
        glVertex2f(0.5, -0.5);
    glEnd();

/* flush GL buffers */

    glFlush();

}


void init()
{

/* set clear color to black */

    glClearColor(0.0, 0.0, 0.0, 0.0);

/* set fill color to white */

    glColor3f(1.0, 1.0, 1.0);

/* set up standard orthogonal view with clipping */
/* box as cube of side 2 centered at origin */
/* This is default view and these statements could be removed */
```

Program 2.2 Second version of `simple.c`   *Continued on next page.*

```
      glMatrixMode(GL_PROJECTION);
      glLoadIdentity();
      gluOrtho2D(-1.0, 1.0, -1.0, 1.0);

int main(int argc, char** argv)
{

/* Initialize mode and open a window in upper left corner of
/* screen */
/* Window title is name of program (arg[0]) */

      glutInit(&argc,argv)
      glutInitDisplayMode(GLUT_SINGLE | GLUT_RGB);
      glutInitWindowSize(500, 500);
      glutInitWindowPosition(0, 0);
      glutCreateWindow("simple");
      glutDisplayFunc(display);
      init();
      glutMainLoop();

}
```

Program 2.2 Second version of `simple.c` (*continued*)

2.11 Primitives and Attributes

Primitives are the atomic entities that we work with in our graphics system. In the one primitive we have seen so far, a polygon, is defined by a set of vertices. The polygon is a geometric primitive. That is, the polygon exists in a space, usually a two- or three-dimensional user-defined space, and can be imaged by our viewing process. Later, we shall see that OpenGL allows us to apply transformations to geometric primitives so that we can move them, resize them, and reorient them. OpenGL also has nongeometric primitives, such as pixels, that are dealt with in quite a different manner. Those primitives are introduced in Chapter 7.

The three basic types of geometric primitives in OpenGL are points, line segments, and polygons. More sophisticated objects can be built out of these primitives, or we can use OpenGL curves and surfaces (Chapter 9). The basic primitives are all determined by vertices. Thus, they are specified as was the polygon in `simple.c`, but the type parameter in `glBegin()` varies.

Each primitive has **attributes**, properties that determine how it is displayed by OpenGL. For example, the polygon in our simple program was drawn in white. A line segment might be drawn in green and be thick or thin. In Chapter 6, we introduce more sophisticated attributes, called material properties, that determine how light interacts with the primitive.

It is important to remember that although we conceptualize attributes as being associated with objects—a red line, a blue point—in fact, OpenGL regards attributes as part of its state. Thus, when we produced a white polygon in `simple.c`, the whiteness of the polygon was determined by the present color, which was part of the state, being white. In Chapter 3, we shall learn how the programmer can better bind attributes to objects.

2.11.1 Points

Points are the simplest primitive. The type in `glBegin()` is GL_POINTS (see Figure 2.2, a). Each vertex determines a point; points that are within the clipping window are displayed using the present point size attribute, which is set by `glPointSize()` and the present color.

> `void glPointSize(GLfloat size)`
>
> Sets the point size state variable. Size is measured in pixels on the screen, and the default is 1.0.

We can thus use the same four vertices we used for our polygons but display those vertices as points in four different colors with the code

```
glPointSize(2.0);
glBegin(GL_POINTS);
    glColor3f(1.0, 1.0, 1.0);
    glVertex2f(-0.5, -0.5);
    glColor3f(1.0, 0.0, 0.0);
    glVertex2f(-0.5, 0.5);
    glColor3f(0.0, 0.0, 1.0);
    glVertex2f(0.5, 0.5);
    glColor3f(0.0, 1.0, 0.0);
    glVertex2f(0.5, -0.5);
glEnd();
```

Note that `glPointSize()` is one of the functions that cannot go between a `glBegin()` and a `glEnd()`.

2.11.2 Lines

There are three choices for type (see Figure 2.2, b, c, and d) for line segments. We can use GL_LINES, GL_LINE_STRIP, and GL_LINE_LOOP, to define one or more line segments between a `glBegin()` and a `glEnd()`.

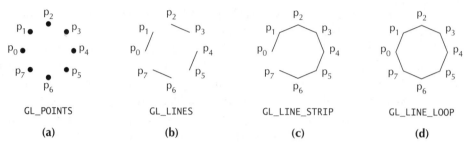

Figure 2.2 Point and line types

GL_LINES: Each successive pair of vertices between glBegin() and glEnd() defines a line segment. Thus, the following code defines two line segments: the first from (-0,5, -0.5) to (-0.5, 0.5) and the second from (0.5, 0.5) to (0,5, -0.5):

```
glBegin(GL_LINES);
    glVertex2f(-0.5, -0.5);
    glVertex2f(-0.5, 0.5);
    glVertex2f(0.5, 0.5);
    glVertex2f(0.5, -0.5);
glEnd();
```

GL_LINE_STRIP: The vertices define a sequence of line segments with the end point of one segment starting the next line segment. Thus, the following code defines three line segments: the first from (-0.5, -0.5) to (-0.5, 0.5), the second from (-0.5, 0.5) to (0.5, 0.5), and the third from (0.5, 0,5) to (0.5, -0.5):

```
glBegin(GL_LINE_STRIP);
    glVertex2f(-0.5, -0.5);
    glVertex2f(-0.5, 0.5);
    glVertex2f(0.5, 0.5);
    glVertex2f(0.5, -0.5);
glEnd();
```

GL_LINE_LOOP: The vertices connect the line segments as in GL_LINE_STRIP, but in addition, the last vertex is connected to the first. Thus, the following code defines a square:

```
glBegin(GL_LINE_LOOP);
    glVertex2f(-0.5, -0.5);
    glVertex2f(-0.5, 0.5);
    glVertex2f(0.5, 0.5);
    glVertex2f(0.5, -0.5);
glEnd();
```

The attributes for line segments are the color, the line thickness, and a pattern, called the **stipple pattern**, that allows us to create dashed and dotted lines.

---

void glLineWidth(GLfloat width)

Sets the width in pixels for the display of lines. The default is 1.0.

---

void glLineStipple(GLint factor, Glushort pattern)

Defines a 16-bit pattern for drawing lines. If a bit in pattern is 1, a pixel on the line is drawn. If the bit is 0, the pixel is not drawn. Successive groups of 1s and 0s in pattern are repeated factor times for values of factor between 1 and 256. The stipple pattern is repeated as necessary to draw the line. The bits are used starting with the lowest-order bits.

For example, the following commands set the drawing color to yellow, define lines as two pixels wide, and define a dashed stipple pattern in which groups of six pixels are not colored and the following six pixels are rendered in yellow:

```
glColor3f(1.0, 1.0, 0.0);
glLineWidth(2.0);
glLineStipple(3, 0xcccc);
```

2.11.3 Enabling OpenGL Features

Stippling is one of many OpenGL features that have to be enabled specifically. The renderer has many capabilities, such as lighting, hidden-surface removal, and texture mapping, although generally each feature will slow down the rendering processing. A user program can turn on—enable—or turn off—disable—each of these features individually with the application program. Some features, such as lighting, may be required in one part of a program but not in others.

---

void glEnable(GLenum feature)
void glDisable(GLenum feature)

Turns the OpenGL option feature on or off.

Line stippling is enabled by

```
glEnable(GL_LINE_STIPPLE);
```

Don't forget to enable features you want to use. Setting the parameters is not sufficient if the feature has not been enabled.

2.11.4 Filled Primitives

The polygon primitive with which we started is one example of a filled primitive, that is, a primitive with an interior that can be filled with a color or a pattern. Figure 2.3 shows the six filled primitives with the type parameters.

GL_POLYGON: Defines a polygon by a sequence of glVertex*() calls between and glBegin() and glEnd().

GL_QUADS: Successive groups of four vertices define quadrilaterals.

GL_TRIANGLES: Treats each successive group of three vertices between a glBegin() and a glEnd() as a triangular polygon. Extra vertices are ignored.

GL_TRIANGLE_STRIP: The first three vertices after a glBegin() define the first triangle. Each subsequent vertex is used with the previous two to define the next triangle. Thus, after the first polygon is defined, the others require only a single glVertex*() call.

GL_QUAD_STRIP: The first four vertices define a quadrilateral. Each subsequent pair of vertices is used with the previous pair of vertices to define the next quadrilateral.

GL_TRIANGLE_FAN: The first three vertices define the first triangle. Each subsequent vertex is used with the first vertex and the previous vertex to define the next triangle.

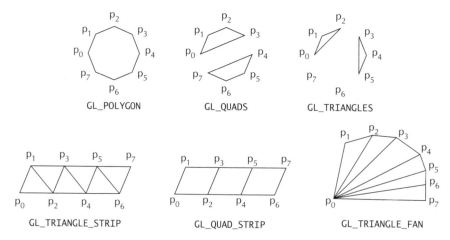

Figure 2.3 Filled types

These multiple polygon types have two advantages. First, a particular OpenGL implementation may have special software and hardware to render triangles or quadrilaterals more quickly than general polygons. Second, many CAD applications generate triangles or quadrilaterals with shared edges. Strip primitives allow us to define these primitives with far fewer OpenGL functions calls than if we had to treat each as a separate polygon. In Chapter 4, we introduce vertex arrays as another way that we can reduce the number of function calls required to define complex objects that share vertices.

2.11.5 Rectangles

OpenGL provides a function, `glRect*()`, for drawing two-dimensional filled rectangles aligned with the axes.

```
void glRect{sifd}(TYPE x1, y1, x2, y2)
void glRect{sifd}v(TYPE *v1, TYPE *v2)
```

Specifies a two-dimensional rectangle, using the standard data types by the x and y values of the corners or by pointers to arrays with these values.

2.11.6 Polygon Stipple

All the filled types are treated as polygons by the rendering process and thus have the same attributes. The simplest way to display a polygon is to fill it with a solid color. As we saw in `simple.c`, we can obtain a solidly colored polygon by using `glColor*()`. We can also fill the polygon with a stipple pattern by enabling polygon stipple by

`glEnable(GL_POLYGON_STIPPLE);`

We then set the pattern by `glPolygonStipple()`.

```
void glPolygonStipple(const Glubyte *mask)
```

Sets the stipple pattern for polygons. The `mask` is a 32 × 32 pattern of bits.

The pattern is used as in line stipple but is two dimensional and is aligned with the window. Thus, if we rotate the polygon by changing its vertices and redrawing it, the stipple pattern will not be rotated.

2.12 Polygon Types

The unfilled primitives, such as lines and line loops, pose no difficulties whether the vertices are defined in two or in three dimensions. Such is not the case for filled primitives, however. Consider a polygon whose edges cross as in Figure 2.4. It is somewhat arbitrary which points we consider to be inside the polygon and which outside. Unless polygons are **simple polygons**—polygons whose edges do not cross—two different OpenGL implementations may render them differently. OpenGL does not check whether a polygon is simple; that is left to the application program.

Two-dimensional polygons have an additional feature: All the vertices lie in the same plane and thus for nonsimple polygons, an interior is well defined. In three dimensions, a set of more than three vertices need not lie in the same plane. Once more, different OpenGL implementations might render such polygons differently. If this situation is a potential problem, it must be dealt with within the application program.

A third issue is that even when all vertices lie in the same plane, rendering a complex polygon with many vertices can present problems for the implementation. **Convex objects** are ones for which if we connect any two points in the object, the entire line segment connecting these points lies inside the object (Figure 2.5). Convex polygons are much easier to render. Because triangles are always convex and every triangle is planar, graphics systems usually work best with triangles.

In OpenGL, a polygon can be displayed in three different ways: filled, by its edges, or just as a set of points (the vertices). In addition, because our two-dimensional polygons are really three-dimensional polygons that are restricted to the plane z = 0, they have two faces: a front face and a back face. OpenGL can render either or both faces.

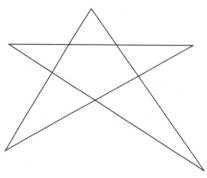

Figure 2.4 Nonsimple polygon

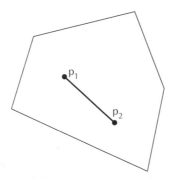

Figure 2.5 Convex polygon

A **front face** is one in which the order of the vertices is counterclockwise when we view the polygon. A **back face** is one in which the vertices are specified in a clockwise order. These definitions make sense for convex polygons. Defining front and back for nonconvex polygons may have difficulties, but OpenGL does not promise anything for such polygons, anyway.

The function `glPolygonMode()` lets us tell OpenGL how to render the faces.

> `void glPolygonMode(GLenum face, GLenum mode)`
>
> Specifies how the faces (GL_FRONT, GL_BACK, or GL_FRONT_AND_BACK) are to be rendered (GL_POINT, GL_LINE, or GL_FILL). The default is to fill both faces.

We can also not render either or both faces by culling the front- or back-facing polygon using `glCullFace()`.

> `void glCullFace(GLenum mode)`
>
> Causes the faces specified by mode (GL_FRONT, GL_BACK, or GL_FRONT_AND_BACK) to be ignored during rendering.

Culling must be enabled by

`glEnable(GL_CULL_FACE);`

OpenGL allows us to change the definition of front and back facing through the function `glFrontFace()`.

> void glFrontFace(GLenum mode)
>
> Allows the specification of either the counterclockwise (GL_CCW) or clockwise (GL_CW) direction for defining a front face.

Suppose that we want to display a polygon both by filling it and by displaying its edges. For example, we might want to display a polygon with yellow edges and filled in red. In OpenGL, the edges of a polygon are part of the inside of the polygon, so we cannot show both the edges and the inside with a single rendering. Instead, we can render the polygon twice: first with the polygon mode set to GL_LINE and the color set to yellow and then with mode set to GL_FILL and the color set to red, as in the code

```
glPolygonMode(GL_FILL);
glColor3fv(yellow);
square();
glPolygonMode(GL_LINE);
glColor3fv(red);
square();
```

In this code, the colors are in arrays, and the polygon is defined in the function square(). But we have a potential problem here. The two renderings of the polygon are on top of each other and even though the edge is drawn after the fill, small numerical errors in the renderer can cause parts of the yellow edge to be hidden by the red fill.

To solve this problem, we can ask OpenGL to move the lines slightly forward by the function glPolygonOffset(). The offset is a linear combination of the two parameters weighted by two internal constants, so it is not simple to set in terms of units of the application. Nevertheless, if you cannot get the desired effects without using the offset, some trial and error with the parameters may give a better image.

> void glPolygonOffset(GLfloat factor, GL float units)
>
> Sets the offset for polygons. The offset can be positive or negative and can be enabled for any of the polygon modes.

Polygon offset can be enabled separately for any of the three polygon modes. For example, the following with a positive offset should work for our example:

```
glEnable(GL_POLYGON_OFFSET_LINES);
```

2.13 **Color Interpolation**

The color used to render a polygon is the present value of the color state variable. When we change colors between calls to glVertex*(), we change the state but conceptually are associating the new color with the next vertex. In OpenGL, we often refer to **vertex colors** when we use them in this manner.

Suppose that we have a line segment defined by

```
glBegin(GL_LINES);
    glColor3f(1.0, 0.0, 0.0);
    glVertex2f(1.0, 0.0);
    glColor3f(0.0, 0.0, 1.0);
    glVertex2f(0.0, 1.0);
glEnd();
```

The vertices are defined as red and blue, but in what color will OpenGL render the points between the vertices? The default is to use **smooth shading**, whereby OpenGL will interpolate the colors at the vertices to obtain the color of intermediate points. Thus, as we go along the line, we see the color starting as red and then passing through various shades of magenta before becoming blue.

For polygons, the same is true except that the interpolation formula must interpolate the vertex colors across the interior of the polygons. Usually, OpenGL renders polygons as a set of triangles, using a simple two-dimensional interpolation formula called **bilinear interpolation**. Interpolating vertex properties will arise in other contexts later, such as in texture mapping and using material properties.

OpenGL also allows us to use the color at the first vertex to determine the properties of the entire primitive. Thus, we could have a solid blue line, or we could obtain a green polygon, even if there were color changes between vertex definitions. This style is called **flat shading** and is set by setting the shading model by the function glShadeModel().

---

void glShadeModel(GLenum mode)

Sets the shading model to smooth (GL_SMOOTH) or flat (GL_FLAT). Smooth shading is the default.

Suppose that you have an application that generates nonconvex, nonplanar polygons. What can you do? You could hope for the best, as OpenGL generally will produce something. Or, you could break up, or **tessellate**, your polygons into triangles within your application. But a problem arises if we wish to display only the

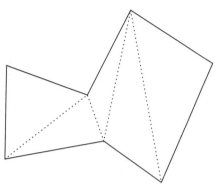

Figure 2.6 Tessellating a polygon

edges. Consider the polygon in Figure 2.6. When we break it up for display into five triangles, we won't have a problem if we fill the five polygons. However, if the polygon mode is set to display edges, we want only the edges corresponding to the original polygon to be displayed, not the new edge created by the tessellation.

```
void glEdgeFlag(GLboolean flag)
void glEdgeFlagv(GLboolean *flag)
```

Sets the edge flag (GL_TRUE, GL_FALSE) that determines if subsequent vertices are the start of edges that should be displayed if the polygon mode is GL_LINE.

We can decide which edges to display by using the function glEdgeFlag*(). If the flag is set to GL_TRUE, each vertex is considered the beginning of a line segment to be displayed. If the flag is set to GL_FALSE, the vertices do not start edges that are to be displayed.

We also have a third option. The GLU library provides a tessellator. The tessellator decides how to break up a general polygon and takes cares of such issues as creating faces that have a consistent facing and setting the edge flags. Use of the tessellator requires a large number of additional functions, and we will not discuss it further.

2.14 Text

Text is not one of the OpenGL primitives. This fact may seem a bit strange, given the importance of text in such applications as producing graphs. However, it is important to remember that OpenGL provides a minimal set of primitives that provide building blocks for the application programmer. We could attempt to build a set of characters from the primitives that we have seen, but that might not be a very appealing task.

In general, text generation presents a few problems that must be confronted. Suppose that we want to create a **font**, a set of characters in a given size and style, such a 10-point Times Roman bold font. The two principal forms for generating such characters are **bitmap characters** and **stroke characters**. Bitmap characters are stored as rectangular patterns of bits in which if a bit is 1, it is displayed; otherwise, it is not displayed. In Chapter 7, we shall study how OpenGL allows the user to define and to output bitmaps. Such characters are very fast to generate, since each can be requested by a single OpenGL call. However, bitmap characters cannot be modified nicely by such operations as scaling. In addition, the patterns will appear differently on windows of different sizes. Stroke characters are generated by using the standard OpenGL primitives, such as lines, polygons, and curves and can be modified by the transformations that we will discuss in Chapter 5. However, stroke characters require more storage and are slower to generate. If you are willing to do the work, you can generate either type of characters. OpenGL supports both.

A simpler approach might be to use the fonts that are provided by most windowing systems. Programs that do so might not be portable to a different environment, but switching to another font in another system does not often present major problems. We can obtain such a font through system specific functions.

GLUT offers a third possibility by providing a few of its own bitmap and stroke fonts. We can obtain a bitmap character through the function `glutBitmapCharacter()`, which uses the patterns from certain fonts in the X Window System.

```
void glutBitMapCharacter(void *font, int char)
```

Renders the character `char`, given by an ASCII code, in the font given by `font`.

Thus, we can get a bitmapped Times Roman 10-point character 'a' by

```
glutBitMapCharacter(GLUT_BITMAP_TIMES_ROMAN_10, 'a');
```

Similarly, we can get an 8×13 bit character for 'a' by

```
glutBitMapCharacter(GLUT_BITMAP_8_BY_13, 'a');
```

But where does the character appear on the screen? In OpenGL, bitmaps are handled differently from our geometric primitives. Bimaps appear in the size specified at a location determined the **raster position**, which is part of the OpenGL state. This position determines where the lower-left corner of the next bitmap will appear on the display. We can set that position with the function `glRasterPos*()`.

```
void glRasterPos{234}{sifd}(TYPE x, TYPE y, TYPE z, TYPE w)
void glRasterPos{234}{sifd}v(TYPE *array)
```

Specifies the raster position. The position is mapped to screen coordinates, using the current model-view and projection matrices.

Thus, we can set the raster position in world coordinates. The current raster position is updated automatically so that the next character will not be rendered on top of the previous one. GLUT provides the helper function `glutBitMapWidth()`, which allows the application program to determine the width of character so that it can determine how to change the raster position if necessary.

```
int glutBitmapWidth(GLUTbitmapFont font, int char)
```

Returns the width in pixels of `char` in the GLUT font named by `font`.

The corresponding functions for stroke fonts are `glutStrokeCharacter()` and `glutStrokeWidth()`.

```
void glutStrokeCharacter(void *font, int char)
```

Renders the character `char`, given by an ASCII code, in the stroke font given by `font`.

```
int glutStrokeWidth(GLUTbitmapFont font, int char)
```

Returns the width in bits of `char` in the GLUT font named by `font`.

The fonts GLUT_STROKE_MONO_ROMAN and GLUT_STROKE_ROMAN are fixed and proportional stroke fonts. However, their sizes are not in bits. Their sizes are approximately 100×100 units in world coordinates. Because they are defined as other geometric primitives, they pass through the geometric pipeline. Consequently, the usual way to position stroke characters is through the OpenGL transformations, such as scaling and translation, as discussed in Chapter 5.

2.15 **Inquiries and Errors**

Thus far, we have assumed that everything works perfectly; our programs compile and run just as we imagined. Now let's consider reality. We make errors; programs may run but not give the results we expect or may run and display nothing. OpenGL provides some error-checking facilities. It also allows us to obtain the values of any part of the state.

The OpenGL state can be inquired through the six functions `glGetBooleanv()`, `glGetIntegerv()`, `glGetFloatv()`, `glGetDoublev()`, `glGetPointerv()`, and `glIsEnabled()`. The first five return a pointer to the proper type. The application program needs to know the parameter it is seeking. We can obtain both present values, which are part of the state, and system parameters. For example, the following returns the current RGBA values to the array, which should have been allocated to hold four floats:

```
glGetFloatv(GL_CURRENT_COLOR, color_array);
```

The following call returns the number of red bits used for color in the implementation.

```
glGetIntegerv(GL_RED_BITS, bits);
```

Later, we will see a few other `get` functions in OpenGL.

```
void glGetBooleanv(GLenum name, GLboolean *value)
void glGetIntegerv(GLenum name, GLint *value)
void glGetFloatv(GLenum name, GLfloat *value)
void glGetDoublev(GLenum name, GLdouble *value)
void glGetPointerv(GLenum name, GLvoid **value)
```

Returns values of parameters in the state or system parameters named by `name` to user variables.

The function `glIsEnabled()` allows a program to check whether a particular feature has been enabled by a `glEnable()`.

```
GLboolean glIsEnabled(GLenum feature)
```

Returns `GL_TRUE` or `GL_FALSE`, depending on whether `feature` is enabled.

Error checking can be done in two parts. We can check if an error has been made by `glGetError()`, which returns an error type or `GL_NO_ERROR` if no error has been made. Errors are measured from initialization until this function is called. When the function is called, the error flag is reset to GL_NO_ERROR. A string for the particular error can be obtained by gluGetErrorString().

`GLenum glGetError()`

Returns the type of the last error since initialization or the last call to glGetError(). If no error has occurred, GL_NO_ERROR is returned.

`GLubyte* gluErrorString(GLenum error)`

Returns a string corresponding to the error returned by glGetError().

The error-reporting mechanism in GLUT is implementation dependent. Generally, if you request a facility that is unsupported, the program will terminate with an error message. GLUT provides a function, glutGet(), that lets the application obtain information about the state of GLUT.

`int glutGet(GLenum state)`

Returns the state of the specified GLUT state variable.

We can also obtain other information. We can determine depth of the color buffer (GLUT_WINDOW_BUFFER_SIZE) or whether the current display mode is supported (GLUT_DISPLAY_MODE_POSSIBLE).

2.16 Saving the State

The OpenGL state determines how primitives are rendered. Virtually all changes we make to attributes and to other items, such as the model-view and projection matrices, change the state. Programs that alter these variables can spend most of their time making state changes, many of which require recalculation of variables. For example, we often have to compute our camera parameters or the colors we wish to use. Rather than recalculate values we have used previously, OpenGL provides two types of stacks on we can store values for later use.

The **matrix stacks** store projection and model-view matrices, with a separate stack for each type. We push and pop matrices with glPushMatrix() and glPopMatrix(). The stack used is the one corresponding to the present matrix mode (GL_MODELVIEW or GL_PROJECTION).

```
void glPushMatrix()
void glPopMatrix()
```

Pushes and pops matrices to the stack for the present matrix mode.

Matrix stacks have two major uses. When we build hierarchical models in Chapter 5, we shall use stacks to traverse the tree data structures that we will use to describe these models. This application involves the model-view matrix. The second use involves the projection matrix. We often have to do a fair amount of calculation or use user input to determine the required projection matrix. Suppose that we then want to zoom in on the scene temporarily. We can do this by altering the present projection matrix in a fairly simple manner. The problem is that when we want to return to the unzoomed view, we do not want to—or may be unable to—recalculate the original projection matrix. Saving it on the stack before we zoom solves the problem. Thus, we often see such code as

```
glMatrixMode(GL_PROJECTION);
glLoadIdentity();
glutPostRedisplay();
glPushMatrix();
/* change the projection matrix */
glutPostRedisplay();
glutPopMatrix();
```

Note the pairing of the push and pop operations: one pop for each push. In hierarchical systems, not having the correct pairing can leave the stack in the wrong state.

 Pushes and pops must be paired in a program to be able to return to the desired state.

OpenGL breaks its attributes into 20 groups corresponding to sets of related attributes. For example, all the polygon attributes are in the group GL_POLYGON_BIT. All the line attributes are in the group GL_LINE_BIT. We can push any groups of attributes or all attributes (GL_ALL_ATTRIBUTE_BITS) onto the attribute stack through the function glPushAttrib() and recover them through glPopAttrib().

```
void glPushAttrib(GLbitfield mask)
void glPopAttrib()
```

Pushes and pops groups of attributes to the attribute stack. The identifiers for the groups are combined with logical OR to form mask.

2.17 The Viewport

So far we have used the entire window for our graphics. We can also restrict OpenGL to draw to any part of the window through the use of a **viewport**. A viewport is a rectangular area of the window on the screen. Its size is measured in pixels. We set the viewport by the function `glViewport()`.

`void glViewport(GLint x, GLint y, GLsizei w, GLsizei h)`

Sets the viewport of width w and height h pixels in the window with its lower-left corner at (x, y). The default viewport is the entire initial window.

One use of viewports is to divide the window so that different types of information can be rendered to different parts of the window. For example, in a CAD application we might use some viewports for menus and instructions and another for constructing the design. Each of these viewports can have its own viewing conditions specified by its own use of `gluOrtho2d()`. By using viewports that do not overlap, we can produce a complex image in a single window with minimum complexity in the code.

In Chapter 3, we use viewports to control the appearance of our images when the user changes the shape of the window.

Chapter 3

Interaction and Animation

Our next step will be to add dynamics to our simple graphics. To do so, we must be able to create or to change objects in a manner that leads to a smooth display process. We also want to be able to interact with our graphics by using menus, pointing to objects, and using the mouse for specifying locations. The extra functions we need will come mostly from the GLUT library.

3.1 The Reshape Callback

One of the most common interactive operations is resizing the screen. Usually, this operation is initiated when the user uses the mouse to move a corner or an edge of the window. This action generates a window event that is handled by the **reshape callback**. The information returned to the callback function is the new height and width, in pixels, of the window. Hence, the programmer identifies a callback function in main() by glutReshapeFunc() and then writes the callback function.

```
void glutReshapeFunc(void (*f) (int width, int height))
```

Invoked whenever the user changes the size of the window by using the mouse. The height and the width of the new window are returned to the function f(). A display callback is invoked automatically by executing f().

The reshape callback is invoked when a window is first created and thus becomes a handy place to put viewing functions. Because the height and the width of the window are returned to the callback, we can have the viewing conditions change as the user alters the size and the shape of the window. GLUT has a default reshape callback, but because the reshape callback can create many different effects, it is common not to rely on the default.

Suppose that our initial window size, as specified by glutInitWindowSize(), is square and the user resizes the window so that it is smaller and no longer square. When the window becomes smaller, the programmer must decide whether the same objects should be displayed at a smaller size or whether fewer objects should be visible. The programmer must also decide whether the shape of the objects should be unchanged, even though the window may no longer be square. Obviously, these decisions depend on the particular application. Let's consider the case in which we want to see the same objects but to ensure that their shapes are not changed. Thus, a circle will still appear as a circle but at a smaller size. We can accomplish both of these tasks by altering the window and the viewport. Consider the typical reshape callback defined by

```
glutReshapeFunc(myreshape);
```

Here, myreshape() is given by

```
GLsizei w, h;

void myreshape(GLsizei w, GLsizei h)
{

/* adjust clipping box */

    glMatrixMode(GL_PROJECTION);
    glLoadIdentity();
    if (w <= h)
        gluOrtho2D(-2.0, 2.0, -2.0 * (GLfloat) h /
        (GLfloat) w,2.0 * (GLfloat) h / (GLfloat) w);
    else
        gluOrtho2D(-2.0 * (GLfloat) w / (GLfloat) h,
                    2.0 * (GLfloat) w / (GLfloat) h);
    glMatrixMode(GL_MODELVIEW);


/* adjust viewport */

    glViewport(0, 0, w, h);

/* set global size for use by drawing routine */

    ww = w;
    wh = h;
}
```

The first part of the function alters the projection matrix. We start, as usual, by loading an identity matrix. The **aspect ratio**, the height-to-width ratio of the window, is used to determine a clipping window. If the screen window is square, the clipping window is a 2.0 × 2.0 window centered at the origin of the world coordinate system. If the screen window is not square, we set a window whose shortest side is 2.0 units. We also set the viewport so that we will use the entire new screen window. We reset the matrix mode back to model-view mode. This step is not necessary but often is a convenience, since programs tend to alter the model-view matrix more than the projection matrix. Note that ww and wh are defined outside the callback as global variables so that the size of the window can be used by other functions.

Consider what happens if our display callback draws a single cube of side length 1.0 units, as in our simple example from the previous chapter. If our initial window is square, we will see in the middle of the window a square whose sides are half the length of the window. Now suppose that we resize the screen window so that it is five times longer than it is wide. The reshape callback will change the clipping window so that its height is still 2.0 units, but its width is now 10.0 units. Our 1.0 × 1.0 cube will still appear in the middle of the window and will still appear as a square. The change to the viewport is necessary so that that the full clipping window set by gluOrtho2D() will be visible regardless of how the screen window is resized. A display callback is generated automatically so that resizing the screen window not only changes the size of the window but also causes all the geometry defined in the display callback to be redrawn.

3.2 The Idle Callback

Suppose that we want to animate our square from the previous chapter. One simple method is to use the **idle callback** function from GLUT. This function is identifed by glutIdleFunc(), which should be located in the main() function. The idle callback identifies the idle callback function, which should be executed whenever the event queue is empty.

```
void glutIdleFunc(void (*f) (void))
```

The function f() is executed whenever no other events are to be handled.

Here is a trivial example. Suppose that we modify our simple program from the previous chapter by adding to the main() function the line

```
glutIdleFunc(myidle)
```

Further, suppose that we define `myidle()` as

```
void myidle()
{
    glutPostRedisplay()
}
```

The new function, `glutPostRedisplay()`, performs a function similar to that of directly invoking the display callback—the function `display()` from the `simple.c` program—but allows the implementation to be smarter in deciding when to carry out the display callback. As GLUT goes through the event loop, more than one event can require that the window be redrawn. If each such event were to call the display function direction, we would have the window redrawn multiple times. Use of `glutPostRedisplay()` ensures that the window gets drawn at most once each time GLUT goes through the event loop. In general, it is a good idea to never call the display callback directly but rather to use the `glutPostRedisplay()` whenever the display needs to be redrawn.

`void glutPostRedisplay()`

Requests that the display callback be executed.

If we make these changes to our `simple.c` program, we will probably see little change on the screen of our display, although you might notice that our computer is doing more work and that the screen may appear to flash. What we have done is ask our computer to redraw the display whenever it has nothing else to do. But as we have not changed what is in the display callback, the computer is drawing the same picture over and over. Thus, we first clear the screen, which accounts for any flashes that we may see, and then we draw our square. More computer resources are being consumed than in our first program, in which we drew the square only once. A more realistic use of the idle callback is to alter some of the data used in drawing the square.

3.3 A Rotating Square

Suppose that we define the four vertices of the square to lie at four equally spaced points on a circle, as in Figure 3.1. In terms of an angle θ, the four points $(\cos\theta, \sin\theta)$, $(-\sin\theta, \cos\theta)$, $(-\cos\theta, -\sin\theta)$, and $(\sin\theta, -\cos\theta)$ form the vertices of a cube, regardless of the value of θ.

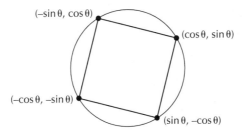

Figure 3.1 Square inside of a unit circle

If we change this angle as part of our idle callback and then redisplay, we should see the cube in a new position each time the cube is redrawn. Thus, consider the idle callback

```
void myidle()
{
    theta += 2.0;
    if(theta >= 360.0) theta -= 360.0;
    glutPostRedisplay();
}
```

Each time that `myidle()` is called, the value of theta is increased 2 degrees. Now, all we need do is rewrite the display callback such that it uses θ for the vertices. We also have to be careful as to where we define the vertices. Because the form of the callbacks is fixed by GLUT, we must define θ as a global to order to use it in both the display callback and the idle callback.

```
#define DEG_TO_RAD 57.29578 /* degrees to radians */
#include <math.h>
GLfloat theta = 0.0;
void mydisplay()
{
    glClear(GL_COLOR_BUFFER_BIT);
    glBegin(GL_POLYGON):
        glVertex2f(cos(DEG_TO_RAD *theta),
            sin(DEG_TO_RAD *theta);
        glVertex2f(-sin(DEG_TO_RAD *theta),
            cos(DEG_TO_RAD *theta);
        glVertex2f(-cos(DEG_TO_RAD *theta),
            -sin(DEG_TO_RAD *theta);
        glVertex2f(sin(DEG_TO_RAD *theta),
            -cos(DEG_TO_RAD *theta);
    glEnd();
    glFlush();
}
```

These modifications leave us with a program that, although inefficient, works. Later, we shall replace the use of trigonometric functions with rotation operations in OpenGL. You may, however, be annoyed with the appearance of the screen. It probably is flashing and does not appear to display a square. This problem comes from the interaction between the application program and the display process. Fortunately, we can handle this problem simply with double buffering.

3.4 Double Buffering

Most graphics displays are built so that the screen you see is redrawn, or **refreshed**, at a fixed rate. This process requires that the display hardware take the contents of the color buffer and use these values to determine the colors in the graphics window on the screen. This refresh process is not controllable from the user program and in fact is uncoordinated, or asynchronous, with it. Consequently, the user program is creating new values in the color buffer at the same time that the display process is taking these values out for display. The values used for display are not those of a single square drawn for a particular value of θ but rather some combination of values from two or more executions of the display callback.

Although we cannot couple the two processes, we can ensure that we will display only a single fully drawn square, through a technique called **double buffering**. The main idea is to use two color buffers, called the **front buffer** and the **back buffer**, rather than one. The front buffer is the one that is displayed by the display hardware, whereas the back buffer is the one into which the application draws. All we need do is swap the two buffers after we have finished constructing an entire square. We can do this swap by replacing the `glFlush()` with `glutSwapBuffers()` in our display callback.

`void glutSwapBuffers()`

Swaps the front and back buffers.

Note that `glutSwapBuffers()` is a GLUT rather than a GL function because the swap involves an interaction with the windowing system. We must request double buffering in our initialization, as single buffering is the default. We do so through

```
glutInitDisplayMode(GLUT_DOUBLE | GLUT_RGB);
```

3.5 **Using the Keyboard**

We now turn to using the two most important interactive devices: the mouse and the keyboard. For the keyboard, events are generated every time we press or release a key. GLUT has a keyboard callback identified through the function glutKeyboardFunc(). This callback is invoked whenever a key is pressed. GLUT ignores releasing of the key, although many window systems allow the application program to respond to key release events.

```
void glutKeyboardFunc(void *f(unsigned char key, int x, int y))
```

Identifies the function f() that is called when any key is pressed on the keyboard. The key pressed is returned to f(), as is the position of the mouse in the window. Note that the position is given in pixels measured from the top-left corner of the window.

The key pressed is returned as a char to the callback function. Generally, the keyboard callback uses a simple control structure, such as if or case to determine whether the key pressed is one that the callback should handle and if it is, how to handle it. For example, suppose that we want to end the program if the user presses a Q or a q or the escape key (ASCII 27). In the main() function, we define a keyboard callback

```
glutKeyboardFunc(mykey);
```

We then write the function

```
void mykey(char key)
{
    if(key == 'q' || key == 'Q' || key == '\27') exit(0)
}
```

The keyboard callback also returns the position of the mouse at the time a key was pressed. We can use these values to have keys have different effects, depending on where the mouse is located. For example, in a drawing program, we might use the keyboard to exit the program except if the mouse is located in the drawing area. Here the keyboard callback might be used to enter text onto the screen. Note that because the mouse position is given as a position on the screen, the values returned are in pixels, measured from the top-left corner of the screen.

GLUT has provisions for using the various special keys, such as the function and arrow keys, that are on most keyboards. These keys are handled through the glutSpecialFunction() callback.

```
void glutSpecialFunction(void (*f) (int key, int x, int y))
```

Specifies the special key callback. The function f() is executed when key is pressed. The mouse position (x, y) is also returned.

Each special key is designated by a string defined in glut.h. Thus, within the callback, we might see such lines as

```
if(key == GLUT_KEY_F1) ...... /* function key 1 */
if(key == GLUT_KEY_UP) ...... /* up arrow key */
```

We can also make use of the **modifier keys**—Control, Alt, and Shift—through the glutGetModifiers() function, which can be called from within the mouse or keyboard callbacks.

```
int glutGetModifiers()
```

Returns one of GLUT_ACTIVE_SHIFT, GLUT_ACTIVE_CTRL, or GLUT_ACTIVE_ALT if that key is pressed at the time a mouse or a keyboard event is generated.

Thus, to have Control-*c* or Control-*C* terminate a program, we could have the following within the keyboard callback:

```
if((glutGetModifiers() == GLUT_ACTIVE_CTRL) &&
    ((key == 'c')||(key == 'C'))) exit(0);
```

The modifiers can be helpful in situations in which we have either a one-button or a two-button mouse and would like to use some of the options that are available with a three-button mouse. For example, with a one-button mouse, we could use a mouse click, a Control-mouse click, and a Shift-mouse click to get all the functionality of the three-button mouse.

3.6 Using the Mouse Callback

For the mouse, we use glutMouseFunc() to identify the mouse callback function.

```
void glutMouseFunc(void (*f)(int button, int state,
    int x, int y))
```

Identifies the mouse callback function f(), which returns the position of the mouse in the window, its state (GLUT_UP or GLUT_DOWN) after the event, and which button caused the event (GLUT_LEFT_BUTTON, GLUT_MIDDLE_BUTTON, or GLUT_RIGHT_BUTTON).

The simplest and most common way a mouse is used is to return a position on the screen to the application program. A **mouse event** occurs when a button on a mouse is pressed or released. The callback returns the position of the mouse in units of pixels measured, as usual, from the top-left corner of the window. The callback also returns which button caused the event and the state of that button after the event. In our examples, we shall consider only events generated by pressing a button, so the state that we shall check for is GLUT_DOWN. Thus, if we want to use the left mouse button to end our program, we can identify a mouse callback in the main() function:

```
glutMouseFunc(mymouse);
```

We can then use the callback function

```
void mymouse(int x, int y, int button, int state)
{
    if(state == GLUT_DOWN && button == GLUT_LEFT_BUTTON)
        exit();
}
```

The mouse callback can also be used interactively to control what is drawn. Suppose that we want to draw a box whose corners are given by two successive mouse clicks with the right mouse button and whose sides are aligned with the screen. The left mouse button will still be used to exit the program.

The first problem we must confront is where in the program we do the drawing. That is, where do we place the OpenGL functions that draw the box? We have two simple strategies. In the first, we do everything within the mouse callback. Thus, the first time the user clicks the right button, we save the position; the second time the user clicks this button, we draw a rectangle. Thus, the mouse callback looks something like

```
int hh; /* global for viewport height */

void mymouse(int button, int state, int x, int y)
{
```

```
static bool first = true;
static int xx, yy;
if(state == GLUT_DOWN && button == GLUT_LEFT_BUTTON)
    exit(0);
if(state == GLUT_DOWN && button == GLUT_RIGHT_BUTTON)
{
    if (first)
    {
        xx = x;
        yy = hh - y;
        first = !first;
    }
    else
    {
        first = !first;
        glClear(GL_COLOR_BUFFER_BIT);
        glBegin(GL_POLYGON);
            glVertex2i(xx,yy);
            glVertex2i(xx,hh-y);
            glVertex2i(x,hh-y);
            glVertex2i(x,yy);
        glEnd();
    }
}
}
```

This code has a few subtleties. The most important one is the necessity of inverting the *y* value returned by the mouse callback. This inversion is required because the values returned to the mouse callback are given in screen coordinates whose origin is at the upper-left corner. The values used for the clipping window and specification of the geometry are in world coordinates, where the origin is at the lower-right corner. However, to carry out the inversion, we need the height of the screen window, a value that can change during the execution of the program if the user resizes the window. We handle this problem by using the global value of the window height (hh), which is updated automatically by the reshape callback.

The vertices specified in our example use the integer form of glVertex2i(). The values used for the locations of the vertices are those obtained from the mouse callback and thus are integers. A little thought will show that the clipping window that we defined in the reshape callback is too small. A better choice for this example would be to use the reshape callback to have the clipping window match the screen window, as in the code

```
int ww, hh; /* globals for viewport height and width */

void myReshape(GLsizei w, GLsizei h)
{
```

```
glMatrixMode(GL_PROJECTION);
glLoadIdentity();
gluOrtho2D(0.0, (GLfloat) w, 0.0,(GLfloat) h);
glMatrixMode(GL_MODELVIEW);
glViewport(0,0,w,h);
ww = w;
hh = h;
}
```

As we have developed the code, no display callback is used; all the work is done in the mouse callback. As a practical matter, GLUT insists that every program have a display callback. We could just put in the dummy display callback:

```
void mydisplay() {}
```

But, although this display callback will work, many application programmers would object to this style.

A more general strategy is to place drawing functions in the display callback and use the other callbacks for state changes. Although in many situations, we may not always be able to do this, we can do it easily for this example through the following two callbacks:

```
GLint x1, y1, x2, y2;
int hh;

void mymouse(int x, int y, int button, int state)
{
    static bool first = true;
    int x1, yy;
    if(state == GLUT_DOWN && button == GLUT_LEFT_BUTTON)
        exit();
    if(state == GLUT_DOWN && button == GLUT_RIGHT_BUTTON)
    {
        if (first)
        {
            x1 = x;
            y1 = hh - y;
            first = !first;
        }
        else
        {
            first = !first;
            x2 = x;
            y2 = hh - y;
        }
        glutPostRedisplay();
    }
}
```

```
void mydisplay()
{
    glClear(GL_COLOR_BUFFER_BIT);
    glBegin(GL_POLYGON);
        glVertex2i(x1, y1);
        glVertex2i(x1, hh - y2);
        glVertex2i(x2, hh - y2);
        glVertex2i(x2, y1);
    glEnd();
}
```

3.7 Mouse Motion

We also generate events when the mouse moves, whether or not the mouse buttons are pressed. If the mouse moves with a button pressed, we call this event a **move event**. If the mouse is moved without a button pressed, a **passive motion event** is generated. We also generate an **entry event** whenever the mouse enters or leaves the window. The motion callback function is specified by glutMotionFunc() and the passive motion callback by glutPassiveMotionFunc(). Both return the position of the mouse.

```
void glutMotionFunc(void (*f) (int x, int y))
void glutPassiveMotionFunc(void (*f) (int x, int y))
```

Specify the motion and passive motion callback functions. The position of the mouse (x, y) is returned to the callback.

Events occur whenever the mouse moves a small system-dependent amount. One use of the motion callback is in programs that can draw curves while the mouse is moved with a button clicked. As long as a button is held down, we can extend a polyline through a line in the callback of the form

```
void mymotion(int x, int y)
{
.
.
.
    if(first_time_called) glBegin(GL_LINE_STRIP);
    glVertex2f(sx* (GLfloat) x, sy * (GLfloat) (h - y));
.
.
.
}
```

In this code, the mouse position is scaled, and the vertical mouse coordinate must be inverted to be in OpenGL's coordinate system. Note also that a `glEnd()` must be generated when the mouse button is released.

The mouse generates an entry event whenever it leaves the OpenGL window.

```
void glutEntryFunc(void (*f) (int state))
```

Specifies the entry callback function. The returned state is either GLUT_ENTERED or GLUT_LEFT.

3.8 Menus

Interactive programs are characterized by far more elaborate types of interactions than the simple uses of the mouse and the keyboard we have discussed so far. All modern windowing systems support a set of **widgets**, which are special types of windows with which the user can interact. Typical widget sets include menus, buttons, slide bars, and dialog boxes. Because GLUT is simple and portable, it provides limited capabilities. Most widgets are provided by system-specific toolkits. Of course, as widgets are graphical objects, we could use OpenGL to create any particular type of widget.

GLUT does provide one important widget: menus. Usually, these menus are implemented as pop-up menus that appear when a particular mouse button is held down. Defining a menu requires three steps. First, we must decide what entries are in the menu, that is, what strings will be displayed in each row of a menu. Second, we must tie specific actions to the rows. Third, we must tie each menu to a mouse button. The menu mechanism works just like other callbacks. When a user releases the mouse button that popped up the menu, an identifier for the row on which the mouse was located is passed to the menu callback function.

Menus are usually created either in `main()` or in an initialization function called from `main()`. Top-level menus are created by `glutCreateMenu()`, which is given the name of the callback function for the menu and returns an integer identifier for the menu.

```
int glutCreateMenu(void (* f) (int value))
```

Creates a top-level menu that uses the callback `f()`, which is passed an integer `value` for the menu entry. A unique identifier is returned for the menu created.

The menu created becomes the current menu. The current menu can be changed by glutSetMenu().

```
void glutSetMenu(int id)
```

Sets the current menu to the menu with identifier id.

Entries are added into the current menu by glutAddMenuEntry(). Each entry consists of two parts: a string displayed for the entry and a value returned when that entry is selected.

```
void glutAddMenuEntry(char *name, int value)
```

Adds an entry with name displayed to the current menu; value is returned to the menu callback.

Finally, we can attach the menu to a mouse button by glutAttachMenu().

```
void glutAttachMenu(int button)
```

Attaches the current menu to the specified mouse button (GLUT_RIGHT_BUTTON, GLUT_MIDDLE_BUTTON, or GLUT_LEFT_BUTTON).

Suppose that we want to use the right mouse button to pop up a menu that will have two entries: one to clear the screen and the other to end the program. We set up our menu in init() or in main() by

```
glutCreateMenu(mymenu);
glutAddMenuEntry("Clear Screen", 1);
glutAddMenuEntry("Exit", 2);
glutAttachMenu(GLUT_RIGHT_BUTTON);
```

Note that with only one menu, we do not need its identifier. Now we write the menu callback function mymenu():

```
void mymenu(int value)
{
    if(value == 1) glClear();
    if(value == 2) exit(0);
}
```

We can also add submenus to a menu. A submenu will have a name that appears as an entry in its parent menu. When the user moves the mouse to this entry, the submenu pops up. We add an entry for a submenu by glutAddSubMenu().

```
void glutAddSubMenu(char *name, int menu)
```

Adds a submenu entry name as the next entry in the current menu. The value of menu is the ID of the submenu returned when the submenu was created.

We create the submenu just as we do the main menu but must do so first so we can pass the identifier of the menu to glutAddSubMenu().

3.9 The NULL Callback

Callback functions can be redefined during execution by simply naming a new callback function in the appropriate function. At times, we want to simply eliminate a callback. For example, suppose that at some point in a program, we no longer want an idle callback defined. We can accomplish this by passing NULL as the name of the new callback function:

```
glutIdleFunc(NULL);
```

3.10 Subwindows and Multiple Windows

In many applications, both interactive and noninteractive, we want to use multiple windows. In a CAD application, for example, we might want one window for creating objects, another for instructions, and perhaps a third for warning messages. We might want windows to be created and destroyed during the execution of our program. The function glutCreateWindow(), which we introduced in the previous chapter, returns an integer identifier for each window that we create. The function glutDestroyWindow() allows us to get rid of windows.

```
int glutCreateWindow(char *name)
```

Creates a top-level window name wand that returns an identifier for it.

```
void glutDestroyWindow(int id)
```

Destroys the top-level window id.

When a window is created, it becomes the current window. Normally, primitives are rendered to the current window. We can change this window by glutSetWindow().

---

void glutSetWindow(int id)

Sets the current window to the window with identifier id.

Each window can have its own properties, referred to as its **context**. Thus, if we precede the creation of a window by a glutInitDisplayMode(properties), the window that we create will have the specified properties. We can also use the control functions, such as glutInitWindowSize(), to affect the current window. Thus, we can have multiple windows, each with the specific properties needed by the application.

We can also create subwindows of any window, including both top-level windows and subwindows. Subwindows can have their own context. Each is defined to be a subrectangle of its parent through the function glutCreateSubWindow().

---

int glutCreateSubWindow(int parent, int x, int y, int width,
    int height)

Creates a subwindow of parent and returns its ID. The subwindow has its origin at (x, y) and has size width by height in pixels.

When it is created, the subwindow becomes the current window.

3.11 Example: single_double.c

Our next example illustrates many of the concepts just introduced. It demonstrates single and double buffering using a rotating cube. We will also be able to stop the rotation at will. Let's start with the main() function:

```
int singleb, doubleb; /* window ID */

int main(int argc, char** argv)
{

    glutInit(&argc,argv);

        /* create a single buffered window */
```

```
glutInitDisplayMode(GLUT_SINGLE | GLUT_RGB);
singleb = glutCreateWindow("single buffered");
myinit();
glutDisplayFunc(displays);
glutReshapeFunc(myReshape);
glutIdleFunc(spinDisplay);
glutMouseFunc(mouse);
glutKeyFunc(mykey);

        /* create a double buffered window */

glutInitDisplayMode(GLUT_DOUBLE | GLUT_RGB);
doubleb=glutCreateWindow("double buffered");
myinit();
glutDisplayFunc(displayd);
glutReshapeFunc(myReshape);
glutIdleFunc(spinDisplay);
glutMouseFunc(mouse);
glutCreateMenu(quit_menu);
glutAddMenuEntry("quit",1);
glutAttachMenu(GLUT_RIGHT_BUTTON);

        /* enter event loop */

glutMainLoop();

}
```

Note that each window has some callbacks defined for it. Although the two windows share some of the callbacks, either can be changed later independently of the other. The spinning cube can be defined as before, using the idle callback SpinDisplay() to spin it:

```
void displays()
{
    glClear(GL_COLOR_BUFFER_BIT);
    glBegin(GL_POLYGON):
        glVertex2f(cos(DEG_TO_RAD*theta),
            sin(DEG_TO_RAD *theta);
        glVertex2f(-sin(DEG_TO_RAD *theta),
            cos(DEG_TO_RAD *theta);
        glVertex2f(-cos(DEG_TO_RAD *theta),
            -sin(DEG_TO_RAD *theta);
        glVertex2f(sin(DEG_TO_RAD *theta),
            -cos(DEG_TO_RAD *theta);
    glEnd();
    glFlush();
}
```

```
void displayd()
{
    glClear(GL_COLOR_BUFFER_BIT);
    glBegin(GL_POLYGON):
        glVertex2f(cos(DEG_TO_RAD*theta),
            sin(DEG_TO_RAD*theta);
        glVertex2f(-sin(DEG_TO_RAD*theta),
            cos(DEG_TO_RAD*theta);
        glVertex2f(-cos(DEG_TO_RAD*theta),
            -sin(DEG_TO_RAD*theta);
        glVertex2f(sin(DEG_TO_RAD*theta),
            -cos(DEG_TO_RAD*theta);
    glEnd();
    glutSwapBuffers();
}

void spinDisplay(void)
{
            /* increment angle */

    theta += 2.0;
    if (theta >= 360.0) theta -= 360.0;

            /* draw single buffer window */

    glutSetWindow(singleb);
    glutPostRedisplay();

            /* draw double buffer window */

    glutSetWindow(doubleb);
    glutPostRedisplay();
}
```

The two windows share the mouse callback function. This function allows the user to stop the rotation in both windows by setting the idle function to NULL and to restore the spinning later. Although the two windows use the same callback, each maintains its own state. Thus, if we stop rotation in one window, we do not alter the state of the other window. To change the callback for the other window, we first must click the mouse in the other window.

```
void mouse(int btn, int state, int x, int y)
{
    if(btn == GLUT_LEFT_BUTTON && state == GLUT_DOWN)
    glutIdleFunc(spinDisplay);
    if(btn == GLUT_MIDDLE_BUTTON && state == GLUT_DOWN)
    glutIdleFunc(NULL);
}
```

The reshape callback is standard and sets up the clipping window.

```
void myReshape(int w, int h)
{
    glViewport(0, 0, w, h);
    glMatrixMode(GL_PROJECTION);
    glLoadIdentity();
    gluOrtho2D(-2.0, 2.0, -2.0, 2.0);
    glMatrixMode(GL_MODELVIEW);
    glLoadIdentity();
}
```

To illustrate two of the other callbacks, we use both a keyboard callback and a menu to end the program. However, each was assigned to only one of the two windows, so each can use a different method to exit.

```
void mykey(int key)
{
    if(key == 'Q' || key == 'q') exit(0);
}

void quit_menu(int id)
{
if(id == 1) exit(0);
}
```

3.12 Display Lists

The standard rendering mode in OpenGL is known as **immediate mode**. Primitives are passed through the OpenGL pipeline as soon as they are defined in the program. They are then no longer in the system; only their image is on the screen. When something changes and the screen needs to be redrawn, we have to regenerate the primitives, typically in the display callback, and pass them through the pipeline again. Depending on the complexity of the scene, this redisplay process can be very time consuming. It can be especially slow when the application program—the **client**—is on one side of a network and the renderer and the display—the **graphics server**—are on the other side. In this situation, all the primitives, whether or not they appear on the screen, must be sent over a slow connection before passing through the pipeline.

In **retained mode**, graphics, collections of primitives, and other information can be stored as objects on the server, thus avoiding costly transfers and regeneration problems. OpenGL's mechanism for defining such objects is through **display lists**. Display lists can be thought of as a type of graphics file in which we can place most OpenGL entities. We open a display list, give it a name, place things in it, and close it. Display lists store their contents in an internal format that makes for fast redisplay. When we form a display list, we are said to be **compiling** it. Display lists reside on the server and are executed by simple OpenGL calls.

Suppose that we want to create a display list with a red square in it. We create the list by glNewList(). We then define the square as usual and end the list with a glEndList().

```
#define RED_SQUARE 1
glNewList(RED_SQUARE, GL_COMPILE);
glPushAttrib(GL_CURRENT_BIT);
glColor3f(1.0, 0.0, 0.0);
glRectf(-1.0, -1.0, 1.0, 1.0);
glPopAttrib();
glEndList();
```

The flag GL_COMPILE causes OpenGL to place the display list on the server, but the display list is not displayed. If we also want it displayed when it is created, we use the flag GL_COMPILE_AND_EXCUTE. Note that we push and pop the current attributes, which include the present color. We must do this to prevent the state change from setting a new color and thus affecting anything we do subsequently. Often, we can prevent unforeseen side effects of state changes by starting a display list by pushing the matrices and the attributes at the beginning of the display list and popping them at the end.

void glNewList(GLuint name, GLenum mode)

Creates a new display list with an unsigned integer ID name. The value of mode (GL_COMPILE, GL_COMPILE_AND_EXECUTE) determines whether the list is placed on the server with or without being executed.

void glEndList()

Ends the definition of a display list.

We execute a display list through the function glCallList().

void glCallList(GLuint name)

Executes display list name.

Most OpenGL functions can be put into display lists. Of the ones that we have seen so far, only functions that return state variables, such as glGet*(), cannot be inside a display list. Display lists can be called from within other display lists, which is one method of creating hierarchical objects.

Display lists cannot be changed once they are created. If we wish to change the contents of a display list, we have to create a new one with the desired contents and to delete the present one by glDeleteLists().

---

void glDeleteLists(GLuint first, GLsizei number)

Deletes number display lists starting with first.

3.12.1 Multiple Display Lists

Usually, we work with more than a single list. We can execute multiple lists with the function glCallLists(). The identifiers of the display lists are counted relative to a list base, set by glListBase(), and are stored in an array.

---

void glListBase(GLuint offset)

Sets the offset used by glCallLists(). The default is 0.

void glCallLists(GLsizei num, GLenum type, GLvoid *lists)

Executes num display lists from the integers stored in the array lists of type. The present offset is added to each integer in lists to obtain the ID of the display list to be executed.

Often when working with multiple display lists, we need some unused IDs for new lists. The function glGenLists() lets us obtain a set of consecutive unused integers for defining new display lists.

GLuint glGenLists(GLsizei n)

Returns the first of n consecutive integer IDs available for new display lists.

3.12.2 Display Lists and Text

Text is often handled efficiently by using a display list for each character. Regardless of whether we are using a stroke or a bitmap font, the descriptions of the characters are on the server. To generate a character string on the display, we do one function call per character.

Suppose that we decide to use the GLUT bitmap proportional 10-point Times Roman font. We need 256 display lists, assuming that we generate display lists even for the nonprinting characters. We can get the required IDs by

```
base = glGenLists(256);
```

We can now set up the display lists.

```
for(i = 0; i < 256; i++)
{
    glNewList(base + i, GL_COMPILE);
    glutBitMapCharacter(GLUT_BITMAP_TIMES_ROMAN_10, i);
    glEndList();
}
```

Because we are using a GLUT bitmap font, the raster position is automatically moved to the right by the width of the character.

We next set the list base:

```
glListBase(base);
```

That lets us refer to each display list by its ASCII code. Now suppose that we have a character string

```
char *text;
```

We can draw it with the single function call

```
glCallLists((GLint) strlen(text), GL_BYTE, text);
```

Here, we have used the standard function `strlen()` to determine the length of the string, which is the number of display lists we must execute. The character string can then be regarded as an array of bytes, each of which is the number—its ASCII code—that has to be added to `base` to obtain the ID of the call list to be executed.

The example would have been essentially the same if we had used a stroke font, except that we would have then had to deal with the problem of moving to the right each time we drew a character. This problem can be dealt with best by using OpenGL transformations, which we introduce in Chapter 5.

3.13 **Picking and Selection Mode**

One operation fundamental to many interactive programs has yet to be discussed. **Picking** is the operation of locating an object on the screen. This operation presents a few difficulties for OpenGL. First, we must define what we mean by an object. One way is through display lists. But we can think of others. We could create a tag system that would give labels to groups of our primitives. A tricky issue is to define exactly what we mean by picking an object. Do we have to click the mouse *on* a primitive or just *close* to it? What do we do if objects overlap? We can come up with a number of, perhaps system-dependent, ways of handing such issues.

A more difficult issue is how to implement picking within the OpenGL pipeline. The problem for a pipeline system is that we cannot go backward directly from the position of the mouse to primitives that were rendered close to that point on the screen. OpenGL provides a somewhat complex process, called **selection mode**, to do picking at the cost of an extra rendering each time we pick. The basic idea of selection mode is that the objects in a scene can be rendered but not to the color buffer. As we render objects, OpenGL can keep track of which objects render to any chosen area by determining whether they are in a specified clipping volume that does not have to be the same as the clipping volume used to render into the color buffer.

A number of steps and functions are required to do picking. We shall examine each step and then put them together in a simple program. The function glRenderMode() lets us select one of three modes: normal rendering to the color buffer (GL_RENDER), selection mode (GL_SELECT), or feedback mode (GL_FEEDBACK). Feedback mode can be used to obtain a list of which primitives were rendered. We will not discuss this mode.

> GLint glRenderMode(GLenum mode)
>
> Chooses a render mode: normal (GL_RENDER), selection (GL_SELECTION), or feedback (GL_FEEDBACK). The return value can be used to determine the number of hits in selection mode or primitives in feedback mode.

When we enter selection mode and render a scene, each primitive that renders within the clipping volume generates a message, called a **hit**, which is stored in a buffer called the **name stack**. We use the function glSelectBuffer() to identify an array for the selection data. Four functions are available for initializing the name stack, for pushing and popping information on it, and for manipulating the top entry on the stack. The information that we produce is called the **hit list** and can be examined after the rendering to obtain the information needed for picking.

```
void glSelectBuffer(GLsizei n, GLunint *buff)
```

Specifies the array buff of size n in which to place selection data.

```
void glInitNames()
```

Initializes the name stack.

```
void glPushName (GLuint name)
```

Pushes name on the name stack.

```
void glPopName()
```

Pops the top name from the name stack.

```
void glLoadName(GLuint name)
```

Replaces the top of the name stack with name.

In general, each object that we wish to identify is a set of primitives to which we assign the same integer name. Before we render the object, we load its name onto the name stack. We cannot load a name onto an empty stack, so we usually enter an unused name onto the stack when we initialize it, through such code as

```
glInitNames();
glPushName(0);
```

We usually use the mouse callback to enter selection mode and leave selection mode before the end of the mouse callback. When we return to render mode, glRenderMode() returns the number of hits that have been processed. We then examine the hit list. We also change the clipping volume within the mouse callback so that we obtain hits in the desired region, usually an area that is close to the location of the mouse.

We can set the clipping volume in two ways. We could simply set the view volume through gluOrtho2D() or use other viewing functions. We would probably first want to save the present clipping volume with a glPushMatrix(). Then any primitive that fell within this new clipping volume would generate a hit regardless of where the mouse is located. This option works for selection, but when we pick, we want only those objects that render near the cursor.

Suppose that we want all the objects that render into a small user-defined rectangle centered at the cursor. The size of the rectangle is a measure of how sensitive we want our picking to be. This rectangle is a small part of the viewport. Given the viewport, the location of the cursor, the size of the rectangle, and the clipping window, we can find a new clipping window such that all the objects in the new clipping window render into the full viewport. Mathematically, this is an exercise in proportions and involves the inverse of the projection matrix. We can let OpenGL do this calculation for us through the GLU function gluPickMatrix(), which is applied before gluOrtho2D() when we are in selection mode.

```
void gluPickMatrix(GLdouble x, GLdouble y, GLdouble w,
    GLdouble h, GLint *vp)
```

Creates for picking a projection matrix that restricts drawing to a w × h area centered at (x, y) in window coordinates within the viewport vp.

Assuming that we have set up the viewing conditions for normal rendering during initialization or in the reshape callback, the mouse callback is of the form

```
void mouse(int button, int state, int x, int y)
{
    GLuint nameBuffer[SIZE]; /* define SIZE elsewhere */
    GLint hits;
    GLint viewport[4];
    If(button == GLUT_LEFT_BUTTON && state == GLUT_DOWN)
    {
            /* initialize the name stack */

        glInitNames();
        glPushName(0);
        glSelectBuffer(SIZE, nameBuffer);

            /* set up viewing for selection mode */

        glGetIntegerv(GL_VIEWPORT, viewport);
        glMatrixMode(GL_PROJECTION);

            /* save original viewing matrix */

        glPushMatrix();
        glLoadIdentity();
```

```
                    /* N x N pick area around cursor */
                    /* must invert mouse y to get in world coords */

            gluPickMatrix((GLdouble) x, (GLdouble)
                (viewport[3] - y), N, N, viewport);

                    /* same clipping window as in reshape callback */

            gluOrtho2D (xmin, xmax, ymin, ymax);

            draw_objects(GL_SELECT);
            glMatrixMode(GL_PROJECTION);

                    /* restore viewing matrix */

            glPopMatrix();
            glFlush();

                    /* return to normal render mode */

            hits = glRenderMode(GL_RENDER);

                    /* process hits from selection mode rendering */

            processHits(hits, nameBuff);

                    /* normal render */

            glutPostRedisplay();
        }
    }

void display()
{
    glClear(GL_COLOR_BUFFER_BIT);
    draw_objects(GL_RENDER);
    glFlush();
}
```

Note that we have to call the function that draws the objects directly rather than use glutPostRedisplay() twice in the mouse callback, because GLUT will do only one execution of the display callback each time through the event loop. Here is a simple function that draws two partially overlapping rectangles:

```
void drawObjects(GLenum mode)
{
    if(mode == GL_SELECT) glLoadName(1);
    glColor3f(1.0, 0.0, 0.0);
```

```
    glRectf(-0.5, -0.5, 1.0, 1.0);
    if(mode == GL_SELECT) glLoadName(2);
    glColor3f(0.0, 0.0, 1.0);
    glRectf(-1.0, -1.0, 0.5, 0.5);
}
```

Note that we need change only the top element on the name stack. If we had a hierarchical object, we could use glPushName() so that we could have multiple names on the stack for a given hit. For an object with multiple parts, all the parts that were close to the cursor would have their names placed in the same stack.

The final piece we need write is the function that examines the name stack. We will have it print out how many were placed in the stack for each left mouse click and the names of any objects that were picked.

The hit buffer contains one record for each hit. Thus, every object that is rendered near the mouse cursor will generate a record. If no names are on the hit list—no primitives were rendered near the mouse cursor—then the hit record has a 0. Otherwise, we find three types of information, all stored as integers. First is the number of names on the name stack when there was a hit. For our example, this number can be only 1. Next are two integers that give scaled minimum and maximum depths for the hit primitive. Since we are working in two dimensions, these values will not provide us with useful information. For three-dimensional applications, we can use these values to determine the front object that was picked. Third are entries in the name stack. For our example, we will find the identifier of either the red or the blue rectangle here (a 1 or a 2). The following function will print out this information:

```
void processHits (GLint hits, GLuint buffer[])
{
    unsigned int i, j;
    GLuint names, *ptr;

    printf ("hits = %d\n", hits);
    ptr = (GLuint *) buffer;

     /* Loop over number of hits */

    for (i = 0; i < hits; i++)
      {
          names = *ptr;

              /*skip over number of names and depths */

        ptr += 3;

              /* check each name in record */
```

```
      for (j = 0; j < names; j++)
        {
        if(*ptr==1) printf ("red rectangle\n");
        else printf ("blue rectangle\n");

            /* go to next hit record */

        ptr++;
      }
    }
  }
```

Chapter 4

Basic Three-Dimensional Programming

This chapter introduces three-dimensional OpenGL programs in a simple way. We use an orthogonal camera to view objects that are defined in a similar manner to our two-dimensional programs. We use the same primitives that we used in two dimensions and introduce some predefined objects contained in the GLU and GLUT libraries. Finally, we discuss perspective views.

4.1 Cameras and Objects

The basic paradigm used to conceptualize image formation by three-dimensional graphics systems is known as the **synthetic-camera model**. With this model, we emulate what is done by most real-world imaging systems, such as cameras and the human visual system. The synthetic-camera model recognizes that to form an image, we need two independent entities: a set of objects and a viewer of these objects. Each can be specified independently of the other.

The image produced from a set of three-dimensional objects and a camera, which is itself a three-dimensional object, is two dimensional. This process is called **projection** and is carried out by OpenGL. Application programs need specify only the camera and the objects. Figure 4.1 shows this process. Lines called **projectors** are drawn from each point on an image and pass through the center of the lens on the camera, the **center of projection**. The place where a projector from a point on an object passes through the film plane is where the image of that point is located. Figure 4.2 is a slightly reorganized view of the information in Figure 4.1. The primary difference is that the film plane has been moved in front of the camera. In computer graphics, the image on the "film plane," or **projection plane**, of the synthetic camera is what we see on the screen. Equivalently, we can

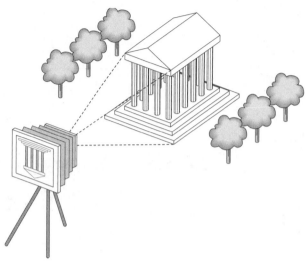

Figure 4.1 Projection

think of the film plane in Figure 4.2 as being ruled into pixel-sized pieces, each pixel corresponding to one or more projectors. The projection process can be described mathematically, but we need not do so to write an OpenGL program in three dimensions. We need only specify the objects and the camera. OpenGL will carry out the projection within its implementation.

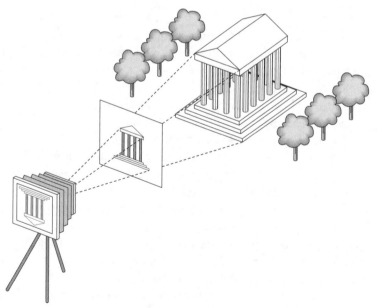

Figure 4.2 Projection with projection plane moved in front of the camera

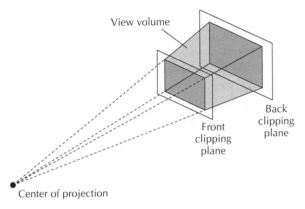

Figure 4.3 Viewing frustum

Three-dimensional objects can be specified in OpenGL through three-dimensional versions of `glVertex*()`, such as `glVertex3f(x, y, z)` and `glVertex3fv(array)`. In this chapter, we specify the points directly. In the next chapter, we use OpenGL's transformations to create more complex objects.

Specifying a camera is not as straightforward as specifying objects. If we think of a real camera, we can set its position and then rotate it in three independent directions. Thus, we need six parameters, or **degrees of freedom**, for the camera position alone. We also have to specify a lens—normal, wide angle, or telephoto—and different cameras use different sizes of film. OpenGL allows us to specify all these parameters for our virtual camera. We shall start, however, with a very simple camera, the one for which our two-dimensional camera is a special case. This simple camera will produce **orthographic projections**, the simplest type of projection.

The projection process has two parts. The first is deciding what is visible. OpenGL's viewing functions define a **viewing**, or **clipping**, **volume** which is analogous to the volume that a real camera would see through its lens. Objects that lie outside this volume do not appear in the image and are said to be **clipped** out of the scene. In the real world, we see only objects that are in front of the camera and even those that can be infinitely far away, as long as they are in front. In computer graphics, we add both a near and a far clipping plane, as in Figure 4.3, so that we see only the objects in a finite volume. Thus, the clipping volume is a truncated pyramid called a **frustum**. The second part of projection is determining where the image of a particular location on the object within the clipping volume lies on the film.

4.2 **Orthographic Projections in OpenGL**

We can think of an orthographic projection as constructing the type of image that we would see with a long telephoto lens. The image would look somewhat flat but would preserve distances and shapes. In terms of the synthetic camera of Figure 4.2, we obtain an orthographic projection when we move the camera an infinite distance from the objects but leave the projection plane near the objects. Moving the camera to infinity makes all the projectors parallel, and the center of projection can be replaced by a **direction of projection**. The viewing frustum becomes a right parallelepiped—a rectangular box—as shown in Figure 4.4.

The fundamental orthographic viewing function is glOrtho(), which we can use to set up the proper viewing matrix.

```
void glOrtho(GLdouble left, GLdouble  right, GLdouble bottom,
     GLdouble top, GLdouble near, GLdouble far)
```

Sets up an orthographic projection matrix and defines a viewing volume that is a right parallelepiped. The distances are measured *from the camera,* so we must have right > left, top > bottom, and far > near.

The viewing volume is shown in Figure 4.4. Note that even though the camera is located at the origin, we can have the near plane or both the near and far planes behind the camera. Such will not be the case for other views.

Viewing with an orthographic camera is particularly simple. Suppose that we want to alter the projection matrix. The glOrtho() function changes the present matrix incrementally, so we usually start by loading an identity matrix. Hence, the code for a cubic clipping volume of side length 2, centered at the origin, is

```
glMatrixMode(GL_PROJECTION):
glLoadIdentity();
glOrtho(-1.0, 1.0, -1.0, 1.0, -1.0, 1.0);
```

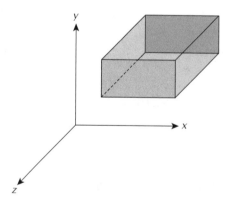

Figure 4.4 Orthographic viewing volume

4.3 Viewing a Cube

We can write a simple three-dimensional program analogous to our first two-dimensional program by defining an object within a display callback. We discuss modeling objects a bit later. For now, we can use an object supplied by GLUT, a wireframe cube. The wireframe cube is composed of line segments. The solid cube is built from polygons. GLUT also has spheres, cones, tori, regular polyhedra—dodecahedra, octahedra, tetrahedra, icosahedra—and a famous graphics object known as the Utah teapot. We examine these actions at the end of this chapter.

```
void glutWireCube(GLdouble size)
void glutSolidCube(GLdouble size)
```

Generates wire frame and solid cubes centered at the origin with sides of length size aligned with the coordinate axes.

Thus, we can display the cube by using the display callback for a double-buffered display:

```
void display()
{
    glClear(GL_COLOR_BUFFER_BIT);
    glutWireCube(0.5);
    glutSwapBuffers();
}
```

4.4 Locating the Camera

The problem with our program is that the camera is pointed at one face of the cube and we will see only that face. If we want to see the other faces of the cube so as to see more of its three-dimensional structure, we have to move either the camera or the object. It turns out that in OpenGL, these operations are the same. Moving an object relative to a fixed camera and moving a camera relative to a fixed object can produce the same image. In computer graphics, the difference between these views is less real than in the real world, in which walking around the side of a building to see the other side and asking someone to rotate the building are obviously different. The mathematical equivalence of these two approaches is implemented through the model-view matrix, whose name expresses this equivalence.

Given this point of view, it would seem to make sense to rotate the cube and perhaps move it away from the origin. We could do this in two ways. We could compute new locations for the vertices of the cube. However, since we are using the cube from GLUT, we do not have direct access to these vertices. The second approach would be to use transformations. We could then rotate the cube and then translate it to the desired new location. However, we have yet to discuss transformations, and computing the parameters for a desired view can be tricky. OpenGL provides a helpful GLU library function, `gluLookAt()`, that provides a simple user interface for many viewing situations.

Suppose that we have some objects whose locations we know. To obtain a desired view, we can position and orient the camera within the world coordinate system. We can decide on a position, called the **eye point**, for the camera and decide where to aim it to by specifying a point at which it is pointing: the **at point**. This situation is shown in Figure 4.5. Note that the two points do not fully fix the camera, because we can still rotate it about the line between the eye and at points and not violate the specifications. We need a third input, the direction we want to consider as up in the image: the **up vector**. Technically, OpenGL will project this vector onto the back of the virtual camera to obtain the up direction. No problem should exist, as long as the vector between the eye and at points is not parallel to the up vector. A simple choice of the up vector is often $(0, 1, 0)$ or the y direction in world coordinates.

```
void gluLookAt( GLdouble eyex, GLdouble eyey, GLdouble eyez,
     GLdouble atx, GLdouble aty, GLdouble atz, GLdouble upx,
     GLdouble upy, GLdouble upz)
```

Determines a matrix that can be used to position and orient the camera using a camera location (the **eye** point), a point (the **at** point) to aim it, and the desired **up** direction.

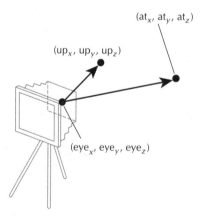

Figure 4.5 Specifying the camera with the `at` vector

The matrix determined by `gluLookAt()` is applied to the existing matrix. Hence, we must first make sure that we are in the desired matrix mode, usually the model-view mode, and have initialized this matrix.

Suppose that we want an isometric view of the cube, which is centered at the origin and aligned with the axes in world coordinates. An isometric view (Figure 4.6) is symmetric with respect to the vertices of the cube. A simple way to obtain such a view is to place the camera on a line passing through the origin and the point $(1, 1, 1)$. Thus, we can set up our viewing by the OpenGL code

```
glMatrixMode(GL_MODELVIEW);
glLoadIdentity();
gluLookAt(1.0, 1.0, 1.0, 0.0, 0.0, 0.0, 0.0, 1.0, 0.0);
```

The implementation of the function `gluLookat()` consists of the required translations and rotations to set up the view.

Putting everything together, we get a minimal three-dimensional program, as follows:

```
#include <GL/glut.h>

void display()
{
    glClear(GL_COLOR_BUFFER_BIT);
    glMatrixMode(GL_MODELVIEW);
    glLoadIdentity();
    gluLookAt(1.0, 1.0, 1.0, 0.0, 0.0, 0.0, 0.0, 1.0, 0.0);
    glutWireCube(0.5);
    glutSwapBuffers();
}

void reshape(int w, int h)
{
    glViewPort(0, 0, w, h)
    glMatrixMode(GL_PROJECTION):
```

Figure 4.6 Isometric image of a cube

```
        glLoadIdentity();
        glOrtho(-4.0, 4.0, -4.0, 4.0, -4.0, 4.0);
}

void init()
{
    glClearColor (0.0, 0.0, 0.0, 0.0);
    glColor3f(1.0, 1.0, 1.0);
}

int main(int argc, char** argv)
{
    glutInit(&argc,argv);
    glutInitDisplayMode(GLUT_DOUBLE | GLUT_RGB);
    glutInitWindowSize(500,500);
    glutInitWindowPosition(0,0);
    glutCreateWindow("cube");
    glutReshape(reshape);
    glutDisplayFunc(display);
    init();
    glutMainLoop();
}
```

Note that we are using the default colors, so we could have left out the color functions in init(). The program is not interactive, so double buffering is not required, and we could have located the camera in init(). However, our choices are probably better, as we want to expand this structure to interactive three-dimensional applications.

Although we could have obtained the same isometric view of the cube by placing the eye point anywhere along the line from the origin through the point (1, 1, 1), if we changed the eye point, we would have also had to change the near and far distances in glOrtho(), because these distances are measured *from the camera*.

 The clipping volume set in glOrtho() is measured from the camera. Thus, the near distance must be less than the far distance.

4.5 Building Objects

Let's redo the example, building our own cube. This time, we will use polygons and give a different color to each face. We will center the cube at the origin and let it have sides of length 2. We could start with code something like this

```
cube()
{
    glColor3f(1.0, 0.0, 0.0);
```

```
glBegin(GL_POLYGON);
    glVertex3f(-1.0, -1.0, -1.0);
    glVertex3f(-1.0, 1.0, -1.0);
    glVertex3f(-1.0, 1.0, 1.0);
    glVertex3f(-1.0, -1.0, 1.0);
glEnd();

/* the other faces   */
.
.
.

}

void display()
{
    glClear(COLOR_BUFFER_BIT);
    cube();
}
```

Note that because we will be filling the polygons, we should be sure to specify the vertices in a counterclockwise manner when each face is viewed from the outside so that we will have the correct interpretation of its orientation: front or back facing.

This code requires 42 function calls within cube() to define the cube. We could do slightly better if we used the type GL_QUADS rather than GL_POLYGON in the first glBegin(). We could then eliminate all subsequent uses of glBegin() and omit all the calls to glEnd() except the last, because each consecutive group of four vertices would determine a quad.

4.5.1 Using Arrays

We can obtain a better structure for the code by putting the colors and the vertices in arrays. This structure will not only make the code clearer but will also prove more flexible for interactive applications.

We number the vertices as in Figure 4.7. The necessary arrays are then

```
GLfloat vertices[][3] = {{-1.0, - 1.0, 1.0}, {-1.0, 1.0, 1.0},
    {1.0, 1.0, 1.0}, {1.0, -1.0, 1.0}, {-1.0,- 1.0, -1.0},
    {-1.0, 1.0, -1.0}, {1.0, 1.0, -1.0}, {1.0, -1.0, -1.0}};

GLfloat colors[][3] = {1.0, 0.0, 0.0}, {0.0, 1.0, 1.0},
    {1.0, 1.0, 0.0}, {0.0, 1.0, 0.0}, {0.0, 0.0, 1.0},
    {1.0, 0.0, 1.0}};
```

We could use the previous code, simply substituting glColor3fv() for glColor3f() and glVertex3fv() for glVertex3f(), but that would not be much

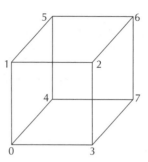

Figure 4.7 Numbering of cube vertices

of a gain. Instead, we add a simple function that draws one polygon in terms of the indices of the vertices.

```
void polygon(int a, int b, int c , int d)
{
    glColor3fv(colors[a]);
    glBegin(GL_POLYGON);
        glVertex3fv(vertices[a]);
        glVertex3fv(vertices[b]);
        glVertex3fv(vertices[c]);
        glVertex3fv(vertices[d]);
    glEnd();
}
```

This function assigns a color to the polygon from the first index, but we could change this choice easily. We can now replace the cube function by

```
void cube()
{
    polygon(0, 3, 2, 1);
    polygon(2, 3, 7, 6);
    polygon(3, 0, 4, 7);
    polygon(1, 2, 6, 5);
    polygon(4, 5, 6, 7);
    polygon(5, 4, 0, 1);
}
```

Although the execution of this code does not save us any function calls, it is a lot cleaner than our previous example. One of its advantages is that the location of each vertex appears only once. In an interactive program, where vertices might be changed by the user during program execution, making changes to vertices is particularly simple.

4.5.2 Vertex Arrays

OpenGL provides **vertex arrays**, a facility that extends the use of arrays in a way that avoids most of the function calls to draw the cube. The main idea is that information stored in arrays can be stored on the clients, or application programs, and accessed by a single function call. We can store the information in a way that retains the structuring that we defined earlier, such as the order in which vertices are called to draw the cube.

Although the facility is called vertex arrays, OpenGL provides support for six types of arrays: vertex, color, color index, normal, texture coordinate, and edge flag. We shall see some of the other types later. Using vertex arrays requires three steps. First, as with other OpenGL features, we must enable their functionality. Second, we must specify the format of the arrays. These two steps are usually part of the initialization phase of our programs. Third, we use the arrays to render the scene.

In our example, we need only color and vertex arrays. We enable them by

```
glEnableClientState(GL_COLOR_ARRAY);
glEnableClientState(GL_VERTEX_ARRAY);
```

The form of the arrays is given by

```
glVertexPointer(3, GL_FLOAT, 0, vertices);
glColorPointer(3, GL_FLOAT, 0, colors);
```

```
void glEnableClientState(GLenum array)
void glDisableClientState(GLenum array)
```

Enables and disables arrays of types GL_VERTEX_ARRAY, GL_COLOR_ARRAY, GL_INDEX_ARRAY, GL_NORMAL_ARRAY, GL_TEXTURE_COORD_ARRAY, or GL_EDGE_FLAG_ARRAY.

```
void glVertexPointer(GLint dim, GLenum type, GLsizei stride,
    GLvoid *array)
void glColorPointer(GLint dim, GLenum type, GLsizei stride,
    GLvoid *array)
```

Provides the information on arrays. The data are in array, dim is the dimension of the data (2,3, or 4), type denotes how the data are stored (GL_SHORT, GL_INT, GL_FLOAT, or GL_DOUBLE), and stride is the number of bytes between consecutive data values (0 means that the data are packed in the array).

The first value (3) denotes three-dimensional data. The second and third parameters indicate that the data are floats packed in the array given by the fourth paramater.

We need a new array that stores the indices in the order in which we want to use them. The following array contains the necessary information:

```
GLubyte cubeIndices[]={0, 3, 2, 1, 2, 3, 7, 6, 0, 4, 7, 3, 1, 2,
    6, 5, 4, 5, 6, 7, 0, 1, 5, 4};
```

Now we can draw the cube through the function glDrawElements().

```
void glDrawElements(GLenum mode, GLsizei n, GLenum type,
    void *indices)
```

Draws elements of type mode using n indices from the array indices for each. The array is of type (GL_UNSIGNED_BYTE, GL_UNSIGNED_SHORT, or GL_UNSIGNED_INT).

If we render each face individually, we can use the loop

```
for(i = 0; i < 6; i++) glDrawElements(GL_POLYGON, 4,
    GL_UNSIGNED_BYTE, cubeIndices);
```

However, recall that when we use the type GL_QUADS, each successive group of four vertices determines a new quad. Thus, a single function call suffices:

```
glDrawElements(GL_QUADS,24,GL_UNSIGNED_BYTE, cubeIndices);
```

But a subtle problem occurs here. When we execute glDrawElements(), all the enable arrays are rendered. Thus, the rendering is equivalent to what we would see from code of the form

```
glColor3fv(color[cubeIndices[0]]);
gl Vertex3fv(vertex[cubeIndices[0]]);
glColor3fv[color[cubeIndices[1]]);
glVertex3fv[vertex[cubeIndices[1]]);
/* etc */
```

Thus, the code is as if there were a color change before each vertex. We avoided one potential problem by making sure that we had the same number of colors as vertices. But we saw in Chapter 2 that the default shading model is smooth. If we assign a different color before each vertex, OpenGL will, by default, interpolate these vertex colors across the face of each polygon. We can avoid this problem by requesting flat shading:

```
glShadeModel(GL_FLAT);
```

Now, although the color array will be used at each vertex, only the first color for each polygon will be used in the rendering. Thus, each time we render the cube by using vertex arrays, we need make but a single function call, which is a dramatic improvement from our original 42 function calls.

We could have also used display lists to reduce the overhead of drawing the cube. If we put the entire cube in one display list, we could have done a single `glCallList()`. Which form we use will depend on the particular requirements of the application.

4.6 Hidden-Surface Removal

Our next problem is how to make sure that surfaces that a viewer would not see are not visible in the rendering image. In Chapter 2, we saw a solution for a special case of this **hidden-surface-removal** problem, namely, that we could cull the back-facing polygons by enabling culling and saying that we want the back faces culled.

```
glEnable(GL_CULL_FACE);
glCullFace(GL_BACK);
```

However, this tactic works only for convex objects. Although the cube is convex, we need a more general approach.

Thus far, we have been working with polygons that are rendered as opaque or solid. In the real world, a viewer of a scene composed of such objects would not see the parts of any polygons that were behind any other polygons. In some situations, such as with convex objects, we can simply not render back-facing polygons. We can also think about stategies based on the painter's algorithm, which says that if we can sort the polygons in terms of the distance from the camera, we can render them back to front, with the front polygons hiding the ones farther back. Aside from issues of efficiency and establishing under what circumstance such an approach will always work, the problem is that this type of approach cannot work with a pipeline renderer. Polygons and other primitives can be generated in an arbitrary order by an application program. With immediate-mode rendering, the default in OpenGL, each polygon is sent down the rendering pipeline as soon as it is defined, and thus our method for doing hidden-surface removal must be independent of this order.

The method used by OpenGL for hidden-surface removal is called the **z-buffer algorithm**. It is based on using some extra storage to store depth information about the polygons the renderer has seen during the rendering process. This extra storage is called the **z** or **depth buffer**. Although users need not know the details of the algorithm, they must enable it and clear the depth buffer before the beginning of the process. Because these operations have to be within the user program, this is the only case in which a user needs to know which algorithm is used in the rendering process. In contrast, for such operations as drawing lines or filling polygons, the user does not need to know anything about the particular algorithms used by the implementation.

In the initialization, we have to request a depth buffer, so a typical `glutInitDisplayMode()` now looks like this:

```
glutInitDisplayMode(GLUT_RGB | GLUT_DOUBLE | GLUT_DEPTH);
```

We have to enable depth buffering by

```
glEnable(GL_DEPTH_TEST);
```

Finally, we usually clear the depth buffer when we clear the color buffer in the display callback.

```
glClear(GL_COLOR_BUFFER_BIT | GL_DEPTH_BUFFER_BIT);
```

For most programs, that's all we need do. For more complex situations, such as when we use translucent materials, we will need a few more functions to give us finer control over the depth buffer, but we need not worry about these issues here.

4.7 GLU and GLUT Objects

We can construct our own objects from the simple set of primitives. Later, we will introduce curves and surfaces so we can escape from the flat world of lines and polygons. In many situations, however, we want a slightly more sophisticated set of objects without introducing the heavy machinery required to deal with curves and surfaces. Of particular importance in many applications are **quadrics**: ellipsoids, including spheres; cones; and cylinders. Both GLUT and GLU provide some of these objects. What they both do is provide polygonal approximations to these objects and let the user determine how many polygons should be used. However, the user can access each object with a single function call, thus avoiding the need to build the objects within the application program.

4.7.1 GLU Quadrics

GLU provides three types of quadrics: spheres, cylinders, and disks. These primitives are stored in a more complex way than the simple primitives that we have seen thus far. In particular, we can create these objects with a desired drawing style, with different styles of normals—which we will use later for lighting calculations—and with texture coordinates, which we will also discuss later. Because they require more complex data structures than do the simple primitives, these objects require a little more effort to define. All can be created and deleted through gluNewQuadric() and gluDeleteQuadric(). Creation returns a pointer to the object, which we can use to enter information into its data structure.

```
GLUquadricObj* gluNewQuadric()
```

Creates a new quadric object and returns a pointer to it.

```
void gluDeleteQuadric(GLUquadricObj *obj)
```

Deletes quadric obj.

We can render a quadric object in four ways: displaying points for the vertices of the polygons used to approximate the quadric, displaying the edges of the polygons, filling the polygons, or in **silhouette mode**, which draws lines between vertices except those between coplanar polygons. These styles are set by gluQuadricDrawStyle().

```
void gluQuadricDrawStyle(GLUquadricObj *obj, GLenum style)
```

Sets the drawing style (GLU_POINT, GLU_LINE, GLU_FILL, or GLU_SILHOUETTE) for quadric object obj.

We can have OpenGL generate the normals for shading by gluQuadricNormals() and the texture coordinates by gluQuadricTexture().

```
void gluQuadricNormals(GLUquadricObj *obj, GLenum mode)
```

Specifies the normal mode for quadric object obj: no normals (GLU_NONE), which is the default; one normal per polygon (GLU_FLAT); or one normal per vertex (GL_SMOOTH).

```
void gluQuadricTexture(GLUquadricObj *obj, GLboolean mode)
```

Specifies whether quadric object `obj` should have texture coordinates generated. The default is `GL_FALSE` for no texture coordinates.

Now we can set which object we would like the quadric to be by using one of the functions `gluSphere()`, `gluCylinder()`, `gluDisk()`, or `gluPartialDisk()`. These objects are shown in Figure 4.8, rendered with lines.

Spheres are approximated, using lines of longitude and latitude to create the approximating polygons. We can use OpenGL transformations to move the sphere, to rotate it, or to reshape it into an ellipsoid.

```
void gluSphere(GLUquadricObj *obj, GLdouble radius, GLint
     slices, GLint stacks)
```

Renders quadric object `obj` as a sphere centered at the origin with the given `radius`. The sphere is approximated with polygons, using `slices` lines of longitude and `stacks` lines of latitude.

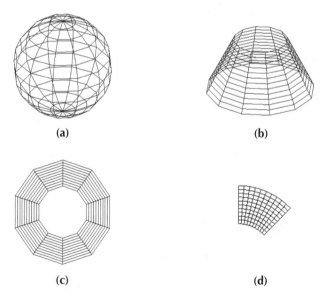

(a)   (b)

(c)   (d)

Figure 4.8 GLU quadrics, (a) sphere, (b) cylinder, (c) disk, and (d) partial disk

The cylinder is aligned with the *z*-axis. Its base is always in the plane $z = 0$, and its height, top radius, and bottom radius are set by `gluCylinder()`. The approximating polygons are determined by the number of stacks we want in *z* and how many slices we want going around it. Just as with the sphere, we can move, orient, or scale it with OpenGL transformations.

```
void gluCylinder(GLUquadricObj *obj, GLdouble base, GLdouble
    top, GLdouble height, GLdouble slices, GLdouble stacks)
```

Renders quadric object `obj` as a centered cylinder of `height` aligned with the *z*-axis whose base is in the plane $z = 0$. The cylinder has the specified `base` and `top` radii. The polygons are determined by using `stacks` lines in the *z* direction and `slices` lines around the cylinder.

Disks are flat and have a hole in the center. They are created in the plane $z = 0$. Disks defined by the radii of the inner and outer circles, are formed from concentric rings that are sliced radially like a pie. Partial disks have a wedge removed. The wedge is specified by the angle at which it starts and how many degrees are in the wedge. Angles are measured from the positive *y*-axis.

```
void gluDisk(GLUquadricObj* obj, GLdouble inner, GLdouble
    outer, GLint slices, GLint rings)
```

Defines a disk in the plane $z = 0$ by its `inner` and `outer` radii. The polygons are formed from concentric `rings` and `slices` around the center.

```
void gluPartialDisk(GLUquadricObj* obj, GLdouble inner,
    GLdouble outer, GLint slices, GLint rings, GLdouble
    start, GLdouble angle)
```

Defines a disk with a wedge of `angle` degrees removed, starting at `start`.

A typical sequence to create a sphere might look like

```
GLUquadricObj mySphere;
mySphere = gluNewQuadric();
gluQuadricDrawStyle(mySphere, GLU_LINE);
```

We could create the sphere in `init()` or `main()`. Now we could draw the sphere of radius 1.0 with 12 divisions for both longitude and latitude in the display callback by

```
gluSphere(mySphere, 1.0, 12, 12);
```

4.7.2 GLUT Objects

GLUT adds a few more objects. These functions generate normals automatically, and all but the teapot do not generate texture coordinates. Rather than attach the rendering style to the object, each type of object has a function that generates it as a wire frame and a second that generates it with filled polygons. In addition to the cube, which we have already seen, are a sphere, a cone, a torus, some regular polyhedra, and the Utah teapot. The wire cone and the wire torus are shown in Figure 4.9, the regular wire polyhedra in Figure 4.10, and the wire teapot in Figure 4.11.

```
void glutWireSphere(GLdouble radius, GLint slices, GLint stacks)
void glutSolidSphere(GLdouble radius, GLint slices, GLint stacks)
```

Generates polygonal approximations to a sphere, centered at the origin with the specified `radius`, through `stacks` lines of latitude and `slices` lines of longitude.

```
void glutWireCone(GLdouble base, GLdouble height, GLint slices,
    GLint stacks)
void glutSolidCone(GLdouble base, GLdouble height, GLint
    slices, GLint stacks)
```

Generates a polygonal approximation to a cone with its `base` in the plane $z = 0$ and the given `height`. Polygons are formed by `stacks` lines of latitude and `slices` lines of longitude.

```
void glutWireTorus(GLdouble inner, GLdouble outer, GLint sides,
    GLint slices)
void glutSolidTorus(GLdouble inner, GLdouble outer, GLint
    sides, GLint slices)
```

Defines a torus aligned with the z-axis by its `inner` and `outer` radii, `sides` divisions for radial sections, and `slices` around the torus.

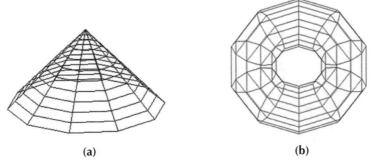

(a)   **(b)**

Figure 4.9 GLUT, (a) cone and (b) torus

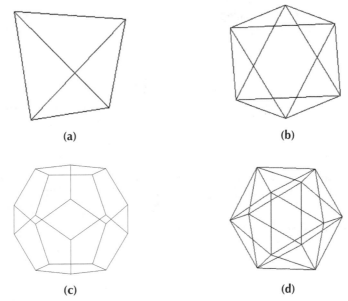

(a)   **(b)**

(c)   **(d)**

Figure 4.10 GLUT Platonic solids, (a) tetrahedron, (b) octohedron, (c) dodecahedron, and (d) icosahedron

Figure 4.11 Utah teapot

The regular polyhedral objects, know as the Platonic solids, are all defined with their vertices on a sphere of radius 1.

```
void glutWireTetrahedron()
void glutSolidTetrahedron()
void glutWireOctahedron()
void glutSolidOctahedron()
void glutWireDodecahedron()
void glutSolidDodecahedron()
void glutWireIcosahedron()
void glutSolidIcosahedron()
```

Generate the regular polyhedra (Platonic solids) with all vertices on the unit sphere.

The Utah teapot is generated by using OpenGL surfaces. The teapot has been used for many years for testing rendering algorithms. It is constructed from 192 vertices. The teapot is generated with both normals and texture coordinates.

```
void glutWireTeapot(GLdouble size)
void glutSolidTeapot(GLdouble size)
```

Generates the Utah teapot of a given size.

4.8 Perspective Projections

Now that we have the basics down, we can look at more general viewing. Perspective viewing implements the synthetic-camera model in Figure 4.1. The viewing volume is limited on the sides by four planes that meet at the center of projection, forming an infinite viewing pyramid. However, just as with orthogonal viewing, we have near and far clipping planes. The resulting clipping frustum is shown in Figure 4.12. Note that the projection plane can be anywhere in front of the camera.

OpenGL provides the function glFrustum() to create the required matrix for perspective viewing. Its parameters are the same as for glOrtho().

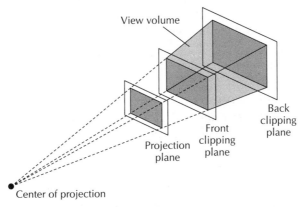

Figure 4.12 Viewing frustum for perspective projections

> void glFrustum(GLdouble left, GLdouble right, GLdouble bottom,
>   GLdouble top, GLdouble near, GLdouble far)

Defines a matrix for perspective projection. The front and back clipping planes are determined by near and far, which are measured from the center of projection and must be positive, with far > near. The bottom-left and top-right corners of the front clipping plane are (left, bottom, near) and (right, top, near) in camera coordinates.

Unlike the orthographic projection, in which the camera can lie inside the clipping volume, in perspective viewing, the viewing frustum must be in front of the camera. All the parameters are in camera coordinates, so both the near and far distances must be positive, with the far distance greater than the near distance.

 Remember that the parameters for viewing are in camera, or viewing, coordinates. The near and far parameters are measured from the camera to the clipping planes.

The matrix calculated by glFrustum() is applied to the current matrix. We must make sure that we are in the proper matrix mode first and usually we start with an identity matrix, so the following sequence is standard:

```
glMatrixMode(GL_PROJECTION);
glLoadIdentity();
glFrustum(left, right, bottom, top, near, far);
```

Just as with orthographic views, the projection matrix defines the clipping volume and the type of projection but not the position and the orientation of the camera. The camera in OpenGL is at the origin pointed in the negative *z* direction. Changes to the viewing via glFrustum() are equivalent to changing the lens on a camera but not its position. To change position or orientation, we must move the objects relative to the camera through the model-view matrix, either through OpenGL transformations or with gluLookAt().

Although the viewing volumes formed by glFrustum() are fairly general, the interface provided by glFrustum() can make it difficult to obtain a desired view. The problem is that as we change the distance between the near and far planes, the angles that the sides of the frustum make with respect to its center can change dramatically. As a user changes these distances to get the desired objects into the scene, objects on the sides can be lost as these angles change. A more natural interface is closer to what we do with a real camera. When we want to see more objects with a camera in a fixed location, we change the lens and get one with a wider angle of view. The function gluPerspective() provides such an interface.

---

void gluPerspective(GLdouble fov, GLdouble aspect, GLdouble
    near, GLdouble far)

Specifies a projection matrix by the angle of view (fov) in the *y* direction, the aspect ratio of the near and far clipping planes, and the distances to the near and far planes.

The near and far clipping planes have the same **aspect** (width to height) ratio. However, if the aspect ratio is not 1, the top and side angles of the frustum are different. The function gluPerspective() uses the angle between the top and bottom of the frustum. Because this clipping volume can be constructed with the correct choice of parameters in glFrustum(), gluPerspective() is in the GLU library. For a user, it is often easiest to set up viewing by positioning the camera, determining the near and far distances, and then using gluPerspective() with a wide angle. Once we are happy with the other parameters, it is easy to narrow the viewing angle.

One potential problem with perspective views is loss of accuracy in depth, which can be noticeable in the display. The problem stems from the limited number of bits in the depth buffer and a nonlinear scaling that is part of the implementation of perspective projections. The problem is worst when the near plane is very close to the center of projection, something we might otherwise want to do so that we can see objects very close to the camera.

 Placing the front clipping plane too close to the camera can lead to numerical problems in depth calculations for perspective views.

Transformations

Transformations are the key to manipulating objects, to animating scenes, and to obtaining the desired views. This chapter presents the fundamentals of transformations in OpenGL. Rather than deriving the various common transformations, such as rotation, translation, and scaling, we concentrate on using the transformation functions in OpenGL. We show how to use transformations to model a variety of phenomena.

5.1 Line-Preserving Transformations

In computer graphics, we work with two fundamental geometric entities: points or vertices, which are locations in space, and directions, or **vectors**. Although each type can be specified in a similar manner, each describes something very different from the other. For example, we can talk about the point $(1, 0, 0)$ and the direction $(1, 0, 0)$ in three dimensions. The point is fixed in space in its coordinate system. The vector points in the positive, x direction but has no location. Both can be transformed. We can move from one point to another, or we can rotate a vector to orient it in another direction.

Transformations map vertices and vectors to other vertices and vectors. We can transform points to points or directions to directions in infinite ways. But in computer graphics, we are interested in one important property for all our transformations: They must preserve lines and line segments. The reasons are both practical and physical.

In the physical world, many of the operations we perform on objects preserve lines. Consider, for example, translations and rotations. If we start with a cube and rotate it about one of its edges, we still have a cube. Likewise, if we pick up the cube and move it somewhere else, we still have a cube. If we carry out any sequence of rotations and translations of this cube, none of its fundamental geo-metric properties, such as its size or its angles, are changed. For this reason, rotations and translations are known as **rigid-body transformations**.

All the primitives we have used so far are defined by vertices. Primitive OpenGL functions use vertices to define line segments that are primitives themselves or that form the edges of polygons. The only entities that flow down the OpenGL pipeline are vertices and vectors. They are assembled into primitives at the end of the pipeline after OpenGL has determined those that they are visible. Consider what would happen if we had to implement a general transformation that could transform, for example, a line segment into a curve. We would have to compute all the intermediate points on the curve from points on the line segment, an operation that would not fit with our pipeline. If we restrict ourselves to trans-formations that preserve line segments, we need transform only the end points—two vertices—of each line segment. We can then let the hardware and the software construct the interior points of the transformed line segment at the end of the pipeline.

Two classes of transformations are of importance to computer graphics that preserve lines: **affine transformations** and **projective transformations**. Affine transformations include such operations as translation, rotation, and scaling. Such transformations preserve parallel lines and are reversible. Projective transformations include the orthographic and perspective projections that we have discussed. Because these transformations project three-dimensional entities into two dimensions, they cannot be inverted. Both affine and projective transfor-mations can be implemented by matrix operations involving vertices and vectors.

5.2 Homogeneous Coordinates

We have seen that many OpenGL functions are the same in two and three dimen-sions. OpenGL has only a single representation of two- and three-dimensional entities. Two dimensions is a special case of three dimensions, with all two-dimen-sional primitives lying in the plane $z = 0$. Thus the two-dimensional point (x, y) is the same as the three-dimensional point $(x, y, 0)$.

In fact, OpenGL works in four dimensions, with three dimensions being a special case. Although you need not know all the mathematics of this system, called **homogeneous coordinates**, it will sometimes make some of OpenGL's functionality a little clearer. Normally, a three-dimensional point is represented internally as $(x, y, z, 1)$ and a two-dimensional point as $(x, y, 0, 1)$. It is possible to create a more general point in four dimensions, either directly or by transformations, in the form (x, y, z, w). Such a point is eventually displayed as the three-dimensional point $(x/w, y/w, z/w)$ as long as w is not 0.

Directions, such as are used for normals, are represented as $(x, y, z, 0)$ and are equivalent to points at infinity.

With this representation, all the transformations that we use for modeling, viewing, and projection are represented by 4×4 matrices that act on the homogeneous coordinate representations of points and directions. When we set up an OpenGL transformation such as rotation or translation, we are setting up 4×4 matrices within OpenGL. We can also set matrices directly by specifying the necessary 16 elements.

5.3 The Model-View and Projection Transformations

A simplified view of the OpenGL pipeline in shown in Figure 5.1 Each vertex passes through two transformations that are defined by the current model view and projection matrices, which are part of the OpenGL state. Initially both are set to 4×4 identity matrices.

Although both of these matrices can be set by the same OpenGL functions, each type is used for a different purpose. The model-view matrix is used to position objects relative to a camera. The projection matrix forms the image through projection and also helps with clipping by mapping vertices to a normalized coordinate system.

5.4 Translation

In Figure 5.2, we see a camera and an object. Suppose that in world coordinates, the object is at the origin. Because the camera in OpenGL is also at the origin, we want to move the object away from the camera or, equivalently, move the camera away from the objects. A simple solution would be to move one or the other along the z-axis. The operation of translation adds a **displacement** to every vertex on the object. Thus, if $(x, y, z, 1)$ is the homogeneous coordinate representation of the vertex at (x, y, z), translation moves this vertex to $(x + d_x, y + d_y, z + d_z, 1)$. We can apply the translation to all the vertices by making the model-view matrix a translation matrix, using glTranslate*().

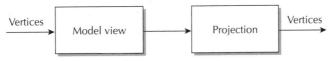

Figure 5.1 Transformation matrices in the OpenGL pipeline

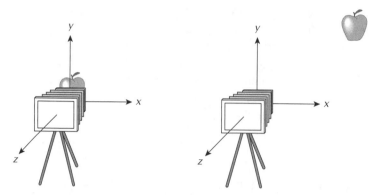

Figure 5.2 Camera and (a) object centered at origin and (b) with object moved away from the camera

```
void glTranslate{fd}(TYPE dx, TYPE dy, TYPE dz)
```

Alters the present matrix by a translation matrix with parameters dx, dy, dz. TYPE is either GLfloat or GLdouble.

Translation is applied to the present matrix, that is, the matrix determined by the present matrix mode (GL_PROJECTION or GL_MODELVIEW). Thus, if we want a pure translation matrix, we first must set the matrix mode, then initialize the matrix to an identity matrix, and finally execute glTranslate(). Thus, if we want to move all the vertices one unit down the negative z-axis, we use the sequence

```
glMatrixMode(GL_MODELVIEW);
glLoadIdentity();
glTranslatef(0.0, 0.0, -1.0);
```

Note that one interpretation of parameters in glTranslate*() is that they represent the distances from a fixed camera at the origin that we want to move the objects. Thus, a positive d_x is a translation to the right of the camera, a positive d_y is a translation above the camera, and a positive d_z is a distance behind the camera. These distances are correct in the right-handed coordinate system in Figure 5.3. Note also that the distances are the same as the ones used for drawing the objects; that is, they are in world coordinates.

 Distances in translation are in a right-handed coordinate sustem. A positive displacement in z can move objects from in front of the camera to behind the camera.

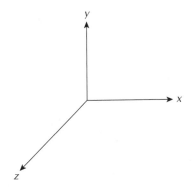

Figure 5.3 Right-handed coordinate system

Now suppose that we want to create a scene with two objects in it, both in front of the camera. We could use the code

```
glMatrixMode(GL_MODELVIEW);
glLoadIdentity();
glTranslatef(0.0, 0.0, -1.0);
glutWireTetrahedron();
glLoadIdentity();
glTranslatef(0.0, 0.0, -3.0);
glutWireCube();
```

Or, we could use the code

```
glMatrixMode(GL_MODELVIEW);
glLoadIdentity();
glTranslatef(0.0, 0.0, -1.0);
glutWireTetrahedron();
glTranslatef(0.0, 0.0, -2.0);
glutWireCube();
```

These two fragments produce the same output. Why? In the first case, we draw two cubes, each centered at the origin. The first is moved one unit from the camera, and the second is moved three units from the origin. As we set the model-view matrix back to the identity matrix before we draw the second cube, the positioning of each cube is completely independent of the other. In the second case, we do not reset the model-view matrix back to an identity matrix. The function glTranslate*() forms a translation matrix that is applied to the *present* matrix. Thus, the two translations are combined, or **concatenated** together, to form a compound transformation. In this case, we know that if we do two translations, the result is a translation by the sum of the displacements. The tetrahedron has only the result of the first translation applied to it, whereas the cube experiences the sum of two translations.

5.5 Rotation

Rotation is more difficult to define, because there are more parameters to specify for a general rotation. If you take an object and rotate, you might note that you can rotate about any axis and that there is a point, not necessarily on the object, that is unaffected by the rotation. We call this point the **fixed point** of the rotation. We also have to specify how many degrees we want to rotate about the chosen axis. Figure 5.4 shows the parameters for a general rotation. Two points, p_1 and p_2, determine a line segment that gives the direction about which we want to rotate. The point p_0 is the fixed point for the rotation and often is the center of the object that is being rotated.

The rotation function in OpenGL, `glRotate*()`, assumes that the fixed point is at the origin. We will see how to deal with a general fixed point later. It forms a rotation matrix about a given axis, which is determined by a vector in three dimensions. The desired amount of rotation about this axis is in a clockwise direction, looking from the positive direction along the given direction back toward the origin. Thus, in a right-handed coordinate system, a 90 degree rotation about the z-axis rotates the positive x-axis into the positive y-axis.

 A positive direction of rotation about a vector is counterclockwise when looking from the positive direction.

Just as with translation, rotations can be specified by using floats or doubles.

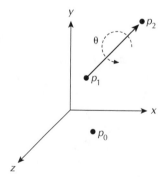

Figure 5.4 Defining a general rotation

```
void glRotate{fd}(TYPE angle, TYPE dx, TYPE dy, TYPE dz)
```

Forms a rotation matrix about the axis given by (dx, dy, dz) with a fixed point of the origin. TYPE can be GLfloat or GLdouble.

We can use both rotation and translation to obtain a rotation about a fixed point other than the origin. The idea is that we can use translation to move the fixed point to the origin. Then we can use glRotate*() to do the desired rotation. At the end, we have to do another translation to move the fixed point back. Thus, if we want to rotate about the direction (d_x, d_y, d_z) with the fixed point (x_f, y_f, z_f), we use the sequence

```
glMatrixMode(GL_MODELVIEW);
glLoadIdentity();
glTranslatef(xf, yf, zf);
glRotatef(angle, dx, dy, dz);
glTranslatef(-xf, -yf, -zf);
```

Note the order of the transformations. In OpenGL, the order in which the transformations are applied is the opposite of the order in which they appear in the program. In other words, *the last transformation specified is the first one applied.* This unintuitive result is a consequence of the fact that each transformation defined in OpenGL is applied to the present matrix by postmultiplication. So for our example, we start with an identity matrix, apply a translation that moves the fixed point to the origin, and then apply the rotation to this matrix. The last translation is by the inverse of the first translation and moves the fixed point back to its original location. Because the vertices postmultiply the model-view matrix, it is this last matrix that is applied first mathematically. Of course, only one model-view transformation is carried out on the vertices; it is the composite of the transformations that we specified.

 Do not forget that the last transformation specified in the program is the first one applied.

It is important to remember that we have set up a model-view matrix that is part of the state. Thus, unless we change that matrix, all primitives that appear later in the program will also be rotated about the same fixed point. This includes any primitives that are in display lists that do not change the present matrices and are executed after the model-view matrix has been changed.

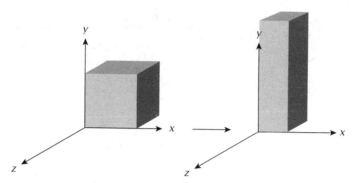

Figure 5.5 Scaling with nonuniform scale factors

5.6 Scaling

The third standard transformation provided by OpenGL is scaling. When we scale an object, we make it bigger or smaller. However, we can scale in multiple ways. Consider the scaling of a cube in Figure 5.5. The cube has been made longer in one direction and shorter in the other. In the first case, the scaling factor is greater than 1, in the second, it is less than 1. We also note that scaling has a fixed point, which is unchanged by the scaling. In Figure 5.5, the fixed point is the origin. The function `glScale*()` allows us to specify different scale factors along the three axes. The fixed point is at the origin, but we can use the same technique as with rotations to obtain any desired fixed point.

```
void glScale{fd}(TYPE sx, TYPE sy, TYPE sz)
```

Sets up a scaling matrix with scale factors `sx`, `sy`, and `sz` and a fixed point of the origin. TYPE is either `GLfloat` or `GLdouble`.

Scale factors less than 0 are allowed and give us reflection about the axes in addition to scaling. For example, `glScalef(1.0, -2.0, 0.5)` will leave the *x* values unchanged, reflect about the *y*-axis and elongate the object along the *y* direction, and shrink the object in the *z* direction.

5.7 Setting Matrices Directly

We can construct any affine transformation from a properly chosen sequence of rotations, translations, and scalings. Generally, we do this construction within the user program. Sometimes, however, we want to construct a model-view or projection matrix directly or use a matrix that we form in our own program to alter an exisiting projection or model-view matrix.

In OpenGL, the matrices are stored in 16-element one-dimensional arrays in column order rather than in 4×4 two-dimensional arrays. Two functions enable us to manipulate our own matrices: `glLoadMatrix*()` and `glMultMatrix*()`. The first function loads a user-defined array as the present matrix. The second postmultiplies the current matrix by a user-defined array.

```
void glLoadMatrix{fd}(TYPE *m)
```

Loads the array m, of TYPE GLfloat or GLdouble, as the current matrix.

```
void glMultMatrix{fd}(TYPE *m)
```

Postmultiplies the current matrix by m, which is of TYPE GLfloat or GLdouble.

One of the important uses of setting our own matrices is to add shear to our fundamental operations. Figure 5.6 illustrates shear applied to a two-dimensional square in the x direction. It is as if we had pulled the front and back faces in opposite directions. This operation is affine, since it preserves lines, and we can see that the fixed point for this transformation is the origin in our figure.

The required matrix is

$$M = \begin{bmatrix} 1 & \cot\theta & 0 & 0 \\ 0 & 1 & 0 & 0 \\ 0 & 0 & 1 & 0 \\ 0 & 0 & 0 & 1 \end{bmatrix}$$

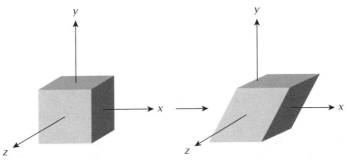

Figure 5.6 Shearing a cube

Its derivation is not needed here. We can form this matrix in our code as follows:

```
GLfloat m[16];
for(i = 0; i < 16; i++) m[i] = 0.0;
m[0] = m[5] = m[10] = m[15] = 1.0;
m[4] = cot(DEG_TO_RAD*theta);

glLoadMatrixf(m);
```

We can apply shear in any of the three directions by adding or substituting cotangent terms above the diagonal in our matrix. In addition to giving us more flexibility in creating objects, shear gives us more flexible viewing. For example, the projection of the cube in Figure 5.7 is known as an **oblique projection**. It is a parallel projection but cannot be obtained directly, because the only parallel projection matrix we have in OpengGL is the one formed from glOrtho(). We can, however, alter the matrix formed by glOrtho() by a shear matrix similar to M to create a view as in Figure 5.7.

```
glMatrixMode(GL_PROJECTION);
glLoadIdentity();
glOrtho(right, left, bottom, top, near, far);
glMultMatrixf(m);
```

More generally, when we use glMultmatrix*(), the matrix that we form is concatenated with other matrices. The following example generates the shadow of a cube from a point light source at (x_1, y_1, z_1) by projecting it onto the plane $z = 0$. The matrix can be formed in three steps. First, we move the light source to the origin; then we do the projection. Finally, we move the light source back. The required projection matrix is given by[1]

$$M = \begin{bmatrix} 1 & 0 & 0 & 0 \\ 0 & 1 & 0 & 0 \\ 0 & 0 & 1 & 0 \\ 0 & -\dfrac{1}{y_l} & 0 & 0 \end{bmatrix}$$

---

1. The details of how we obtain this matrix and those in the next two examples can be found in E. Angel, Interactive Computer Graphics (Reading, MA: Addison-Wesley, 2000). These details are not necessary to follow the code.

Figure 5.7 Oblique projection of a cube

The required code to set up the matrix is

```
GLfloat m[16];
for(i = 0; i < 15; i++) m[i] = 0.0;
m[0] = m[5] = m[10] = 1.0;
m[7] = -1.0/y1;
```

This time we want to render the cube twice. First, we render the cube with whatever model-view matrix we have set up. We then change the color to that assigned for the shadow and alter the model-view matrix by the two translations and the shadow projection matrix. We apply these transformations to the existing matrix as whatever transformations we applied to locate and orient the cube, which must also apply to the shadow.

```
glMatrixMode(GL_MODELVIEW);

/* set up model-view matrix and attributes for cube */

cube();

/* save matrix and color */

glPushMatrix();
glPushAttrib(GL_CURRENT_BIT);

glTranslate(x1, y1, z1);
glMultMatrix(m);
glTranslate(-x1, -y1, -z1);

/* draw shadow in black */

glColor3f(0.0, 0.0, 0.0)
cube();

/* restore matrix and color */

glPopMatrix();
glPopAttrib();
```

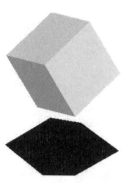

Figure 5.8 Cube and its projected shadow

Note the necessity of saving (pushing) both the current color and the current model-view matrix so we can proceed with drawing other objects or redrawing the cube if it is moving. An image generated by this procedure is shown in Figure 5.8.

5.8 Transformations and Coordinate Systems

We have seen that OpenGL uses a variety of coordinate systems. Every change of coordinate systems is equivalent to a transformation. Thus, we can take two equivalent views of what the model-view transformation does. We can look at it as a transformation that moves objects relative to the camera. Or, we can think of it as an operation that takes specifications of objects in world coordinates and gives their representation in camera coordinates. Both points of view are valid. From the application programmer's perspective, the first view is probably more useful. The second point of view is best suited to understanding what happens internally.

The two points of view help explain why the parameters in the viewing functions, glOrtho(), glFrustum(), and gluPerspective(), are measured from the camera. These transformations are almost always used to form the projection matrix. The vertices that this matrix is applied to have already been transformed by the model-view matrix and thus are already in camera coordinates. Hence, the parameters of any functions that are applied at this stage should also be in camera, or eye, coordinates.

If we apply the same reasoning to the projection transformation, we see that it transforms the representation of objects in camera coordinates to a representation in **clip coordinates**. Clip coordinates retain the information in homogeneous form and map vertices to a normalized volume. Once the division is done, in case the w term is not unity, vertices are in a three-dimensional coordinate system called **normalized device coordinates**. Although the mathematical process of projection maps vertices in a three-dimensional world to locations on the two-dimensional view surface, OpenGL retains three-dimensional information as long as possible so that operations, such as hidden-surface removal, lighting, and texture mapping, can be done as late as possible. Finally, the entities that are visible are mapping through the viewport transformation to **window coordinates**, where the units are in pixels.

5.9 Modeling with Transformations

Although they can be applied to either the model-view matrix or the projection matrix, transformations are, in practice, used primarily to model objects via the model-view matrix. We shall examine two strategies. The first uses a set of standard objects to build scenes. Each object must be sized, oriented, and placed in the scene individually. In the second, we build objects that have interconnected parts that must move together. Here, we use transformations to encapsulate these relationships.

5.9.1 Instancing

Suppose that we start with a collection of common objects, such as cubes and spheres, for which we might have the code, or they many be objects supplied by GLUT or GLU. We can build other objects by applying affine transformations to them. Often these base objects are called **symbols**, and each occurrence of one in our code is an **instance** of that symbol.

If we start with a cube, we can create any right parallelepiped by scaling it. If we also allow shear, we can create any parallelepiped from the cube. We can create any ellipsoid by scaling a sphere. We can apply rotation matrices to orient these objects and translation matrices to position them. The matrix that brings the object into the model with the desired size, orientation, and position is called the **instance transformation**.

Generally, the basic objects that we use to build our models are sized, located, and oriented in a convenient manner. For example, spheres are often of a unit radius with the center at the origin. Cubes may have a side of length 1 and their sides aligned with the coordinate axes. The GLU cylinder was aligned with the z-axis and had its base in the plane $z = 0$. With such a starting point, we almost always want to scale the object to its desired size, then orient it, and finally translate it to its desired position in that order. Consequently, a typical instancing sequence looks like

```
glMatrixMode(GL_MODELVIEW);
glLoadIdentity();
glTranslatef(x, y, z);
glRotatef(theta, dx, dy, dz);
glScalef(sx, sy, sz);
```

Note again the order of the transformations.

5.9.2 Hierarchical Models

In many applications, the parts of a model depend on one another. If we move one part of the model, it causes other parts to move. In the majority of such applications, including figure animation and robotics, the models are hierarchical. The parts of such models can be arranged as a tree data structure composed of nodes and links. Each node except for the top, or root, node has a parent, and all nodes except for the terminal nodes or leaves, have one or more children. Figure 5.9 shows a simple robot arm (a) and its hierarchical representation (b). Figures 5.10 and 5.11 show a simple figure we might want to animate and its hierarchical representation. In these hierarchies, the position and the orientation of an object can be affected by the position and the orientation of its parent and its parent's parent and so on. Both of these examples have parts that are connected by joints that rotate, thus reducing animation and motion to computing a set of joint angles and then rerendering the scene when one or more of these angles change.

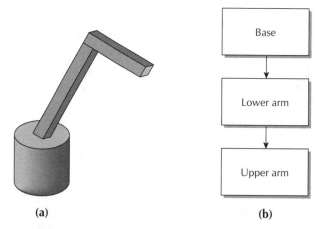

(a) (b)

Figure 5.9 (a) A simple robot arm and (b) its hierarchical representation

Figure 5.10 A figure constructed from GLU spheres and cylinders

From an OpenGL perspective, we would like to represent these models by using transformations. The instance transformations that we just presented are not quite right because they place each symbol in the scene independently of the others. However, if we recall that OpenGL transformations are applied to the existing matrix, we can observe that each transformation represents a *relative* change from one scaling, position, and orientation to another.

Consider the simple robot arm (Figure 5.9). It consists of three parts: a base, a lower arm, and an upper arm. Each part can be described in its own coordinate system, using standard OpenGL objects, such as cylinders and scaled cubes, as shown in Figure 5.12.

Suppose that we use a cylinder for the base and scaled cubes for the upper and lower arms. We can define the parts through three functions: `base()`, `lower_arm()`, and `upper_arm()`. Note that the quadric object has to be created

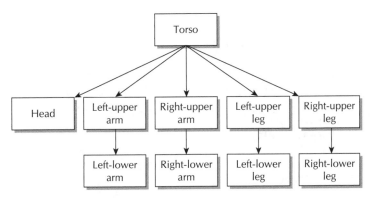

Figure 5.11 Hierarchical representation of Figure 5.10

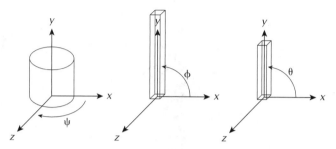

Figure 5.12 Robot parts

within `main()` or `init()` and that the various parameters describing the various lengths are defined elsewhere in the program. The use of `glPushMatrix()` and `glPopMatrix()` allows us to use the present model-view matrix to locate the entire figure while still preserving it for drawing other objects.

```
GLUquadricObj   *p; /* pointer to quadric object */


void base()
{
    glPushMatrix();

/* rotate cylinder to align with y-axis */

    glRotatef(-90.0, 1.0, 0.0, 0.0);

/* cylinder aligned with z-axis, render with 5 slices for base and
    5 along length */

    gluCylinder(p, BASE_RADIUS, BASE_RADIUS, BASE_HEIGHT, 5, 5);
    glPopMatrix();
}

void upper_arm()
{
    glPushMatrix();
    glTranslatef(0.0, 0.5*UPPER_ARM_HEIGHT, 0.0);
    glScalef(UPPER_ARM_WIDTH, UPPER_ARM_HEIGHT, UPPER_ARM_WIDTH);
    glutWireCube(1.0);
    glPopMatrix();
}

void lower_arm()
{
```

```
    glPushMatrix();
    glTranslatef(0.0, 0.5*LOWER_ARM_HEIGHT, 0.0);
    glScalef(LOWER_ARM_WIDTH, LOWER_ARM_HEIGHT, LOWER_ARM_WIDTH);
    glutWireCube(1.0);
    glPopMatrix();
}
```

The base can rotate independently of the rest of the robot. The lower arm is attached to the base and can rotate relative to it. However, when the base rotates, it also rotates the lower arm. The upper arm can rotate with respect to the lower arm but is also affected by the rotation of the base and the lower arm. The lower arm is also positioned on top of the base so must be translated up. The upper arm has to be translated up the height of the base and the length of the lower arm. The following display callback captures all these relationships. The code is incremental, and matrices need not be recomputed.

```
void display(void)
{

    glClear(GL_COLOR_BUFFER_BIT);
    glMatrixMode(GL_MODELVIEW);
    glLoadIdentity();
    glColor3f(1.0, 0.0, 0.0);
    glRotatef(theta[0], 0.0, 1.0, 0.0);
    base();
    glTranslatef(0.0, BASE_HEIGHT, 0.0);
    glRotatef(theta[1], 0.0, 0.0, 1.0);
    lower_arm();
    glTranslatef(0.0, LOWER_ARM_HEIGHT, 0.0);
    glRotatef(theta[2], 0.0, 0.0, 1.0);
    upper_arm();
    glutSwapBuffers();
}
```

We can complete this program with animation in a number of ways. One method is to use a menu attached to one of three mouse buttons to choose which angle to change and to use the other two buttons to increase or decrease that angle. Alternatively, we could use the keyboard to choose an angle and increment or decrement it with either the keyboard or the mouse.

Our first example did not require us to save any information about the model-view matrix as we went through the display callback, because the transformations accumulated. If we look at the tree in Figure 5.9(b), we see that it is a very simple one in which no node has more than one child. The figure in Figure 5.10 is more complex. It consists of parts connected to a torso. Each arm and leg consists of two parts, but each arm and leg depends on the location and orientation of the torso but not on each other. Let's assume that we can build the individual parts and put that information in a set of functions, such as head(), torso(), and left_upper_arm(). Each part can be located with respect to its parent by a translation and one or more rotations, depending on how the part is connected to its parent.

The display callback must traverse the tree in Figure 5.11. That is, we must visit every node, drawing the objects for that node, using the correct model-view matrix. A standard preorder traversal travels down the left of the tree, visiting each node. When we can go no further, we back up to the first right branch and repeat the process recursively. Let us see how that process works with the figure model.

First, we draw the torso. It has one angle associated with it, which allows us to rotate the torso about an axis in the y direction. We then go on to the head. However, we note that we will have to come back up to the torso to get to the arms and legs. Any matrix that we apply to draw the head is not required for the arms or legs. Rather than recompute the matrix that we apply at the torso node, we can save it on the stack with a glPushMatrix(). We can then go to the node for the head, changing the model-view matrix as necessary to draw the head, which uses two joint angles. When we come back to the torso node, we recover the model-view matrix with a glPopMatrix(). We will have to come back up to the torso after dealing with the left arm, so we must go to a glPushMatrix() immediately after the pop to keep a copy of the same model-view matrix. Although the following code may appear somewhat convoluted, the rule is very simple. Every time we go to the left at a node with another unvisited right child, we do a push; every time we return to that node, we do a pop. Note that we must do a pop at the end so that the total number of pushes and pops is the same.

```
void display()
{
    glClear(GL_COLOR_BUFFER_BIT|GL_DEPTH_BUFFER_BIT);
    glMatrixMode(GL_MODELVIEW);
    glLoadIdentity();
    glColor3f(1.0, 0.0, 0.0);

    glRotatef(theta[0], 0.0, 1.0, 0.0);
    torso();
    glPushMatrix();

    glTranslatef(0.0, HEADX, 0.0);
    glRotatef(theta[1], 1.0, 0.0, 0.0);
    glRotatef(theta[2], 0.0, 1.0, 0.0);
    glTranslatef(0.0, HEADY, 0.0);
    head();
```

```
glPopMatrix();
glPushMatrix();
glTranslatef(LUAX, LUAY, 0.0);
glRotatef(theta[3], 1.0, 0.0, 0.0);
left_upper_arm();

glTranslatef(0.0, LLAY, 0.0);
glRotatef(theta[4], 1.0, 0.0, 0.0);
left_lower_arm();

glPopMatrix();
glPushMatrix();
glTranslatef(RUAX, RUAY, 0.0);
glRotatef(theta[5], 1.0, 0.0, 0.0);
right_upper_arm();

glTranslatef(0.0, RLAY, 0.0);
glRotatef(theta[6], 1.0, 0.0, 0.0);
right_lower_arm();

glPopMatrix();
glPushMatrix();
glTranslatef(LULX, LULY, 0.0);
glRotatef(theta[7], 1.0, 0.0, 0.0);
left_upper_leg();

glTranslatef(0.0, LLLY, 0.0);
glRotatef(theta[8], 1.0, 0.0, 0.0);
left_lower_leg();

glPopMatrix();
glPushMatrix();
glTranslatef(RULX, RULY, 0.0);
glRotatef(theta[9], 1.0, 0.0, 0.0);
right_upper_leg();

glTranslatef(0.0, RLLY, 0.0);
glRotatef(theta[10], 1.0, 0.0, 0.0);
right_lower_leg();

glPopMatrix();
glutSwapBuffers();
}
```

We can complete this program and animate in a manner similar to the robot example. For example, we can use a menu to choose which of the 11 angles to change and either two mouse buttons or two keys to increment and to decrement the chosen angle.

We can generalize this code by defining a node data structure, such as the left-child right-sibling structure, as follows:

```
typedef struct treenode
{
    GLfloat m[16];
    void (*f)();
    struct treenode *sibling;
    struct treenode *child;
} treenode;
```

This structure allows us to store the matrix that is applied to the parent at each node and the function to be drawn at the node. For example, we can define the torso node by using OpenGL to compute the rotation matrix that we used earlier and by storing it in a node, along with the other information.

```
treenode torso_node;
glLoadIdentity();
glRotatef(theta[0], 0.0, 1.0, 0.0);
glGetFloatv(GL_MODEL_VIEW_MATRIX), torso_node.m);
torso_node.f = torso;
torso_node.sibling = NULL'
torso_node.child = &head_node;
```

Once we have defined all the nodes—say, in init()—we can traverse the data structure in the display callback by calling code such as the following:

```
void traverse(treenode *root)
{
    if(root == NULL) return;
    glPushMatrix();
    glMultMatrix(root->m);
    root->f();
    if(root.child != NULL) traverse(root->child);
    glPopMatrix();
    if(root->sibling != NULL) traverse(root->sibling);
}

void display()
{
    glClear(COLOR_BUFFER_BIT|GL_DEPTH_BUFFER_BIT);
    glMatrixMode(GL_MODELVIEW);
    glLoadIdentity();
    traverse(&torso_root);
    glutSwapBuffers();
}
```

We can also create dynamic structures by using dynamically created nodes. For example, we can define

```
typedef treenode* tree_ptr;
```

We can then define

```
tree_ptr torso_ptr;
torso_ptr = malloc(sizeof(treenode));
```

Tree nodes are defined in almost the same way, using pointers, and the traversal accomplished recursively in same way as before:

```
traverse(torso_ptr);
```

One advantage of using this approach is that we can create and delete nodes within the application program, allowing us great flexibility in how we can work with our models.

Chapter | **6**

Lights and Materials

The colors that we see in the real world are based on the interaction between the materials of which the objects are comprised and the lights that illuminate them. OpenGL mimics this process, using a lighting model that incorporates diffuse, specular, ambient, and emissive terms. OpenGL allows us to define a variety of light sources and material properties. We shall also consider the fourth color component in RGBA color, the alpha value, and show how to use it to display translucent surfaces.

6.1 Light/Material Interactions

Thus far, we have achieved color in a scene by simply assigning a color to an object. If the object is visible, this color is the one that we display. But this situation is not physically realistic, as the colors that we see in the real world are based on the interaction between light coming from sources and the materials of which the objects are composed. What is perhaps worse is that if we assign a fixed color to a three-dimensional object, we risk not seeing its three dimensionality in the image. In a two-dimensional photograph or painting, objects appear to be three dimensional because we see small variations, or **shades**, in the colors of rendered objects. These shades are determined by light/material interactions. If we simply display a red sphere in OpenGL by giving it a single color, the sphere will appear as a uniformly colored disk. What we need to add to our OpenGL functionality is the ability to shade objects in a manner that is visibly close to what we see in images created by photographs.

In the physical world, the shades that we see are the result of a multitude of complex interactions between light and materials. Light from sources strikes objects. Some of this light is absorbed by the surfaces and some is reflected. Objects appear in a color because of the colors of the light striking them and which frequencies in the light are reflected. The light that is reflected from an object can be scattered over a narrow or a broad range of angles, depending on the smoothness of the surface. Reflected light may then strike other surfaces, where it is in turn partially absorbed and partially reflected. If we have highly reflective materials in the scene, a significant percentage of the light will go through many such reflections before most of it is absorbed.

Consequently, for a renderer to do physically-correct shading, we need a global calculation, one that uses information about all the objects and lights in the scene to compute the shade for any point. OpenGL does not work this way. It uses a pipeline architecture in which each primitive is passed down the pipeline independently and is rendered independently if it is visible. Thus, in OpenGL, shading is done locally on a polygon-by-polygon basis.

In most situations, we can do a reasonably good job with OpenGL, although scenes full of highly reflective objects probably will not render well. We can also use many tricks within OpenGL to give good approximations to global calculations. For example, shadows for general scenes require a global calculation. However, we saw in the previous chapter that for the special case of a shadow on a flat surface, we could do a second rendering to obtain shadows. Nevertheless, for scenes consisting of objects that are not highly reflective, we can do a fairly good job of shading on a polygon-by-polygon basis.

6.2 The Phong Model

Many physically-based models exist showing how light interacts with a material. Phong proposed an approximate model that is easy to compute and that has been very useful in computer graphics. The Phong model is used in OpenGL for its shading calculations.

Suppose that we start with the light from an ideal point source illuminating a surface. The Phong model is based on using the four vectors in Figure 6.1.

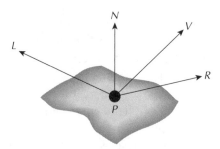

Figure 6.1 Vectors used in the Phong model

Consider a point P on the surface. The direction to the light source is given by the vector L. The viewer is located in the direction V. Note that either or both the viewer and the light source could be an infinite distance from the surface. The direction that reflected light leaves the surface depends on both the direction it came from and the orientation of the surface. The local orientation at a point is given by the **normal** vector N, which is perpendicular to the surface. If the surface is highly reflective, it will act like a mirror, and most of the light will go off in the direction of a perfect reflector R. In OpenGL, the direction V is known from the viewing specifications and points toward the camera. We specify L, the direction to the light source, through our light source functions. The local orientation will have to be supplied by the user program. The vector R can be computed within OpenGL from N and L. The Phong model considers four types of contributions to the shade at a point: **diffuse reflections**, **specular reflections**, **ambient reflections**, and **emissive light** from the material. The Phong model uses RGB color and is applied independently to each of the primaries.

6.2.1 Diffuse Reflection

In a diffuse interaction, the light that strikes a point is partially absorbed and partially reflected. The reflected light is scattered equally in all directions. A diffuse surface appears the same to all viewers, so the calculation does not depend on V. However, the amount of light reflected does depend on the angle between the light source and the normal (see Figure 6.2). Diffuse surfaces tend to look dull, like plastic. We characterize the surface by the fraction of the incoming light reflected by each of the RGB components. When illuminated by white light, a surface has a color because the surface absorbs more light at some frequencies than at others. In the Phong model, this means that each of the RGB components can have different properties.

Figure 6.2 Diffuse reflections

6.2.2 Specular Reflections

A specular surface also absorbs some of the light striking it and reflects the rest. However, a specular surface is smooth, and the reflected light is concentrated along the direction R that a perfect reflection would travel. Because this reflected light is concentrated, what the viewer sees depends on the angle between R and V (see Figure 6.3).

The smoother the surface is, the more concentrated the reflected light. The Phong model characterizes this concentration with a **shininess coefficient**. We must also specify what fraction of the incoming light is reflected. Specular surfaces include polished materials, such as metals, and are responsible for the bright highlights that we often see in images.

6.2.3 Ambient Reflection

The Phong model is based on using ideal point light sources. However, the real world is characterized by sources that have a finite area. In addition, global phenomena, such as multiple reflections, result in light from many directions striking each point. One simple way to deal with this light is to add a constant amount of light to every point in the scene. We call this light **ambient light**, and it is similar to the effect that we see in a room with multiple lights and diffusers that spread out the light. Ambient light is also partially absorbed and partially reflected, but the light that we see does not depend on any of the four vectors, only on the incoming light intensity and the fraction that is reflected.

6.2.4 Emission

In the real world, light sources have a finite area and thus often are visible in a scene. In addition, a surface may both emit light and reflect light that strikes it. In the Phong model, we can add on an emissive term that is not affected by incoming light and can help model visible light sources. The emissive contribution from a surface is not used to calculate shading. Thus, a purely emis-

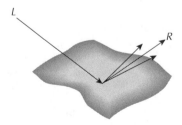

Figure 6.3 Specular reflections

sive surface appears the same, regardless of any other sources or materials. Emissive light is unaffected by the position of the viewer.

6.3 **OpenGL Lighting**

A real light source not only has a finite area but also has a set of frequencies with corresponding strengths at which it emits light. In addition, the source may emit light differently in different directions. Such sources are far too difficult to model in a system that tries to do lighting calculations in real time. Consequently, OpenGL provides a limited variety of light sources and leaves it to the user to approximate the world by carefully controlling these sources.

In OpenGL, we can have point sources, spotlights, and ambient sources. Sources can be located either at a finite distance from the objects or at infinity. Each source can have separate diffuse, specular, and ambient properties.

Each source has separate diffuse, specular, and ambient RGB parameters. It may appear strange that each light has multiple parameter sets. After all, a real light source has but one color and cannot be characterized as being both a blue diffuse source and a white ambient source. However, because we cannot do global lighting in OpenGL, we can use this added flexibility to give better approximations. For example, suppose that we have a white light in a red room. The light that hits a surface directly from the source will be white, but reflections from the red wall will add an ambient component that is red or pink. We can model this global contribution in OpenGL by using white diffuse and specular components and a red ambient component for the light source.

Materials are modeled in a complementary manner. For each surface, we must give separate ambient, diffuse, and specular components or use default values. These parameters are the fraction of the incoming light of each type that is reflected. We can also give an emissive component to the surface. Each parameter has separate RGB values.

Lighting calculations must be enabled, and each light source must be enabled individually. For a single source, we could use

```
glEnable(GL_LIGHTING);
glEnable(GL_LIGHT0);
```

Enabling lighting asks OpenGL to do the shading calculations. All colors will be assigned based on light sources and material properties not by glColor*(). Individual lights must be turned on and off separately.

 Once lighting is enabled, colors assigned by glColor*() are no longer used.

Lights and materials are part of the OpenGL state. So are normal vectors. Thus, the user generally must supply the normal vectors through `glNormal*()`. Some functions, such as `glutTeapot()`, will compute normals for you. Normals are usually computed for each vertex or once for each polygon.

```
void glNormal3{bsidf}(TYPE dx, TYPE dy, TYPE dz)
void glNormal3{bsidf}v(TYPE norm)
```

Defines the present normal to be the vector (dx, dy, dz) of TYPE or a pointer to the array norm.

6.4 Specifying a Light Source

The main function for creating light sources is `glLight*()`. The two forms are for scalar and vector (array) parameters.

```
void glLight{if}(GLenum light, GLenum param, TYPE value)
void glLight{if}v(GLenum light, GLenum param, TYPE *value)
```

Sets scalar and vector parameters for OpenGL light source `light`, parameter `param` to `value`.

For a point source, we can set its (x, y, z) location (GL_POSITION), and its diffuse (GL_DIFFUSE), specular (GL_SPECULAR), and ambient (GL_AMBIENT) RGBA components. The colors properties use RGBA colors. For now, we will always have the fourth component set to 1.0 since we will be working with opaque surfaces.

The defaults are slightly different for light 0 and all the other sources. The default for all lights is no ambient light. For light source 0, the default is white— (1.0, 1.0, 1.0, 1.0)—diffuse and specular components. For all the other light sources, these defaults are black—(0.0, 0.0, 0.0, 1.0). These values allow simple lighting from one source without specifying any parameters. The default value of the position is (0.0, 0.0, 1.0, 0.0). This value is in world coordinates, so it is behind the default camera. Note that this position is in homogeneous coordinates and that the 0 for the w component indicates that the source is at infinity because $w = 0$ indicates that it is the representation of direction rather than of a point. We call such a source a **distant source**, and it corresponds to parallel light from the specified direction.

We can set up a spotlight by giving it a direction and an angle, as in Figure 6.4. The parameter name for the direction is GL_SPOT_DIRECTION and its default is in the negative z direction. Note that the direction is specified by the triplet (dx, dy, dz). A spotlight has an angle (GL_SPOT_CUTOFF) that is measured from the spotlight direction and forms a cone of light. The default is 180 degrees, for which the spotlight is a point source. The amount of light within a spotlight can be made to drop off exponentially from its center by giving it a nonzero value for GL_SPOT_EXPONENT.

The light from a point light source drops off as the inverse of the distance squared from the light to the surface. This attenuation should be applied to the specular and diffuse terms. However, an ideal point source is only an approximation to real distributed light sources, and use of a purely quadratic drop-off can produce images with too much contrast. A softer, more realistic image can be obtained by using a more general term of the form $1/(a + bd + cd^2)$, where d is the distance as computed by OpenGL and a, b, and c are the constant (GL_CONSTANT_ATTENUTATION), linear (GL_LINEAR_ATTENUATION), and quadratic (GL_QUADRATIC_ATTENUATION) factors. The default is no attenuation ($a = 1$, $b = c = 0$).

The position of a near light source and the direction of a distant one are given in homogeneous coordinates and are passed down the OpenGL pipeline, just as are other geometric entities. Thus, they are subject to the model-view transformation in effect when they are defined. Consequently, depending on where in the code we define a light source's position or direction, we can have a light source fixed in position as the viewer or objects move, a light source that moves around while the objects and viewer are stationary, or have the viewer, the objects, and the light source all moving independently.

Consider the following code fragments for an application with an initialization function, init(); an idle callback, idle(); and a display callback,

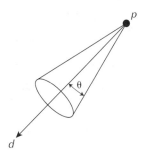

Figure 6.4 Spotlight at p pointing in direction d

display(). If we want the light source to remain stationary, we set its location in init() and never change it.

```
void init()
{
    GLfloat light_pos[] = {1.0, 2.0, 3.0, 1.0}

        /* rest of init() */

    glEnable(GL_LIGHTING);
    glEnable(GL_LIGHT0);
    glMatrixMode(GL_MODELVIEW);
    glLoadIdentity();
    glLightfv(GL_LIGHT0, GL_POSITION, light_pos);
}
```

The position of both the camera and the objects can be altered later in the program by altering the model-view matrix, but the light position is defined only in init(), so it will not change.

Now suppose that we have an idle callback that simply increments an angle and want to rotate the light source about the objects.

```
GLfloat light_pos[] = {1.0, 2.0, 3.0, 1.0};
GLfloat theta = 0.0;

void idle()
{
    angle += 2.0;
    if(angle > 360.0) angle -= 360.0;
}

void display()
{
    glClear(COLOR_BUFFER_BIT | GL_DEPTH_BUFFER_BIT);
    glMatrixMode(GL_MODELVIEW);
    glLoadIdentity();
    glLookAt(1.0, 1.0, 1.0, 0.0, 0.0, 0.0, 0.0, 1.0, 0.0);
    glPushMatrix()
    glRotatef(angle, dx, dy, dz);
    glLightfv(GL_LIGHT0, GL_POSITION, light_pos);
    glPopMatrix();

        /* draw objects here */

    glutSwapBuffers();
}
```

In this code, we push the model-view matrix before we add the rotation. After the rotation, we set a new light position, which is altered by the rotation and the previous model-view matrix. We pop the matrix before we draw the objects, so they are unaffected by the rotation.

If we removed the push and pop in the code, both the light source and the objects would have rotated. By altering the model-view matrix in different parts of the code and inserting pushes and pops, we can have both the objects and the light source move in different ways.

Suppose that we position the light source at the origin before we set the model-view transformation, so that the model-view transformation is an identity matrix. We have then fixed the location of the light source at the origin in eye coordinates or, equivalently, at the eye point. We can then use a gluLookAt() in the form

```
gluLookAt(eyex, eyey, eyez, 0.0, 0.0, 0.0, upx, upy, upz);
```

The effect will be the same as keeping the viewpoint at the origin in eye coordinates and moving the objects by (-eyex, -eyey, -eyez), but because we have not changed the position of the light source, which was already at the origin in eye coordinates, we have effectively tied the light source to the eye point. Of course, simply repositioning the light source at the eye point each time that it changed would accomplish the same effect.

In the following code, we set up a light source that has a bright red diffuse component, a bright white specular component, and a small amount of gray ambient light. The source is at infinity and shines from behind the camera in the upper-right corner.

```
GLfloat position0[] = {1.0, 1.0, 1.0, 0.0);
GLfloat diffuse0[] = {1.0, 0.0, 0.0, 1.0);
GLfloat specular0[] = {1.0, 1.0, 1.0, 1.0};
GLfloat ambient0[] = {0.1, 0.1, 0.1. 1.0};

glEnable(GL_LIGHTING);
glEnable(GL_LIGHT0);

glMatrixMode(GL_PROJECTION);
glLoadIdentity();
glLightfv(GL_LIGHT0, GL_POSITION, position0);
glLightfv(GL_LIGHT0, GL_DIFFUSE, diffuse0);
glLightfv(GL_LIGHT0, GL_SPECULAR, specular0);
glLightfv(GL_LIGHT0, GL_AMBIENT, ambient0);
```

A few additional calls to glLight*() will change the source from a point source to a spotlight and add attenuation.

6.5 Specifying a Material

Materials properties match the lighting properties. A material has reflectivity properties for each type of light. However, although each light source in the OpenGL state has light properties, the state contains only one set of materials properties. The functions for setting these properties are in glMaterial*().

```
void glMaterial{if}(GLenum face, GLenum name, TYPE value)
void glMaterial{if}v(GLenum face, GLenum name, TYPE *value)
```

Sets scalar and vector parameters for materials for the face (GL_FRONT, GL_BACK, and GL_FRONT_AND_BACK). Parameter name is of TYPE.

As we have seen, polygons have both front and back faces. These faces can have the same or different properties. For each face, we can set its diffuse (GL_DIFFUSE), specular (GL_SPECULAR), and ambient (GL_AMBIENT) properties. Often, the ambient and diffuse properties are the same and can be set together, using GL_AMBIENT_AND_DIFFUSE. These parameters are four dimensional. Here, the fourth component is the opacity, which can be used to simulate translucent materials. This component is 1.0 for opaque surfaces. The default surface parameters correspond to a gray surface with a small amount of ambient reflection (0.2, 0.2, 0.2, 1.0), high diffuse reflectivity (0.8, 0.8, 0.8, 1.0), and no specular reflectivity (0.0, 0.0, 0.0, 1.0). Each surface can also emit light (GL_EMISSION). This term is not subject to lighting calculations and thus appears the same regardless of the light sources. The final is for shininess parameter (GL_SHININESS). The higher the value of this parameter, the shinier the material appears, as the specular highlights are concentrated in a smaller area near the angle of a perfect reflection.

We can make individual function calls for each property. If we change materials often—for example when have many objects or each face of an object has different properties—we can put the calls that set parameters inside functions. Another strategy is to set up a structure that contains the material properties:

```
typedef struct materialStruct {
    GLfloat ambient[4];
    GLfloat diffuse[4];
    GLfloat specular[4];
    GLfloat shininess;
} materialStruct;
```

Now we set up our materials:

```
materialStruct brassMaterials = {
    {0.33, 0.22, 0.03, 1.0},
    {0.78, 0.57, 0.11, 1.0},
```

```
        {0.99, 0.91, 0.81, 1.0},
        27.8
};
materialStruct redPlasticMaterials = {
        {0.3, 0.0, 0.0, 1.0},
        {0.6, 0.0, 0.0, 1.0},
        {0.8, 0.6, 0.6, 1.0},
        32.0
};
materialStruct whiteShineyMaterials = {
        {1.0, 1.0, 1.0, 1.0},
        {1.0, 1.0, 1.0, 1.0},
        {1.0, 1.0, 1.0, 1.0},
        {100.0}
};
```

We also set up a function to assign them to the faces:

```
void materials(materialStruct *materials)
{
        /* define material properties for front face of all polygons */
        glMaterialfv(GL_FRONT_AND_BACK, GL_AMBIENT,
            materials->ambient);
        glMaterialfv(GL_FRONT_AND_BACK, GL_DIFFUSE,
            materials->diffuse);
        glMaterialfv(GL_FRONT_AND_BACK, GL_SPECULAR,
            materials->specular);
        glMaterialf(GL_FRONT_AND_BACK, GL_SHININESS,
            materials->shininess);
}
```

Now when we want to set up the material properties for, say, the red plastic material, we can make the single function call

```
materials(redPasticMaterials);
```

The same strategy will work if we have light sources whose properties change during the execution of the program.

6.6   Controlling the Lighting Calculation

Shading calculations require a significant amount of resources. In many situations, OpenGL can avoid some of the calculations with little or no effect on the resulting image. The functions glLightmodel*() allow us to tell OpenGL how to carry out its lighting calculations.

Recall that because normals are reversed for back faces and the front and back faces can have different material properties, calculating shading for back faces can

```
void glLightModel{if}(GLenum param, TYPE value)
void glLightModel{if}v(GLenum param, TYPE *value)
```

Sets light model properties for param (GL_LIGHT_MODEL_AMBIENT,
GL_LIGHT_MODEL_LOCAL_VIEWER, and GL_LIGHT_MODEL_TWO_SIDE).

require extra work. In many situations, we work with models in which back faces
are not displayed. For example, we saw earlier that for convex objects, we cannot
see any back faces. OpenGL can take advantage of this situation and not do any
lighting calculations for back faces. If we really need two-sided lighting
calculations—for example, when we can see inside an object—we can request
OpenGL to do the calculation by

glLightModeli(GL_LIGHT_MODEL_TWO_SIDED, GL_TRUE);

 Light for back faces will not be correct unless the light model is set to two sided.

OpenGL can make additional simplifications that are appropriate for some
circumstances. For example, if the viewer is far from the objects, the vector from
any point on the object to the viewer, which is used for calculating the specular
term, is almost unchanged as we move along the object. Thus, suppose that we tell
OpenGL that the viewer is an infinite distance from the scene by

glLightModeli(GL_LIGHT_MODEL_LOCAL_VIEWER, GL_TRUE);

This part of the lighting calculation will be done only once for each polygon.

When we discussed ambient light, it was part of each light source. The reasoning was that a physical light source causes ambient light because much of the light
that it emits reflects from surfaces in the environment. Thus, if all light sources are
disabled, there will be no ambient light. However, often we would like there to be
a little ambient light even when all the sources are turned off. We can do this by
setting up a global ambient light source by

glLightModelfv(GL_LIGHT_MODEL_AMBIENT, global_ambient);

The array global_ambient contains the RGBA values.

6.7 Smooth Shading

Lighting calculations are made on a vertex-by-vertex basis. OpenGL uses the present state to compute vertex colors, using the Phong model. If the shading model,

Figure 6.5 Flat and smooth shading for polygonal approximations to a sphere

set by glShadeModel(), is set to flat (GL_FLAT), a color is computed for only the first vertex in a polygon, and each polygon will appear in a solid color. This situation is appropriate when we are working with objects, such as the cube, that are composed of flat polygons. In this case, even if the object has the same material properties, each polygon will have a different shade, as each has a different orientation with respect to the lights and the viewers.

However, if the polygons are being used to approximate a curved object, such as with the GLU quadrics, giving each polygon a constant shade will only emphasize that what we see is a polygonal approximation to a curved surface. However, OpenGL can interpolate vertex colors across polygons. Consequently, if we set the parameter in glShadeModel() to GL_SMOOTH, OpenGL will perform the lighting calculation at each vertex and will then interpolate these vertex colors across the polygon. Figure 6.5 shows the difference between smooth and flat shading for a polygonal approximation to a sphere.

You may be disappointed with smooth shading if you are using large polygons. Suppose that we use one large rectangle for a wall in a room and want the rectangle to show variations of light across its surface. Hence, we use smooth shading. What we may see is that the center of the wall is very dark compared with the corners. This appearance is a consequence of the interpolation of the colors at the four corners, all of which can be farther from the viewer than from the center. The usual solution to such problems is to tessellate large polygons into smaller ones.

 Shading may be unsatisfactory if you use large polygons, owing to the interpolation of vertex shades across a large area.

6.8 **Working with Normals**

To a large degree, the quality of shading depends on the normals, which we usually have to compute ourselves. A flat polygon has across its surface a constant normal, which can be computed from the first three vertices. However, when we want smooth shading, the normal for each polygon is not what we need.

Smooth shading is sometimes called **Gouraud shading**. This is slight misnomer, however. What Gouraud proposed is that at each vertex, we compute a normal that is the average of the normals of the polygons that meet at that vertex. Because it processes each polygon independently, OpenGL does not have the information to compute vertex normals based on surrounding polygons. Thus, it is the application that must "know" about the surrounding polygons and compute normals correctly. For the smooth image in Figure 6.5, we were able to use the fact that we were trying to approximate a sphere to obtain the exact normals at the vertices, which for the sphere always point directly out from its center to the points on its surface.

The lighting calculations require that the normal vector have unit length; that is, the sum of the squares of the three components must equal 1. Usually, it is more efficient to enforce this requirement within the application program. However, we can also enable automatic normalization by

```
glEnable(GL_NORMALIZE);
```

As this function will be executed on each normal every time we go through our display process, we incur a performance penalty for using it.

When we do transformations, rotations and translations do not affect the length of the normals, but scalings do. Consequently, the normals may no longer have unit length and the shading calculations will be wrong.

 Lighting calculations require that normals have unit length.

 Scaling changes the lengths of normals.

6.9 Transparency

We now turn to working with the fourth color component, the A in RGBA color. This component, the **alpha value**, is ignored in normal rendering. The alpha value will have meaning, however, if we first enable blending, by

```
glEnable(GL_BLEND);
```

Although we can use the alpha value in many ways, its usual use is to determine the degree of opacity of a color or a material. An opacity of 1.0 indicates that a material is opaque and hides anything behind. A value of 0.0 indicates that the material is completely transparent and cannot be seen. Values in between indicate that the material is translucent and that some of the color of objects behind it blends with its color; the value of alpha determines the weight of its contribution to the color assigned at a point in the image.

The use of alpha allows for many additional capabilities but also more options and a few places where one has to be careful. The basic problem is that when we blend translucent polynomials for display, the order in which they are rendered matters. In contrast, when we render only opaque polygons, the z-buffer algorithm for hidden-surface removal ensures that we get the same image regardless of the order in which the polygons are rendered.

Suppose that we have two polygons that we want to blend. Let's start without lighting and assume that each polygon has an RGB color and an alpha value. We start with a color buffer that has been cleared to the clear color set by glClearColor(). Recall that the clear color is an RGBA color, so if we have enabled blending, the initial display, before we render any polygons, may be translucent and show other windows behind the OpenGL window. For now, we can assume that the initial window color is blue and opaque, having been set by

```
glClearColor(0.0, 0.0, 1.0, 1,0);
```

Now suppose that the first polygon is defined by the code

```
glColor3f(1.0, 0.0, 0.0, 0.5);
glBegin(GL_POLYGON);

/* vertices go here */

glEnd();
```

Assuming that this polygon is visible, its color must be blended with the color already in the color buffer, so that it appears translucent. We must decide not only on a new RGB to put in the color buffer where the polygon is rendered but also a new A. The new A will indicate how translucent the blending of the polygon and the background color is.

OpenGL provides a variety of constants that determine how to blend colors and alpha values. The model is based on the idea that the color buffer is the **destination** where we place our colors and that the state values that are used for the polygon colors are the **source**. When blending is disabled, the source color simply replaces the destination color. However, when blending is enabled the new destination color is a combination of the old destination color and the source color, as shown in Figure 6.6.

Suppose that the color buffer contains the values (R_d, G_d, B_d, A_d) at some point where the polygon is to be rendered. Let (R_s, G_s, B_s, A_s) be the polygon color. By blending, we form a new destination color by multiplying the source

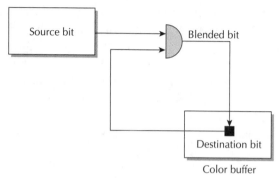

Figure 6.6 Writing model for blending

color by a **source blending factor**, multiplying the destination color by a **destination blending factor**, and adding the results. Thus, the new destination color is $(S_r R_s + D_r R_d, S_g G_s + D_g G_d, S_b B_s + D_b B_d, S_a A_s + D_a A_d)$. (S_r, S_g, S_b, S_a) and (D_r, D_g, D_b, D_a) are the source and destination blending factors, respectively. In OpenGL, we set these factors by the function `glBlendFunc()`.

`void glBlendFunc(GLenum source, GLenum destination)`

Sets the `source` and the `destination` blending factors.

Of the 15 possible blending factors, some can apply to only the source, some to the destination, and others to either. We shall consider some of the most important cases.

When we draw polygonal surfaces, the most common choice is for the source factor to be `GL_SRC_ALPHA` and the destination factor to be `ONE_MINUS_SRC_ALPHA`. Consider what happens when initially, the color buffer is cleared to an opaque color $(R_c, G_c, B_c, 1)$. When we blend in a polygon with color (R_s, G_s, B_s, A_s), the resulting destination color where the polygon is rendered is $(A_s R_s + (1 - A_s)R_c, A_s G_s + (1 - A_s)G_c, A_s B_s + (1 - A_s)B_c, A_s^2 + (1 - A_s)A_c) = (R_d, G_d, B_d, A_d)$.

We can establish a few important properties of the new color. If the original color components are each in the range (0.0, 1.0), so are the new RGBA values. Thus, we can never overflow or underflow a color. If the polygon is transparent $(A_s = 0)$, the new color is the same as the background color. If the polygon is opaque, the new color is the same as the polygon color. These results are what we would expect from real materials.

Now suppose that we add in a second polygon with color $(R_{s'}, G_{s'}, B_{s'}, A_{s'})$. The color where the two polygons overlap will be $(A_{s'}R_{s'} + (1 - A_{s'})(A_sR_s + (1 - A_s)R_c),$ $A_{s'}G_{s'} + (1 - A_{s'})(A_sG_s + (1 - A_s)G_c), A_{s'}B_{s'} + (1 - A_{s'})(A_sB_s + (1 - A_s)B_c), A_{s'}^2 +$ $(1 - A_{s'})(A_s^2 + (1 - A_s)A_c)$. Although this expression is a bit messy, we can verify that the new values of RGB and A will still be in the range (0.0, 1.0). However, the order in which we render the polygons matters. If we switch the order in which we render the two polygons, we get slightly different final colors. Not only is the situation physically unrealistic, but because we usually cannot guarantee the order in which polygons will flow down the OpenGL pipeline, we get different images when the order changes.

We can ensure that the rendering does not depend on the order in which the polygons pass down the pipeline by using the source and destination factors GL_SRC_ALPHA and GL_ONE, respectively. Consider the same example. When we blend in the first polygon, over the opaque background we obtain the color $(A_sR_s + R_c, A_sG_s + G_c, A_sB_s + B_c, A_s^2) = (R_d, G_d, B_d, A_d)$. These colors could overflow, but we can avoid the problem by setting the clear color to black, resulting in the colors $(A_sR_s, A_sG_s, A_sB_s, A_s^2)$. When we blend in the second polygon, we obtain $(A_sR_s + A_{s'}R_{s'}, A_sG_s + A_{s'}G_{s'}, A_sB_s + A_{s'}B_{s'}, A_s^2 + A_{s'}^2)$. The problem here is that the resulting image can be dimmer if the alphas are small, because the color components are scaled rather than blended. If the values of A are large, the colors can overflow.

As far as realism is concerned, the most difficult situation occurs when some of the polygons are opaque and others are translucent. Although we may be willing to accept the order dependency of blending translucent polygons, we must handle opaque polygons correctly. Every opaque polygon must block all polygons behind it.

We can use the depth buffer to keep track of whether a polygon is in front of all polygons that have been rendered so far. However, we must handle translucent polygons differently with respect to changing the values in the depth buffer. When it goes down the pipeline, a translucent polygon will be rendered if it is in front of any polygon found thus far. However, such a polygon should not affect the contents of the depth buffer, as it does not block polygons behind it. OpenGL provides a function, glDepthMask(), that can make the depth buffer read-only (GL_FALSE) or writeable (GL_TRUE).

```
void glDepthMask(GLboolean flag)
```

Makes the depth buffer read-only (GL_FALSE) or writeable (GL_TRUE), the default.

Suppose that we consider the color cube again, but this time, some of the sides are translucent. We can define the vertices as before but this time use RGBA color for the sides, making the first three colors translucent.

```
GLfloat vertices[][3] = {{-1.0, -1.0, 1.0}, {-1.0, 1.0, 1.0},
    {1.0, 1.0, 1.0}, {1.0, -1.0, 1.0}, {-1.0, -1.0, -1.0},
    {-1.0, 1.0, -1.0}, {1.0, 1.0, -1.0}, {1.0, -1.0, -1.0}};
```

```
GLfloat colors[][4] = {1.0, 0.0, 0.0, 0.5},
    {0.0, 1.0, 1.0, 0.5}, {1.0, 1.0, 0.0, 0.5},
    {0.0, 1.0, 0.0, 0.5}, {0.0, 0.0, 1.0, 1.0},
    {1.0, 0.0, 1.0, 1.0}};
```

We can render the cube as before, using the functions polygon() and cube(), making sure that we check each polygon to see whether it is opaque before we render it.

```
void polygon(int a, int b, int c , int d)
{
    glColor4fv(colors[a]);
    if(colors[a][4] != 1.0) glDepthMask(GL_FALSE);
        else glDepthMask(GL_TRUE);
    glBegin(GL_POLYGON);
        glVertex3fv(vertices[a]);
        glVertex3fv(vertices[b]);
        glVertex3fv(vertices[c]);
        glVertex3fv(vertices[d]);
    glEnd();
}

void cube()
{
    polygon(0,3,2,1);
    polygon(2,3,7,6);
    polygon(3,0,4,7);
    polygon(1,2,6,5);
    polygon(4,5,6,7);
    polygon(5,4,0,1);
}
```

We must remember to enable blending and to set the blending factors in main() or init().

```
glEnable(GL_BLEND);
glBlendFactor(GL_SRC_ALPHA, GL_ONE_MINUS_SRC_ALPHA);
```

Chapter 7

Images

Thus far, we have worked with geometric entities that flow down OpenGL's geometric pipeline and are subject to the model-view and projection transformations. OpenGL also allows us to work directly with bits and groups of bits, or pixels, that flow down a parallel pipeline to the frame buffer. We can read bits from the frame buffer and write bits to the frame buffer. We can also take advantage of a variety of features OpenGL provides within the pixel pipeline.

7.1 Pixels and Bitmaps

The back end of every graphics system is the frame buffer, where the image is formed. The frame buffer is really a collection of buffers. For each x, y value in screen space, a corresponding group of bits can be thought of as a generalized picture element, or **pixel**.[1] Such a pixel might have 32 bits for the front-buffer RGBA values, 32 bits for the back-buffer RGBA values, and 64 bits for the front- and back-depth values. If the implementation supports other buffers, such as the accumulation buffer, stencil buffer, and extra color buffers, a pixel will have many more bits. We can envision the frame buffer as in Figure 7.1. It consists of one-bit planes, each of which has the resolution of the screen. Groups of planes correspond to the various OpenGL buffers. All the bits for a given x, y in screen coordinates form a pixel.

From the perspective of an application program that wants to access these buffers directly, we need the ability to read and write rectangular arrays of pixels.

---

1. Most graphics textbooks use the term *frame buffer* to refer to the buffer in which the RGB or RGBA image is formed. A pixel is, then, a group of bits that give the RGB or RGBA value for an x, y location in screen space. OpenGL uses *color buffer* to refer to these bits and the *frame buffer* is the collection of all the buffers, including the color buffer(s) and the depth buffer. OpenGL usage of the terms is closer to how graphics systems are implemented.

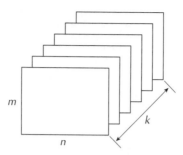

Figure 7.1 An $m \times n$ frame buffer shown with k parallel bit planes

However, we usually manipulate only specific groups of bits in the generalized pixel at one time, namely, those that correspond to one of the OpenGL buffers. Consequently, we shall use the term *pixel* to denote a group of bits, usually an integral number of bytes, at an x, y location in the frame buffer. With this definition, we can write depth pixels or RGBA pixels, depending on where in the frame buffer we do the write operation. Our OpenGL functions will allow us to read or write rectangular blocks of such pixels with a single function execution, an operation called a **bit block transfer operation**, or a **bitblt**.

We also want to be able to work with rectangular arrays of bits, called **bitmaps**. Although they can be thought of as special types of pixel rectangles, bitmaps are used in very different ways, and thus separate functions exist for manipulating pixels and bitmaps. In OpenGL, pixels and bitmaps are the two fundamental nongeometric primitives.

Figure 7.2 shows a simple view of the architecture of a graphics system. The application program runs in the standard processor, as does any other program. The graphics subsystem enters the picture when the application program executes a function that alters the state of the graphics subsystem or generates a graphics primitive, such as a vertex. Geometric primitives flow down the geometric pipeline, which handles transformations—viewing, modeling, projection—lighting, and

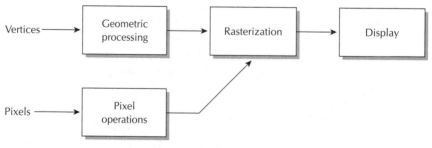

Figure 7.2 Simplified OpenGL architecture showing parallel pipelines

clipping. Eventually, those geometric primitives that are visible are rasterized into a color buffer. Nongeometric primitives flow through a parallel pipeline. The two pipelines merge at the rasterization stage.

At a conceptual level, working with bitmaps and pixels is simple. We can define them in our programs or read them in from files. We then move them to the desired place in the frame buffer. Reading pixels involves going to the correct place in the frame buffer and extracting the values that we find there. Unfortunately, things are not quite so simple in the real world. We have to worry about the differences in how pixels are formatted in the application program, within files, and inside the frame buffer. We also have to worry about the complications owing to different architectures storing discrete data in different ways.

We will also have to account for the different types of pixels. From the perspective of the application program, a pixel might represent an RGB color, an RGBA color, a luminance value, or a depth value. On the application side, these values may be represented in a multitude of ways. For example, colors may be given as bytes, integers, or floats.

In addition, OpenGL has a sequence of operations that can be performed within the pixel pipeline, each with multiple options. For example, we can rescale pixels as they flow down the pipeline. We can also write into the frame buffer in different ways. Fortunately, we will be able to use the default settings for many parameters, and we can get started without introducing too much complexity.

7.2 Bitmaps

Bitmaps are rectangular arrays of bits. The most popular use of bitmaps is for displaying raster text, that is, text composed of characters that are defined by small rectangular blocks of bits. Figure 7.3 shows a few bitmapped characters. Each fits inside a 7 × 9 rectangular array. As we saw in Chapter 2, depending on whether we are working with a fixed width or a proportional font, the boxes may be of different

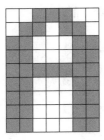 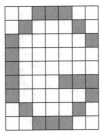

Figure 7.3 Bitmapped characters

sizes. Also, a character may have extra bits around it to aid in spacing the characters correctly when we want to display strings of characters.

Bitmaps are also used for entities, such as cursors and cross hairs in interactive applications, and as **masks** that determine whether something else should happen at a location. For example, we might want to form a bitmap that has the same dimensions as the screen window and use its values to determine whether corresponding pixels in a color buffer should be displayed.

7.2.1 Displaying a Bitmap

The simplest thing that we can do with a bitmap is to display it as a pattern of two colors. Suppose that we have a bitmap that we define in our program. For example, the following code generates 4,096 bits.

```
GLubyte wb[2] = {0 x 00,0 x ff};
GLubyte check[512];
int i, j;
for(i = 0; i < 64; i++) for(j = 0; j < 8; j++)
    check[i*8 + j] = wb[(i/8 + j)%2];
```

Note that we have put the bits into a one-dimensional array. When we display these bits through glBitMap(), we display them as a two-dimensional bitmap for which we can decide how many rows and columns to use. If we interpret these bits as a 64 × 64 square, we get the 8 × 8 checkerboard pattern in Figure 7.4.

We can display this pattern by the function call

```
glBitmap(64, 64, 0.0, 0.0, 0.0, 0.0, check);
```

Each bit in the bitmap is mapped to a pixel on the display, but *which* pixels? The current raster position can be set by the function glRasterPos*(), which we introduced in Chapter 2. The third and fourth parameters (x0 and y0) are added

Figure 7.4 A 64 × 64 bitmap displayed as an 8 × 8 checkerboard pattern

to the current raster position to determine where in the color buffer the lower-left corner of the bitmap is drawn. After the bitmap is drawn, the raster position is increased by the fifth and sixth parameters (xi and yi). In our example, the pattern is simply drawn starting at the present raster position and the raster position, is left unchanged.

The major reason for adding these parameters has to do with creating text. Bitmap characters are stored as rectangular patterns. Some fonts use the same-size boxes; others use different sizes for different characters. However, even if all the characters are stored in the same-size box say—for example, as a 5×7 character set—there are potential complications. For example, a possible uppercase A is shown in Figure 7.5. The **baseline** of the text, where we would want to start printing it, is at the lower-left corner. Note that this character has a column of blank space at the beginning of the character; that space would separate the character from the previous character. Hence, for the A, a choice of 0.0 for both x0 and y0 would seem appropriate. Now consider the lowercase g in Figure 7.5. It also fits in the 5×7 box but the character has a **descender**, which indicates that part of the character should be below the baseline. Thus, for this character to appear correctly, we need a negative value of y0. The exact value of y0 depends on the viewing conditions, as they affect the raster position. We shall return to this issue in the next section. Note that we could have used a larger character set in which the baseline of the characters differed among characters. But such a character set would require more blank spaces within each character box and would require more storage. It is more efficient to use x0 and y0.

When we want to display a string of characters, we have to space them. Here is where xi and yi enter the picture. They are used to increment the raster position after each call to glBitmap(). If we execute glBitmap() for each character with the correct increments, the raster position is set automatically at the beginning of the next character.

A few additional subtleties control where a bitmap appears on the screen and how it appears. First, we address the issue of where the bitmap appears.

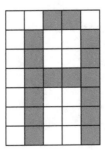 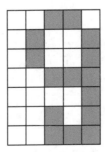

Figure 7.5 Two 5×7 characters

```
void glBitmap(GLsizei r, GLsizei c, GLfloat x0, GLfloat y0,
    GLfloat xi, GLfloat yi, GLubyte *bits)
```

Draws a bitmap of r rows by c columns from the array bits. The bitmap is started offset by x0, y0 from the current raster position. After the bitmap is drawn, the current raster position is incremented by xi, yi.

7.2.2 Mixing Bitmaps and Geometry

Recall from Chapter 2 that the raster position can be specified in two, three, or four dimensions, using floats or integers. This position passes through the geometric pipeline. Thus, the raster position is transformed by both the model-view and projection matrices before it eventually yields a position in screen coordinates. If the resulting position does not lie within the viewport, the bitmap will not be drawn. Note that a mixing of the geometric pipeline, which determines the raster position, and the pixel pipeline, through which the bitmap flows, affects where and whether a bitmap appears. If we want to display only pixels and bitmaps, we could use a window and viewport that match the screen. For example, if w and h are the width and height of the viewport as set by the reshape callback, we could use

```
gluOrtho2D(0.0, (GLfloat) w, 0.0, (GLfloat) h);
```

Now, if the model-view matrix is left as an identity matrix, the raster position can be set by

```
glRasterPos2i(x, y);
```

This sets a position in window coordinates that is the same as the position in the viewport where the generating of the bitmap will begin.

If we want to use both raster primitives and geometric primitives in the same program, setting the raster position can be tricky, as the proper viewing condition for the polygons in the scene may not make it clear how to increment the raster position to place characters in the correct position. One solution to this problem is to use two sets of viewing conditions: one for the geometry and the other for the bitmaps. Within the application program, we can redefine the necessary transformations as needed or use the matrix stacks to save and to recover transformations.

7.2.3 Colors and Masks

In our example, we regarded 1 bits as black and 0 bits as white. In fact, the bitmap is a **mask**. If the bitmap has a 1, we see a color based on the present **raster color**, which is part of the OpenGL state. If the bitmap has a 0, the color of the bitmap does not affect the corresponding pixel in the frame buffer; thus, we see what is "underneath" a 0 bit when the bitmap is placed on top of the color buffer. Suppose that we set the clear color to red and the present drawing color to green. If we clear the screen and draw the bitmap, as in the following code, we will see a red-and-green checkerboard:

```
glClearColor(1.0, 0.0, 0.0, 1.0);
glColor3f(0.0, 1.0, 0.0);
glClear(GL_COLOR_BUFFER_BIT);
glBitmap(64, 64, 0.0, 0.0, 0.0, 0.0, check);
```

In the preceding code, we set the raster color in the same manner that we set the color in our geometric programs, and here it affected the color of the bitmap. OpenGL stores *both* a present drawing color and a present raster color as part of its state. Both colors are set by glColor*(). However, the present raster color is locked by the use glRasterPos*(). Thus, in the following code, the first polygon is drawn in red and the second in green.

```
glColor3f(1.0, 0.0, 0.0);
glBegin(GL_POLYGON))
  .
  .
glEnd();
glRasterPos2i(xr, yr);
glColor3f(0.0, 1.0, 0.0);
glBitmap(64, 64, 0.0, 0.0, 0.0, 0.0, check);
glBegin(GL_POLYGON))
  .
  .
glEnd();
```

The checkerboard is drawn in red because the raster color is the color that was in effect the last time the function glRasterPos2i() was executed.

7.3 Drawing Modes

In our examples thus far, the black bits in the bitmap became pixels colored with the present raster color. We have made two assumptions. First, the buffer that we draw into is the same color buffer into which we draw our geometric primitives. Unless we alter the "drawing buffer" explicitly, this will be the case by default. Second, when we use the present color to draw a pixel, this color is the one that goes into the frame buffer. Again, this is the default case, but we have more control over how bits and pixels are drawn into the frame buffer.

OpenGL uses a drawing model similar to that shown in Figure 7.6. This model is essentially the same as the model we used for blending in Chapter 6. When we want to write pixels or bitmaps, we first look at what is contained in the location at which we wish to draw. What we draw can depend on the value that we find there. Consider a single bit from the bitmap. When we render the bitmap, each bit in the bitmap corresponds to a pixel on the screen. We call this bit the **source bit**. If this bit is 1, OpenGL uses the present raster color to affect the destination pixel. We can think of this color as the **source color**, or **source pixel**.[2] The corresponding pixel in the frame buffer is called the **destination pixel**. In the simplest case, for each location in the frame buffer that corresponds to a 1 bit in the bitmap, the source pixel replaces the destination pixel in the frame buffer. However, if we can first look at the destination pixel, we can make the new value of the destination pixel be some function of the source and destination pixels. In OpenGL, this function operates on a bit-by-bit basis between the source and destination pixels. We can apply any of the 16 possible logical operations between two bits, using the function `glLogicOp()` to select the function.

`void glLogicOp(GLenum op)`

Selects which of the 16 logical operations between the source and destination pixels are combined in the frame buffer if logic operations (GL_COLOR_LOGIC_OP) are enabled. Choices include GL_COPY—the default—GL_OR, and GL_XOR.

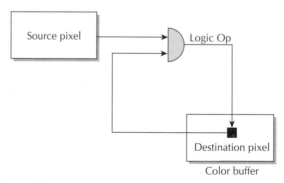

Figure 7.6 Writing model for bitmaps

---

2. Although this definition may seem odd, it will make more sense when we write multibit pixels to the frame buffer.

We must first enable logic operations by

```
glEnable(GL_COLOR_LOGIC_OP);
```

The default (GL_COPY) produces the same result as we would get without enabling logic operations; the source pixel simply replaces the destination pixel. The other possible operations are more interesting. For example, we could always replace the source pixel by the logical OR of the two pixels, taken bitwise, using GL_OR, or by the complement of the source, again taken bitwise, using GL_COPY_INVERTED. Many of these options may leave unexpected colors on the display because logic operations are applied bit by bit. If we use GL_OR between a blue pixel and a yellow pixel, the resulting color may not have any clear relationship to either blue or yellow.

Of all the operations, the most interesting and useful is the exclusive OR operation (GL_XOR). Most of its applications are dependent on the property that, if we apply the operation twice, we get back to the starting state. Thus, if $\oplus$ denotes XOR and x and y are bits,

$$x = x \oplus y \oplus y$$

Hence, if x is the value of a bit in the frame buffer and we draw bit y at the same place, using exclusive OR mode, we get the value $x \oplus y$. When we draw y a second time, we get the value x again.

Suppose that we want to remove an object from the screen. We could clear the color buffer and then redraw all the other objects. This strategy requires that we either go through all the code that defines the other objects or use display lists. If we use XOR, we simply draw the same object a second time at the same place that we drew it the first time. The second draw undoes the first. Here is a simple mouse callback that redraws the checkerboard at the original mouse position each time the left mouse button is clicked and then draws it again at the position of the mouse:

```
void mouse(int btn, int state, int x, int y)
{

    if(btn == GLUT_LEFT_BUTTON && state == GLUT_DOWN)
    {
        glBitmap(64, 64, 0.0, 0.0, 0.0, 0.0, check);
        glRasterPos2i(x, ww - y);
        glBitmap(64, 64, 0.0, 0.0, 0.0, 0.0, check);
        glFlush();
    }
}
```

Here, ww is the height of the window as returned by the reshape callback, which we save as a global variable:

```
void reshape(int w, int h)
{
    glViewport(0, 0, w, h);
    glMatrixMode(GL_PROJECTION);
    glLoadIdentity();
    gluOrtho2D (0.0,   (GLfloat) w, 0.0, (GLfloat) h);
    ww = w;
    glMatrixMode(GL_MODELVIEW);
    glLoadIdentity();
}
```

The mode was set in main() as

```
glEnable(GL_COLOR_LOGIC_OP);
glLogicOp(GL_XOR);
```

In this sample code, the bitmap is drawn initially at the lower-left corner of the window in the display callback:

```
void display()
{
    glClear(GL_COLOR_BUFFER_BIT);
    glColor3f(1.0, 0.0, 0.0);
    glRasterPos2f(0.0, 0.0);
    glBitmap(64, 64, 0.0, 0.0, 0.0, 0.0, check);
    glFlush();
}
```

Subsequently, each time the left mouse button is clicked, the checkerboard pattern is drawn in the position first, because the raster position has not been changed. This operation erases the previous instance of the checkerboard. Then the raster position is updated to match the mouse location, and the checkerboard is rendered in the new position.

Applications of this simple idea include moving a cursor around the screen, rubberbanding lines and rectangles, and implementing pop-up menus. All these applications involve drawing an object, perhaps on top of other objects, and then returning the screen to its original state.

7.4 Reading and Writing Pixels

We now turn to reading and writing arrays of pixels in the frame buffer. Conceptually, the process is simple. Consider writing. We have image data that are either defined in the application program or read from a file. We have to move these data to the frame buffer. We can use the OpenGL function `glWritePixels()`. Reading is the inverse process. We move pixels from the frame buffer to the application, using `glReadPixels()`. However, we must worry about a host of small problems. Most arise from the differences between how pixels are represented within the frame buffer and how they are represented within processor memory. These problems are exacerbated by the differences in how numbers are represented in different architectures. In addition, we want to be able to use multiple ways of representing pixel data, including ints, bytes, and floats, regardless of how our data are eventually stored in the frame buffer.

We can envision the process as in Figure 7.7. Pixels pass through a pipeline, where they are **unpacked** from their original format in processor memory as they go from the application program to the frame buffer. Pixels can be altered as they go from the program to the frame buffer through **pixel transfer operations**. For example, we might want to scale pixels to go over the range allowed in the frame buffer. We can also apply **pixel mapping** operations, which will allow us to use tables to map pixel values to other values. We might use mapping operations for color-conversion operations between different color systems or to do color balancing to adjust for the properties of our display. We can then apply scaling operations to the pixels to replicate pixels as they are placed in the frame buffer. Finally, a series of tests are performed on each pixel before it is placed in the frame buffer.

A similar but simpler process applies when we read pixels from the frame buffer. Of particular concern is the format conversion, **packing**, that determines how information in the frame buffer is placed in processor memory.

We can also choose which buffers to use for reading and writing. We can write RGB or RGBA pixels to the front or back color buffers; we can read or write depth values; we can also read pixels from one of the buffers that compose the frame buffer and write them to another buffer, even the one from which we are reading.

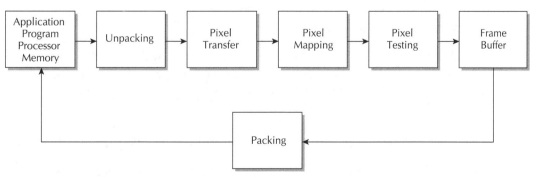

Figure 7.7 Pixel pipeline

This architecture suggests that we can use OpenGL not only to display discrete data, such as pictures and text, but also to process images.

7.4.1 Writing Pixels

The fundamental pixel-writing function is `glDrawPixels()`, which draws pixel rectangles at the current raster position. We must specify the format of the pixels that we are drawing. For example, suppose that we have an RGB image that we form in our program as

`GLubyte image[ROWS][COLUMNS][3];`

We use `GL_RGB` for the format and `GL_UNSIGNED_BYTE` for the type. We draw by

`glDrawPixels(ROWS, COLUMNS, GL_RGB, GL_UNSIGNED_BYTE, image);`

This format specifies that the data are RGB triplets. If the data is provided in separate arrays, we can use `GL_RED`, `GL_GREEN`, and `GL_BLUE` and access three arrays. Other formats are `GL_RBGA` and `GL_DEPTH_COMPONENT` to write into the depth buffer. The type parameter can be most of the standard types (`GL_INT`, `GL_FLOAT`) or be of some packed types that are used to compress image data. For example, the type `GL_UNSIGNED_BYTE_3_3_2` corresponds to some situations in which 1 byte is used to store an RGB value, using 3 bits each for red and green and 2 bits for blue.

`void glDrawPixels(GLsizei w, GLsizei h, GLenum format, GLenum type, GLvoid *array)`

Draws a rectangle of pixels w × h from `array` at the present raster position. The pixels are in the specified `format`, using data of `type`.

7.4.2 Reading Pixels

We can move pixels from the frame buffer to memory with `glReadPixels()`. The parameters are the same as for `glDrawPixels()` but are used in the reverse way. Thus, the following function call will read `rows` * `columns` RGB pixels, starting at the lower-left corner of the frame buffer:

`glReadPixels(0, 0, rows, columns, GL_RGB, GL_UNSIGNED_BYTE, image);`

These values will be returned as unsigned bytes, regardless of how they are represented in the frame buffer.

> void glReadPixels(GLint x, GLint y, GLsizei w, GLsizei h,
>   GLenum format, GLenum type, GLvoid *array)
>
> Reads a rectangle of pixels w × h from the frame buffer, starting at (x, y) into array. The pixels are in the specified format and are written as data of type.

Reading pixels can produce some unexpected results unless we pay careful attention to the resolution of the frame buffer. When we write pixels, we usually can specify a color and not worry about how many bits are in the frame buffer for displaying the color. The implementation will do the best it can with whatever resolution it has. Many systems use a method called **dithering**, which varies low-order bits as they are displayed to smooth out transitions between colors that would otherwise be visible in a low-resolution display. However, when we read from a color buffer, what is returned depends on how much resolution there is. Hence, we might write a pixel where the red has a value between 0 and 255 but read back only 16 different values because the display has only 4 bits for red. If the display is dithered, we might write the same values over a large area and read back a variety of slightly different values. In addition, the number of bits in the display may be different for single- and double-buffered displays on the same system.

 When reading pixels, make sure that you know the resolution of the display and account for possible dithering.

 How pixels are stored within an OpenGL implementation may bear little relation to how they are stored in processor memory.

Hence, when we read pixels, we should check the number of bits of resolution; for example,

glGetIntegerv(GL_RED_BITS, &nbits);

We should also turn off dithering:

glDisable(GL_DITHER);

7.4.3 Copying Pixels

Sometimes, we want to move pixels from one part of the frame buffer to another. We could do a glReadPixels() followed by a glDrawPixels() but that would require using processor memory for a frame buffer–to frame buffer–operation.

The function glCopyPixels() allows us to accomplish this operation without going through processor memory. We set the starting point of the copy as in glReadPixels(), using the present raster position to determine where to place the copy. If we are working with RGB or RGBA colors, the buffer parameter is set to GL_COLOR.

```
void glCopyPixels(GLint x, GLint y, GLsizei w, GLsizei h,
    GLenum buffer)
```

Copies a block of pixels w × h starting at (x, y) from buffer, starting at the present raster position.

7.5 Selecting Buffers

When we read and write RGBA values, we are working with a color buffer in the frame buffer. When we work in single-buffer mode, reading and writing will, by default, be in the front color buffer (GL_FRONT). In double-buffer mode, we use the back color buffer (GL_BACK) by default. These are the same buffers in which geometric primitives are normally placed.

However, most OpenGL implementations support additional color buffers. For example, an implementation that supports double-buffered stereo images has four color buffers: GL_RIGHT_FRONT, GL_LEFT_FRONT, GL_RIGHT_BACK, and GL_LEFT_BACK—or just GL_RIGHT and GL_LEFT for single-buffered stereo. We might also have auxiliary color buffers (GL_AUX0, ..., GL_AUXn) that can be used for other purposes.

We can select which buffer to use for reading by glReadBuffer() and which to use for writing by glDrawBuffer().

```
void glReadBuffer(GLenum buffer)
```

Selects buffer for reading.

```
void glDrawBuffer(GLenum buffer)
```

Selects buffer for drawing.

In some are cases in interactive applications, we want to write into both the front and back buffers. We can do so by selecting GL_FRONT_AND_BACK for the drawing buffer.

There are many examples of how we can use extra buffers. One example is an alternative to the picking mechanism we presented in Chapter 3. In this mechanism, we render each object in a distinct color into a color buffer, one that is not displayed. We can then use the mouse position returned in the mouse callback to determine where to read a color in this color buffer. We then map the color that we read to the identifier of the object. Consider, for example, a shaded sphere. The sphere that we see on the display will show many shades, whereas the rendering of the sphere into the other buffer will be in a constant shade. This technique requires an extra rendering but provides a simple picking strategy. We could also have rendered the scene twice into the back buffer before swapping buffers, once in distinct colors for the picking and the second time as we wish to display the objects.

Another application is when we need renderings using multiple cameras. For example, if a mirror is in a scene, we can first render the scene with a camera behind the mirror into an extra buffer. We can then read that buffer and texture map it—as we shall discuss in Chapter 8—to the face of the mirror when we render the scene normally.

7.6 Pixel Store Modes

Depending on your system, moving data between processor memory and the frame buffer may or may not work correctly. The problem is that OpenGL may need additional information about how bytes are arranged in processor memory. For example, systems differ in the order of bytes in a short or in an int. Some machines may require that data be aligned on 4-byte boundaries in memory. In some cases, despite more than one allowable method of arranging image data, those methods may have great differences in efficiency. OpenGL provides the function glPixelStore*() to allow programs to define how image data are stored in the processor.

```
void glPixelStore{fd}(GLenum param, TYPE value)
```

Sets the pixel store mode parameter param to value.

The values of the parameters account for the many possible situations on different machines. Two of the more common options are

```
glPixelStorei(GL_UNPACK_SWAP_BYTES, TRUE);
glPixelStorei(GL_PACK_SWAP_BYTES, TRUE);
```

These functions reorder the bytes from least significant to most significant for shorts and ints without changing the order of bits in a byte. Other important options are

```
glPixelStorei(GL_UNPACK_ALIGNMENT, 1);
glPixelStorei(GL_PACK_ALIGNMENT, 1);
```

These options pack and unpack the data, always using the next byte. Note that we can control the reading of pixels from the frame buffer—packing—and the writing of pixels to the frame buffer from processor memory—unpacking—independently.

 If pixel functions give unexpected results, check your pixel store modes.

Fortunately, if you are working on a single architecture, you usually need not worry about these options and can use the default values for parameters. You can also often avoid problems, as we did in our program, by using bytes and unsigned bytes as much as possible.

7.7 Displaying a PPM Image

When we use images from the outside, they are usually in a standard format, such as JPEG, TIFF, GIF, or PPM. The multiplicity of these formats stems, in large part, from the multiple types of image data. Images can be RGB, indexed color, RGBA, or luminance. The data may be stored as integers, bytes, or floats. In addition, the data may be compressed to reduce the size of the image file. One of the reasons that OpenGL lacks functions to handle images in standard formats is that so many formats exist. Consequently, we often have to write our own code to read image files and to take images that we form in the frame buffer and save them in a standard format. Often, we can use standard software, such as Photoshop or xv, to convert from one standard format to another, rather than creating a large number of image readers and writers.

We can illustrate the basic ideas, as well as the use of various pixel functions in OpenGL, by writing a program that will read an image in a standard format and use OpenGL to display it. We will do this for a Portable Pixel Map (PPM) file. This format is uncompressed and very simple. The example will cover most issues for uncompressed formats. Working with compressed formats is beyond the scope of this chapter.

PPM files, as do most image files, start with a header that identifies the type of the file, the size and format of the image, and some optional comments. The header is followed by the data. PPM files store RGB images as successive RGB pixels, each component represented by an integer in ASCII form. The header looks like this:

```
P3
# comment 1
# comment 2
        .
# comment n
rows columns max
```

The P3 identifies the file as a PPM file and is followed by an arbitrary number of comment lines, each beginning with a #, and each can be at most 70 characters long. The next three values are integers for the number of rows, columns, and the maximum value of the RGB values in the data. The minimum value is assumed to be 0. These are followed by the data as a sequence of RGB values; each RGB value is a string of ASCII characters for three integers. The PPM format ignores whitespace characters—spaces, tabs, newlines.

We will write the program so it prompts the user for the file name of the PPM file. There are a few tricks in reading the header, because we do not know how many comment lines there will be. We allocate a buffer into which we can read data.

```
FILE *fd;
char c;
char b[70];

printf("enter file name\n");
scanf("%s", b);
fd = fopen(b, "r");

fd = fopen(argv[1], "r");
fscanf(fd,"%[^\n]", b);
if(b[0] != 'P'|| b[1] != '3')
{
    printf("%s is not a PPM file!\n", argv[1]);
    exit(0);
}
```

After we read the first line, we check whether the first two characters are P3. Then, we read the first character on the next line. If the character is a #, we know that it is a comment line and we can read the rest of the line into the buffer. If this character is not a #, we can put it back into the file stream, using ungetc(). Now, we can read the three integers for the number of rows and columns and for the maximum value of the color components.

```
fscanf(fd, "%c", &c);
while(c == '#')
{
    fscanf(fd, "%[^\n]", b);
    printf("%s\n", b);
    fscanf(fd, "%c", &c);
}
ungetc(c,fd);
fscanf(fd, "%d %d %d", &n, &m, &k);
```

We can use the rows and columns to set the size of the window:

```
glutInitWindowSize(n, m);
```

We use a dynamic array so that the program will work for any size image. We now allocate a one-dimensional array of 3*rows*columns unsigned bytes:

```
GLubyte *image;
nm = n*m;
image=malloc(3*sizeof(GLuint)*nm);
```

When using dynamic arrays with OpenGL, it is important to allocate one-dimensional arrays of data rather than arrays of pointers to arrays of data. If we tried the latter, we could not pass the array to an OpenGL function, such as glDrawPixels(). We will use an array of unsigned bytes to store the image data. Although OpenGL can use a variety of types, we usually cannot see at a greater resolution, even if the display has more than 8 bits per color component. However, the data are given as integers, so we must scale them by the factor

```
s=255./k;
```

We can now read the data. If the value of s is 1.0, we can skip the scaling step.

```
if (k == 255) for(i = 0; i < nm; i++)
{
    fscanf(fd, "%d %d %d", &red, &green, &blue);
    image[3*nm - 3*i - 3] = red;
    image[3*nm - 3*i - 2] = green;
    image[3*nm - 3*i - 1] = blue;
}
else for(i = 0; i < nm; i++)
{
```

```
        fscanf(fd, "%d %d %d", &red, &green, &blue);
        image[3*nm - 3*i - 3] = red*s;
        image[3*nm - 3*i - 2] = green*s;
        image[3*nm - 3*i - 1] = blue*s;
    }
```

Finally, we can display the image in the display callback.

```
void display()
{
    glClear(GL_COLOR_BUFFER_BIT);
    glRasterPos2i(0, 0);
    glDrawPixels(n, m, GL_RGB, GL_UNSIGNED_BYTE, image);
    glFlush();
}
```

Note that this program has no geometric functions. By choosing the OpenGL window to match the size of the image, we fill the window when we display the image, as in Figure 7.8. However, when we resize the window, we will see only part of the image if we make the window smaller or extra blank space if we make the window larger, as in Figure 7.9. We cannot avoid this problem if we draw pixels. This situation is fundamentally different from what is possible for displaying

Figure 7.8 Display of PPM image when window size matches image size

Figure 7.9 Display of PPM image after window size has been changed

geometric entities. When we display a scene with polygons, we can change the projection matrix within the reshape callback whenever the window is resized, so that the entire image fills the viewport. The present situation is owing to pixels flowing through their own pipeline, which is unaffected by the projection and model-view matrices. We can rescale images so that they change size when we change the window if we use the images to define texture maps, the topic of the next chapter.

One tempting change to our program would be to use integers rather than bytes for the the array image:

```
GLuint *image;
nm = n*m;
image=malloc(12*sizeof(GLuint)*nm);
```

We would then use glDrawPixels() with integers:

```
glDrawPixels(n, m, GL_RGB, GL_UNSIGNED_INT, image);
```

We could then use pixel transfer operations

```
glPixelTransferf(GL_RED_SCALE, s);
glPixelTransferf(GL_GREEN_SCALE, s);
glPixelTransferf(GL_BLUE_SCALE, s);
```

In this case, the scaling would be done by OpenGL rather than inside the application. However, we must be sure that we are using the correct pixel store mode.

Here is the PPM reader again, using pixel transfer and pixel store operations. The code prints the contents of the header.

```
#include <stdio.h>
#include <stdlib.h>

#include <GL/glut.h>

int n;
int m;


GLuint *image;

void display()
{
    glClear(GL_COLOR_BUFFER_BIT);
    glRasterPos2i(0, 0);
    glDrawPixels(n, m, GL_RGB, GL_UNSIGNED_INT, image);
    glFlush();
}


void myreshape(int h, int w)
{
    glMatrixMode(GL_PROJECTION);
    glLoadIdentity();
    gluOrtho2D(0.0, (GLfloat) n, 0.0, (GLfloat) m);
    glMatrixMode(GL_MODELVIEW);
    glLoadIdentity();
    glViewport(0, 0, h, w);
}


int main(int argc, char **argv)
{
    FILE *fd;
    int  k, nm;
    char c;
    int i;
    char b[70];
    float s;
    int red, green, blue;

    printf("enter file name\n");
    scanf("%s", b);
    fd = fopen(b, "r");
    fscanf(fd, "%[^\n]", b);
    if(b[0] != 'P'|| b[1] != '3')
    {
        printf("%s is not a PPM file!\n", b);
        exit(0);
```

```
    }
    printf("%s is a PPM file\n", b);
    fscanf(fd, "%c", &c);
    while(c == '#')
    {
        fscanf(fd, "%[^\n]", b);
        printf("%s\n", b);
        fscanf(fd, "%c", &c);
    }
    ungetc(c,fd);
    fscanf(fd, "%d %d %d", &n, &m, &k);

    printf("%d rows   %d columns   max value = %d\n", n, m, k);

    nm = n*m;

    image = malloc(3*sizeof(GLuint)*nm);

    s = 255./k;

    for(i = 0; i < nm; i++)
    {
        fscanf(fd, "%d %d %d", &red, &green, &blue);
        image[3*nm - 3*i - 3] = red;
        image[3*nm - 3*i - 2] = green;
        image[3*nm - 3*i - 1] = blue;
    }
    printf("read image\n");
    glutInit(&argc, argv);
    glutInitDisplayMode(GLUT_SINGLE | GLUT_RGB);
    glutInitWindowSize(n, m);
    glutInitWindowPosition(0, 0);
    glutCreateWindow("image");
    glutReshapeFunc(myreshape);
    glutDisplayFunc(display);
    glPixelTransferf(GL_RED_SCALE, s);
    glPixelTransferf(GL_GREEN_SCALE, s);
    glPixelTransferf(GL_BLUE_SCALE, s);
    glPixelStorei(GL_UNPACK_SWAP_BYTES, GL_TRUE);
    glClearColor(1.0, 1.0, 1.0, 1.0);
    glutMainLoop();
}
```

7.8 Using Luminance

In many applications, we work with images that consist only of shades of gray. Often these images are referred to as **luminance** images. Luminance images can be stored in an array, using only scalars for the elements rather than RGB triplets. Such gray-scale images are often captured from the real world, and the gray-scale values can be related to the red, green, and blue color components that we might measure with a black-and-white camera. Equivalently, the gray values can be thought of as the values we might see on a monochrome television.

The relationship between luminance and the color components of a standard RGB display is given by the equation

$$L = 0.30 \ R + 0.59 \ G + 0.11 \ B$$

Thus, what we see on a monochrome display is dominated by the green component. This equation is determined both by the characteristics of the display, such as the relative strengths of the phosphors in a CRT, and the properties of our visual systems. We have very low sensitivity to blue, which is at the end of the visible part of the spectrum, but very high sensitivity to green. Consequently, to handle luminance correctly, we can use pixel scaling with the correct factors when we go between RGB and luminance.

7.9 Pixel Mapping

One weakness of our use of RGB is that it does not take account of the differences in RGB systems among display technologies, including cathode-ray tubes (CRTs), film, and projectors. A given RGB pixel can appear differently on different systems, owing to differences between, for example, film dyes and phosphors. We can mitigate some of these problems in OpenGL by **pixel mapping**. This feature allows each pixel to be altered by a user-defined table. We can apply the features in a variety of modes. We can use a separate table for each of red, green, and blue. Thus, the blue table would alter each blue value as it goes into the frame buffer. If we wish to use the color maps, we first use

```
glPixelTransferi(GL_MAP_COLOR, GL_TRUE);
```

We then set up the maps, using `glPixelMap*v()`.

`void glPixelTransfer{if}(GLenum name, TYPE value)`

Sets the pixel transfer mode parameter `name` to `value`. Various options allow enabling color mapping (GL_MAP_COLOR) and scaling and biasing the scaling.

```
void glPixelMap{ui us f}v(GLenum map, GLint size, TYPE *array)
```

Sets up a pixel map for pixels of type (unsigned int, unsigned short, or float) to map from pixel as specified by map. The map is of length size with values in array. The values of map include GL_PIXEL_MAP_I_TO_R (or G or B) for mapping color indices to colors and GL_PIXEL_MAP_R_TO_R (or G_TO_G or B_TO_B) for rescaling RGB colors.

Generally, the size parameter is determined by how much memory is allocated for each component of a pixel. Thus, if we use 8 bits for each RGB component and we want to map blue values to blue values, we might see a function call of the form

```
float bluemap[256];
glPixelMapfv(GL_PIXEL_MAP_B_TO_B, 256, bluemap);
```

Here, the values of blue on both input to and output from the map would normally be in the range (0, 1). We would have similar lines of code for the green and red maps.

Another common example of the use of pixel maps occurs with **pseudocolor**. Here, we start witth a luminance image but use color to display the gray values. This technnique has many similarities to using indexed color; however, the processing is done on luminance values that have meaning within the application. A typical use might look something like

```
for(i = 0; i < 256; i++)
{
    redmap[i] = i/255.0;
    if(i < 128) greenmap[i] = i/128.0;
    else greenmap[i] = 1.0 - (i - 128.0)/127.0
    blue_map[i] = 1.0 - i/255.0;
}
glPixelMapfv(GL_PIXEL_MAP_I_TO_R, 256, redmap);
glPixelMapfv(GL_PIXEL_MAP_I_TO_R, 256, greenmap);
glPixelMapfv(GL_PIXEL_MAP_I_TO_R, 256, bluemap);
```

Here, black is mapped to blue, white is mapped to red, and grays in the middle are mapped to colors that are shades of green.

7.10 Pixel Zoom

When we are working with pixels, most geometric transformations such as rotation and translation are not practical because pixels are discrete entities and must lie at fixed locations in the frame buffer. If we were to rotate a block of pixels, we could only approximate their appearance on the display. However, scaling of blocks of pixels along the directions of the window can make sense. For example, if we have a raster set of characters and want to make a character twice as large, we can **replicate** its pixels; that is, we can render each pixel in the font four times, as in Figure 7.10.

OpenGL provides the function `glPixelZoom()` for this purpose. We can use it to replicate pixels, thus enlarging the image. We can also use it for reducing the size of the image. If the scale factors are negative, we flip the image.

---

void glPixelZoom(GLfloat sx, GLfloat sy)

Magnifies or reduces pixels by the scale factors sx and sy when pixels are drawn. Negative values flip the image in that direction, in addition to the magnification or reduction.

Note that although fractional factors are allowed, you may notice defects in the image when the pixels are rendered. If we look back at our example of the PPM reader, we flipped the image as we read it to account for how OpenGL displays its pixels. Instead, we could have read in the pixels in order:

```
for(i = 0; i < nm; i++)
{
    fscanf(fd, "%d %d %d", &red, &green, &blue);
    image[3*i] = red;
    image[3*i + 1] = green;
    image[3*i + 2] = blue;
}
```

We would then use the pixel zoom:

```
glPixelZoom(1,0, -1.0);
```

Figure 7.10 Replicating pixels to form larger characters

In some applications, we have images of one size but need to work with images of another. For example, when we work with textures in the next chapter, all the texture maps must have sizes that are powers of 2. We could use a combination C code and OpenGL functions to produce these images but the utility library has a function, gluScaleImage(), to help us.

```
void gluScaleImage(GLenum format, GLint win, GLint hin, GLenum
    typein, void *imagein, GLint wout, GLint hout, GLenum
    typeout, void *imageout)
```

Takes a win × hin image imagein of format and typein and produces a wout × hout image imageout of format and typeout.

7.11 Imaging Processing in OpenGL

With this wealth of functionality, we can write programs to use OpenGL to accomplish many of the operations associated with digital image processing, including histogram computations, filtering (convolution), and color table manipulation. Although all these operations could be done within the user program, we would like to use the OpenGL processing capabailities that are often implemented in hardware.

One approach to doing image processing in OpenGL is to create a set of functions using the pixel functions that we have just presented. Much of this has already been done and comprises the **imaging subset** of OpenGL, which is documented in the *OpenGL Programming Guide*. These functions are an OpenGL extension and thus are not supported on all OpenGL implementations. However, they are so useful that they are supported on many.

Another approach to image processing is to use texture maps, the topic of the next chapter. Texture mapping combines the pixel and geometric pipelines and allows us to use our transformation capabilities on pixels by first converting our images to texture maps.

Chapter 8

Texture Mapping

Texture mapping combines pixels with geometric objects to provide images of seemingly great complexity but without the overhead of building large geometric models. Implementation of texture mapping uses both the geometric and pixel pipelines. Although the basics of how we apply texture maps to objects are simple, doing it well requires careful setting of a variety of parameters. We shall start with a simple example and then add to it in subsequent sections.

8.1 Texels and Textures

At this point, we have two fundamental ways to display objects on the screen. Either we can model them as geometric objects, typically as polygons in three dimensions, and pass them through the geometric pipeline, or we can display blocks of pixels. Each approach has its limitations. Pixels can show great detail but lack three-dimensional properties. Although we can process polygons at rates measured in millions of polygons per second on systems that implement the geometric pipeline in hardware, even these systems cannot process polygons quickly enough to model many natural phenomena, such as fire, grass, water, or clouds.

What we can do, however, is attempt to combine the best features of each approach, using a method called **texture mapping**. Suppose that we have an $n \times m$ array of pixels. Instead of regarding the array as discrete elements, we can think of it as a continuous array. A point in this array is defined by variables s and t. Thus, as in Figure 8.1, we have for each (s, t) pair a value that is the value of a pixel, usually either a luminance value or an RGB or RGBA value. This continuous array is a two-dimensional **texture**. When we refer to the original elements, we call them **texels**, or texture elements, rather than pixels.

Now consider a geometric object in three dimensions. Each point on its surface corresponds to coordinates (x, y, z) in three-dimensional world

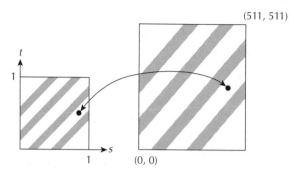

Figure 8.1 Texture map as a continuous image in (*s, t*) space and as a discrete image

coordinates. We can associate each (*x, y, z*) point in world coordinates with a point (*s, t*) in **texture coordinates** through a pair of functions:

$$s = f(x, y, z)$$
$$t = g(x, y, z)$$

We then could use the color or luminance from the texture to determine the color that we use for the point on the surface, if it is visible. This process is shown in Figure 8.2 and shows the essence of texture mapping.

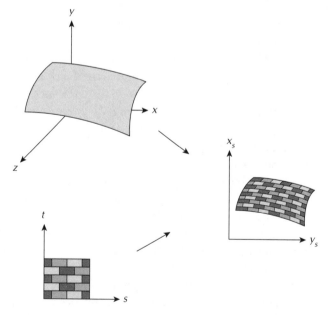

Figure 8.2 Combining a texture with a surface to color pixels in screen coordinates

At this point, texture mapping is rather abstract and not coupled to how OpenGL processes pixels and geometry. The main difficulties are that the pixels (texels) and the geometry flow down different pipelines and that at the point at which we need the texture value, we are in the rasterization stage. Thus, it is not clear how we match points on the surface with texels. OpenGL handles this problem by forcing the application program to define texture coordinates for each vertex. More specifically, texture coordinates, like colors and normals, are part of the OpenGL state; when a vertex is defined, it uses the present texture coordinates. Thus, we never define functions f and g explicitly. Rather, we provide samples of their values in our programs by defining texture coordinates for vertices. OpenGL uses interpolation to determine the texture coordinates that it needs during rasterization by interpolation.

8.2 Constructing a Texture Map

Using a texture map requires three basic steps. First, we must identify the image that we want to use for the texture map. This image can be one that we read in, as in Chapter 7, or it can be defined within the program. The image can also be read out of one of the OpenGL color buffers. Second, we define parameters that determine how the texture should be applied. Third, we define texture coordinates for the vertices in the program.

However, as with other OpenGL functionality, the large variety of options available affects both the efficiency of the process and the appearance of the image. Let's proceed with a simple example, and then we can worry about the options.

OpenGL supports one-, two-, and three-dimensional texture mapping. In two-dimensional texture mapping, the most familiar case, we map images to the surfaces of geometric objects, such as polygons. However, we could also use a one-dimensional texture to create a pattern of colors for a line segment or a curve. Three-dimensional textures use three-dimensional volumes of texels. OpenGL can map the values in this texture volume to surfaces. Conceptually, a three-dimensional texture map is similar to sculpting the shape of a three-dimensional object from a block of material with the specified texture.

Suppose that we have a two-dimensional three-color image in our program. We need not worry from where this image came. We can make this image into a two-dimensional texture map by

```
GLubyte myimage[64][64][3];
glEnable(GL_TEXTURE_2D);

glTexImage2D(GL_TEXTURE_2D, 0, 3, 64, 64, 0, GL_RGB,
    GL_UNSIGNED_BYTE, myimage);
```

First, texture mapping must be enabled. Note that we have to separately enable one-, two-, and three-dimensional mapping. Next, we use glTexImage2D() to specify the texture image. Most of the parameters should be clear. But let's examine them in order.

- GL_TEXTURE_2D: Tells OpenGL that we are specifying a two-dimensional texture. The only other possible option here, GL_PROXY_TEXTURE_2D, is useful if we want to determine whether we have the resources available to support the size texture that we want to use.
- 0: Sets the level of the texture map. OpenGL supports a facility called *mipmapping*, discussed later, that enables us to use a sequence of texture images at different resolutions to increase efficiency. Level 0 is the highest level, and we specify this value when we do not want to use mipmapping.
- 3: Gives the internal format of the image data. The constant 3 identifies the image data as coming from an RGB image. We could have used the symbolic constant GL_RGB instead of the 3. Other values allow us to specify that the image data are in luminance form (1 or GL_LUMINANCE), RGBA (4 or GL_RGBA) or one of many other formats that store image data using other than 8 bits per component.
- 64: Specifies the number of rows in the texture. The number of rows (and columns) must be a power of 2.
- 64: Specifies the number of columns in the texture.
- 0: Sets the border width. A texture map optionally can have a border of one pixel around it, which can be used to create smooth texture maps.
- GL_RGB: Specifies the type of texels that are to be used. This parameter and the next have the same options as for pixel data that we discussed in Chapter 7.
- GL_UNSIGNED_BYTE: Identifies the format of the texels to be used.
- myimage: Identifies pointer to the array of image data.

```
void glTexImage2D(GLenum target, GLint level, GLint iformat,
    GLsizei width, GLsizei height, GLint border, GL enum
    format, GLenum type, GLvoid *texels)
```

Sets up a two-dimensional texture of height × width texels of type and format. A border of b texels can be specified. The image data is of format iformat.

Although this function has many parameters, most of what we are doing here is similar to what we did for images. Texture mapping takes image data from the application program and passes them through the pixel pipeline, just as we do when we draw pixels. Thus, OpenGL must know how these data are formatted in processor memory before it takes them and puts them into texture memory. Consequently, we may also have to set up options via `glPixelFormat*()`. However, a few differences occur at the end of the pixel pipeline. First, texels go into texture memory. Depending on the implementation, texture memory may be part of the same memory that is used for the frame buffer, or it might be special memory. But just as with the frame buffer, OpenGL can use its own format to store texels, and the transfer of texels from the application program to texture memory can take a significant amount of time for large textures. Moreover, texture memory tends to be a limited resource.

 The dimensions of texture images must be powers of 2.

 A significant amount of time may be needed to move a texure image from processor memory to texture memory.

We can set up one- and three-dimensional texture maps in a similar manner, using `glTexImage1D()` and `glTexImage3D()`. Each must be enabled separately (GL_TEXTURE_1D or GL_TEXTURE_3D).

```
void glTexImage1D(GLenum target, GLint level, GLint iformat,
    GLsizei width, GLint border, GL enum format, GLenum type,
    GLvoid *texels)
void glTexImage3D(GLenum target, GLint level, GLint iformat,
    GLsizei width, GLsizei height, GLsizei depth, GLint
    border, GL enum format, GLenum type, GLvoid *texels)
```

Sets up one- and three-dimensional texture maps.

8.3 Texture Coordinates

The mapping between points on geometric objects and texels is done through the functions `glTexCoord*()`. Texture coordinates are part of the OpenGL state. Just as with vertices, texture coordinates are represented internally in four dimensions, which conventionally use the letters (s, t, r, q) to denote the coordinates. If we specify fewer than the full four dimensions, the defaults are $t = r = 0, q = 1$.

```
void glTexCoord{1234}{sifd}(TYPE scoord,....)
void glTexCoord{1234}{sifd}v(TYPE *coord)
```

Sets the current texture coordinates to coord.

In two dimensions, the array of texels that we specified in glTexImage2() is assumed to range over the continuous (s, t) rectangle with coordinates in the range $(0, 1)$. Thus, even if the array does not have the same number of rows and columns, it still has texture coordinates such that $(0, 0)$ is the lower-left corner and $(1, 1)$ is the upper-right corner, as in Figure 8.3.

Now suppose that we want to map our entire texture to a quadrilateral. We set the texture coordinates before each specification of a vertex as in the code

```
glBegin(GL_QUADS);
    glTexCoord2f(0.0, 0.0);
    glVertex3fv(vertex[0]);
    glTexCoord2f(0.0, 1.0);
    glVertex3fv(vertex[1]);
    glTexCoord2f(1.0, 1.0);
    glVertex3fv(vertex[2]);
    glTexCoord2f(1.0, 0.0);
    glVertex3fv(vertex[3]);
glEnd();
```

Effectively, we have defined a texture coordinate for each vertex. In the rendering, OpenGL obtains texture values for interior points by interpolating the values in the array of texels. This method is similar to how OpenGL constructs smooth colors and shades. However, because the texels are discrete, we might see some artifacts of the interpolation. OpenGL provides some parameters that give us some control over the interpolation. We shall discuss these parameters later.

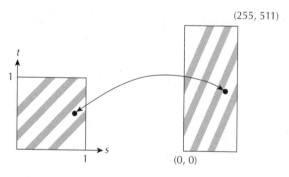

Figure 8.3 Texture coordinates and texture array for a 256 × 512 image

Figure 8.4 Applying a checkerboard texture to quadrilaterals

Figure 8.4 shows two examples of checkerboard textures mapped to a quadrilateral. Checkerboards are especially useful for demonstrating the various options and seeing how OpenGL implements texture mapping. If the quadrilateral is a square aligned with the viewer, we get the image on the left. If we move one of the corners of the quadrilateral, so it is no longer a square, we get the image on the right. In both cases, the texture map is stretched to fit the quadrilateral, and the interior values are obtained from the texture map by interpolation. But we can see from Figure 8.4 that the interpolation can cause distortions to the texture. We can also see that OpenGL renders the quadrilateral as two triangles, which results in the distinct distortion pattern.

Internally, texture coordinates are stored in four dimensions, as are vertices. To complete the analogy with vertices, a 4×4 texture matrix, initially set to an identity matrix, multiplies the present texture coordinates. We can alter this matrix by setting the matrix mode

```
glMatrixMode(GL_TEXTURE);
```

We then use the same techniques that we used for the model-view and projection matrices. Thus, we can use the texture matrix to rotate and scale a given texture by transforming texture coordinates.

8.4 **Texture Parameters**

Although `glTexCoord*()` and `glTexImage*()` are the core routines in texture mapping, we must also set some required parameters. Other optional parameters give us more control over how the texture is applied to the surface. All texture parameters are set by `glTexParameter*()`.

```
void glTexParameter{if}(GLenum target, GLenum name, TYPE value)
void glTexParameter{if}v(GLenum target, GLenum name, TYPE *value)
```

Sets the parameter name to value for texture of type target (GL_TEXTURE_1D, GL_TEXTURE_2D, GL_TEXTURE_3D).

The required parameters determine what happens when values of *s, t, r*, or *q* go outside the range (0, 1) and how the interpolation is applied.

Although the texture map is assumed to be defined for values of *s, t, r*, and *q* over (0, 1), we can use any values in glTexCoord*(). We use the parameter GL_TEXURE_WRAP_* to tell OpenGL what to do if values are out of that range. The first possibility is to let the values repeat (GL_REPEAT), that is, to use the fractional part for positive values and to increase any negative values by the smallest integer that makes them positive. We can make separate decisions for each texture coordinate. The other option is to clamp the values (GL_CLAMP) at 0.0 and 1.0; that is, negative values use 0.0, and values greater than 1.0 use 1.0. A typical usage for two-dimensional texture might look like

```
glTexParameteri(GL_TEXTURE_2D, GL_TEXTURE_WRAP_S, GL_REPEAT);
glTexParameteri(GL_TEXTURE_2D, GL_TEXTURE_WRAP_T, GL_REPEAT);
```

Mapping a texture map to a surface takes place during rendering. Hence, it is not really applied to the surface but rather to a pixel that is the projection, in screen coordinates, of a small region of the surface. Looked at another way, each pixel corresponds to a small area of a geometric surface and to a small region of texture space—sometimes called the **preimage** of the pixel. Depending on the values of the texture coordinates, the size of the surface, and the viewing conditions, each texel may cover multiple pixels (**magnification**), or each pixel may cover multiple texels (**minification**), as in Figure 8.5.

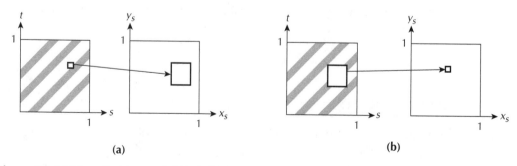

(a)   (b)

Figure 8.5 (a) Magnification and (b) minification

The situation is further complicated because the pixels and texels need not be aligned, and if we are working with perspective or with curved surfaces, the preimage of a texel may not be rectangular. The simplest solution to this problem is through **point sampling**. The center of each pixel is mapped to a point in texture space, using interpolation, and OpenGL uses the value at this point. Although this method is simple and fast, it can lead to unacceptable visual effects that are an example of an aliasing error. A smoother appearance can be obtained by using the average of a group of texels around the point sample to obtain the value of the texture. This averaging is a form of linear filtering. OpenGL uses a 2×2 array of neighboring texels for its filter. We specify these options separately for magnification and minification. The parameters are GL_TEX_MAG_FILTER and GL_TEX_MIN_FILTER, and we can choose between GL_NEAREST and GL_LINEAR. If we want the fastest implementation, we would set these parameter as follows in our initialization:

```
glTexParameteri(GL_TEXTURE_2D, GL_TEXURE_MAG_FILTER, GL_NEAREST);
glTexParameteri(GL_TEXTURE_2D, GL_TEXURE_MIN_FILTER, GL_NEAREST);
```

Texture mapping presents the programmer with many choices between efficiency and smooth textures. A problematic area is with perspective viewing. The fastest methods of interpolating textures do not handle the shape distortion caused by the perspective transformation. Most of the time, you probably will not notice the problem, but you might with regular textures, such as stripes and checkerboards. Some OpenGL implementations can, if asked, adjust their renderers for perspective. The function glHint() can be used to ask the implementation to produce a better-looking image, even if the rendering is slower.

```
glHint(GL_PERSPECTIVE_CORRECTION_HINT, GL_NICEST);
```

The option GL_FASTEST is the alternative to GL_NICEST.

```
void glHint(GLenum option, GLenum hint)
```

Requests that the hint be applied to option.

Hints can be requested for other rendering options, such as for antialiasing lines and polygons (GL_LINE_SMOOTH_HINT, GL_POLYGON_SMOOTH_HINT).

8.5 A Rotating Cube with Texture

The following simple program puts a checkerboard texture on the rotating cube, using the modeling and interaction techniques discussed in Chapters 3 and 4.

Note that very few changes are needed to add texture if we use the standard defaults.

```
#include <stdlib.h>
#include <GL/glut.h>


GLfloat vertices[][3] = {{-1.0, -1.0, 1.0}, {-1.0, 1.0, 1.0},
    {1.0, 1.0, 1.0}, {1.0, -1.0, 1.0}, {-1.0, -1.0, -1.0},
    {-1.0, 1.0, -1.0}, {1.0, 1.0, -1.0}, {1.0, -1.0, -1.0}};

GLfloat colors[][3] = {{{1.0, 0.0, 0.0},
    {0.0, 1.0, 1.0}, {1.0, 1.0, 0.0}, {0.0, 1.0, 0.0},
    {0.0, 0.0, 1.0}, {1.0, 0.0, 1.0}}};

void polygon(int a, int b, int c , int d)
{

/* draw a polygon via list of vertices */

        glBegin(GL_POLYGON);
            glColor3fv(colors[a]);
            glTexCoord2f(0.0, 0.0);
            glVertex3fv(vertices[a]);
            glColor3fv(colors[b]);
            glTexCoord2f(0.0, 1.0);
            glVertex3fv(vertices[b]);
            glColor3fv(colors[c]);
            glTexCoord2f(1.0, 1.0);
            glVertex3fv(vertices[c]);
            glColor3fv(colors[d]);
            glTexCoord2f(1.0, 0.0);
            glVertex3fv(vertices[d]);
        glEnd();
}

void colorcube(void)
{

/* map vertices to faces */

        polygon(0, 3, 2, 1);
        polygon(2, 3, 7, 6);
        polygon(3, 0, 4, 7);
        polygon(1, 2, 6, 5);
        polygon(4, 5, 6, 7);
        polygon(5, 4, 0, 1);
}
```

```
static GLfloat theta[] = {0.0,0.0,0.0};
static GLint axis = 2;

void display(void)
{

    glClear(GL_COLOR_BUFFER_BIT | GL_DEPTH_BUFFER_BIT);
    glLoadIdentity();
    glRotatef(theta[0], 1.0, 0.0, 0.0);
    glRotatef(theta[1], 0.0, 1.0, 0.0);
    glRotatef(theta[2], 0.0, 0.0, 1.0);

    colorcube();

    glutSwapBuffers();
}

void spinCube()
{

    theta[axis] += 2.0;
    if(theta[axis] > 360.0) theta[axis] -= 360.0;
    glutPostRedisplay();
}

void mouse(int btn, int state, int x, int y)
{
    if(btn == GLUT_LEFT_BUTTON && state == GLUT_DOWN) axis = 0;
    if(btn == GLUT_MIDDLE_BUTTON && state == GLUT_DOWN) axis = 1;
    if(btn == GLUT_RIGHT_BUTTON && state == GLUT_DOWN) axis = 2;
}

void myReshape(int w, int h)
{
    glViewport(0, 0, w, h);
    glMatrixMode(GL_PROJECTION);
    glLoadIdentity();
    if(w <= h)
        glOrtho(-2.0, 2.0, -2.0 * (GLfloat) h / (GLfloat) w,2.0 *
            (GLfloat) h / (GLfloat) w, -10.0, 10.0);
    else
        glOrtho(-2.0 * (GLfloat) w / (GLfloat) h, 2.0 * (GLfloat) w /
            (GLfloat) h, -2.0, 2.0, -10.0, 10.0);
    glMatrixMode(GL_MODELVIEW);
}

void
main(int argc, char **argv)
{
```

```
GLubyte image[64][64][3];
int i, j, r, c;
for(i = 0; i < 64; i++)
{
    for(j = 0; j < 64; j++)
    {
        c = (((((i & 0 x 8) == 0) ^ ((j & 0 x 8)) == 0))*255;
        image[i][j][0]= (GLubyte) c;
        image[i][j][1]= (GLubyte) c;
        image[i][j][2]= (GLubyte) c;
    }
}
glutInit(&argc, argv);
glutInitDisplayMode(GLUT_DOUBLE | GLUT_RGB | GLUT_DEPTH);
glutInitWindowSize(500, 500);
glutCreateWindow("colorcube");

glutReshapeFunc(myReshape);
glutDisplayFunc(display);
glutIdleFunc(spinCube);
glutMouseFunc(mouse);
glEnable(GL_DEPTH_TEST);
glEnable(GL_TEXTURE_2D);

glTexImage2D(GL_TEXTURE_2D, 0, 3, 64, 64, 0, GL_RGB,
    GL_UNSIGNED_BYTE, image);
glTexParameterf(GL_TEXTURE_2D, GL_TEXTURE_WRAP_S, GL_CLAMP);
glTexParameterf(GL_TEXTURE_2D, GL_TEXTURE_WRAP_T, GL_CLAMP);
glTexParameterf(GL_TEXTURE_2D, GL_TEXTURE_MAG_FILTER,
    GL_NEAREST);
glTexParameterf(GL_TEXTURE_2D, GL_TEXTURE_MIN_FILTER,
    GL_NEAREST);
glutMainLoop();
}
```

8.6 Applying Textures to Surfaces

We have not yet addressed how textures are applied in the rendering process. If you run the preceding program, you will notice that the color at each point is a mixture of the interpolated colors from the vertex colors and the colors in the texture matrix. But this is not the only option. You might also try combining texture with blending by redefining the colors to have four components with translucency by

```
GLfloat colors[][4] = {{1.0, 0.0, 0.0, 0.5}, {1.0, 1.0, 0.0, 0.5},
    {0.0, 1.0, 0.0, 0.5}, {0.0, 0.0, 1.0 , 0.5},
    {1.0, 0.0, 1.0, 0.5}, {0.0, 1.0, 1.0, 0.5}};
```

Then we would use glColor4f() in our polygon function and not enable depth buffering but instead enable blending:

```
glEnable(GL_BLEND);
glBlendFunc(GL_SRC_ALPHA, GL_ONE_MINUS_SRC_ALPHA);
```

We would then see a more interesting mixture of the texture and polygon colors.

This mode of operation is called **modulation**. Other methods can be set by glTexEnv*(). The most important mode is **replacement** mode, in which only the texture color determines the color we see in the frame buffer. We set these modes through the function glTexEnv*().

```
void glTexEnv{if}(GLenum target, GLenum param, TYPE value)
void glTexEnv{if}v(GLenum target, GLenum param, TYPE *value)
```

Sets texture parameter param to value; target must be GL_TEXTURE_ENV.

The default modulation mode is equivalent to executing

```
glTexEnvi(GL_TEXTURE_ENV, GL_TEXTURE_ENV_MODE, GL_MODULATE);
```

If we use GL_REPLACE rather than GL_MODULATE, we use only the texture color.

Two other options (GL_BLEND and GL_DECAL) determine how blending takes place if you are also using the alpha channel or you specify an environmental color through

```
glTexEnvfv(GL_TEXTURE_ENV, GL_TEX_ENV_COLOR, color);
```

This option combines an environmental color with the object shade and the texture color.

8.7 Borders and Sizing

One difficulty that arises when we use linear filtering is what happens at the texture edges, where we lack one or more texels to use in the filtering. One solution to this problem is to specify texture map with a border of one additional texel on each side through glTexImage*(). Thus, a texture map must be of size $2^m + 2^b \times 2^n + 2^b$, where b is either 0 or 1. Alternatively, we can specify a border color that will be used automatically by

```
glTexParameter3fv(GL_TEXTURE_BORDER_COLOR, color);
```

OpenGL requires that textures have sizes, less any border, that are a power of 2. As we pointed out in Chapter 7, we can use the function glScaleImage() to covert an image to acceptable size for a texture map. We can also obtain a texture map from an image in the frame buffer by the function glCopyTexImage2D().

```
void glCopyTexImage2D(GLenum target, GLint level, GLint iformat,
    GLint x, GLint y, GLsizei columns, GLsizei rows, GLint border)
```

Copies an image from the present drawing buffer to texture memory. The parameters are as in glCopyPixels(), and target is GL_TEXTURE_2D. The parameter level is 0 except if using mipmaps.

You can also copy pixels into parts of an existing texture, using the function glTexSubImage2D().

```
void glTexSubImage2D(GLenum target, GLint level, GLint xoffset,
    GLint yoffset, GLsizei columns, GLsizei rows, GLenum
    format, GLenum type, GLvoid *texels)
```

Copies rows × columns texels described by type and format into texture memory, starting at (xoffset, yoffset).

The function glCopyTexSubImage() replaces part of a texture from the frame buffer.

```
void glCopyTexSubImage2D(GLenum target, GLint level, Glint
    xoffset, Glint yoffset, GLint x, GLint y, GLsizei columns,
    GLsizei rows)
```

Copies pixels from the frame buffer, starting at (x, y), to texture memory. The other parameters are as in glTexSubImage2D().

8.8 Mipmaps

One of the difficulties with texture maps is the time required to interpolate the values of the texels to find the color to apply to a pixel. Often, much of this effort is wasted because a large part of the texture array corresponds to a single pixel in the image. This situation happens, for example, in perspective viewing when a small object is far from the camera. In addition, whether we use point sampling or filtering, the value that we get from the texture map is still only an approximation of the desired texture values. We would prefer to have a texture value that is the average of the texel values over a large area of the texture. One possible way we could accomplish this would be to form smaller texture maps by averaging groups of texels. For example, we could create a 32×32 texture map from a 64×64 texture map by average groups of 4 texels. We could then create a 16×16 texture map by repeating the process. However, once we created these new texture arrays, it would then be problematic to determine which of these maps to use. The OpenGL option called **mipmapping** automates this process.

Suppose that we have a sequence of images, each time by merging 4 pixels into 1. If we start with a 64×64 image, we create 32×32, 16×16, 8×8, 4×4, 2×2, and 1×1 images.[1] The first image has level 0, the second has level 1, and so on. We can now call `glTexImage2D()` for each of these images, each with its own level and dimensions, as in the code

```
GLubyte image0[64][64];
GLubyte image1[32][32];
        .
        .
Glubyte image5[1][1];
glTexImage2D(GL_TEXTURE_2D, 0, GL_RGB, 64, 64, GL_RGB,
    GL_UNSIGNED_BYTE, image0);
glTexImage2D(GL_TEXTURE_2D, 1, GL_RGB, 32, 32, GL_RGB,
    GL_UNSIGNED_BYTE, image1);
        .
        .
glTexImage2D(GL_TEXTURE_2D, 5, GL_RGB, 1, 1, GL_RGB,
    GL_UNSIGNED_BYTE, image5);
```

To use these images, we just need to set the minification filter:

```
glTexParameteri(GL_TEXTURE_2D, GL_TEXTURE_MIN_FILTER,
    GL_NEAREST_MIPMAP_NEAREST);
```

This is the fastest option. OpenGL will use the closest image in which the texel size matches the pixel size and use the closest texel. We can, at a speed penalty, use the closest image and linear filtering (`GL_LINEAR_MIPMAP_NEAREST`), the closest texel but linear filter between the closest images (`GL_NEAREST_MIPMAP_LINEAR`), or do both (`GL_LINEAR_MIPMAP_LINEAR`). Although the usual use of mipmapping uses a set of images that are reduced-size versions of the one image, there is no reason

---

1. If the original image is not square, we halve each dimension, until the smaller is reduced to 1 and then continue halving the other dimension.

we need do so. Hence, we can do something, such as use a simple texture when a surface projects to a small area on the screen but have a detailed view revealed when we move the viewer closer, by using different images at different levels.

However, if we want to start with one image and produce a set of mipmaps from it, we can use OpenGL to produce these images through the GLU function `gluBuild2DMipmaps()`. This function loads the images into texture memory, so we need not call `glTexImage2D()`. Because the mipmap images are in texture memory, no extra storage is required in the application.

```
int gluBuild2DMipmaps(GLenum target, GLint iformat, GLint columns,
    GLint rows, GLenum format, GLenum type, void *texels)
```

Builds and loads set of mipmaps. The parameters are the same as in `glTexImage2D()`. Returns 0 if successful.

8.9 Automatic Texture Coordinate Generation

Although we need to set many parameters if we are to use texture maps efficiently, the essence of two-dimensional texture mapping is fairly simple. We map an image to a surface. Once you become familiar with the parameters and options, the most difficult problem is in determining texture coordinates for vertices. The problems are both practical and theoretical. Keep in mind two helpful analogies: maps of the earth and wallpapering.

One problem in mapping is to represent something that is round—the earth—on a flat surface. We cannot do this without some shape distortion. In the standard Mercator projection, we put the majority of the shape distortion at the poles. However, if you look at an atlas, you will find other types of maps that handle the distortion in other manners. The two-dimensional texture-mapping problem is the inverse of this map problem. Given a rectangular "map," how do we wrap it around a curved surface? There must be some distortion. How we assign texture coordinates determines where the distortion takes place.

Wallpapering also has problems with distortion if we try to put wallpaper on a curved surface. But even on a flat surface, wallpapering has the problem of what to do when we have to use another roll. Matching the new roll to edges of the old roll is problematic. We saw that the use of borders in texture mapping can help, but an additional issue is related to the size of the areas we want to wallpaper or to texture map. In graphics, we often work with surfaces that are defined by groups of polygons. Although we may have a simple method for assigning texture coordinates to any polygon, each polygon may have a different size. Imagine how distorted an image we would obtain if the same checkerboard texture were mapped to each polygon, regardless of its size.

Consider again the problem of generating texture maps for a sphere. One way of describing the points on the sphere is through the equations

$$x(u) = r \cos u \sin v$$
$$y(u) = r \cos u \cos v$$
$$z(u) = r \sin v$$

As u goes over 360 degrees and v goes over 180 degrees, we generate a sphere of radius r centered at the origin. We can generate polygons from these equations by taking evenly spaced values in u and v. This is what the GLU and GLUT quadric objects do. Constant values of u and v generate lines of longitude and latitude. If we want to use a single texture to cover the sphere, we could use texture coordinates

$$s = u/360.0$$
$$t = v/180.0$$

This assignment will work, albeit with distortion of the texture. If we used another method to generate the sphere, we would see a different distortion pattern.

All quadric surfaces can be described by two parameter functions, similar to those for the sphere. For OpenGL quadrics, we can use the GLU function `gluQuadricTexture()` to enable automatic generation of texture coordinates. The texture distortion will be determined by the particular mathematical equations used to define each quadric.

`void gluQuadricTexture(GLUquadricObj *obj, GLboolean mode)`

Turns on (`GL_TRUE`) or off (`GL_FALSE`) automatic texture coordinate generation for quadric object `obj` based on the value of `mode`.

In Chapter 9, we shall introduce OpenGL curves and surfaces. OpenGL supports Bézier surfaces, which can be described by polynomial functions of two variables. OpenGL provides a mechanism, called *evaluators,* which will allow us to compute as many points on these surfaces as needed to make a polygonal model as close as we desire to the curved surface. We can also use evaluators to generate normals for shading and texture coordinates. Thus, the process is automated, if we are willing to accept the scaling and distortion that are determined by our use of this particular scheme. You can see one example of this automatic coordinate generation by using `glutSolidTeapot()` with textures. You need only define a texture map and its parameters, enable texture mapping, and render the teapot. For the checkerboard texture, we get the image in Figure 8.6. The checks on the teapot are of different sizes because the teapot is made up of 32 separate surfaces, each of which has its own size. The automatic texture generation for the surfaces in `glutSolidTeapot()` uses the same range of s and t in for each surface.

OpenGL provides another option for automatic texture coordinate generation. Often, the desired texture coordinates can be expressed in terms of points in (x, y, z) space. OpenGL allows us to generate texture coordinates that are measured as distances from a plane in either object space or eye space. Remember that vertices are represented internally in four-dimensional homogeneous coordinates. Hence, internally every vertex is stored as (x, y, z, w) where usually, but not always, w is equal to 1. The value $ax + by + cz + dw$ is proportional to the distance from (x, y, z, w) to the plane determined by (a, b, c, d). For example, consider the plane

$$x + 2y + 3z + 4 = 0.$$

It has coefficients $(1, 2, 3, 4)$. For any point (x_0, y_0, z_0, w_0) in homogenous coordinates, $x_0 + 2y_0 + 3z_0 + 4w_0$ is proportional to the distance to this plane. OpenGL allows us to generate a texture value for any texture coordinate ($s, t, r,$ or q), using this formula, each with its own plane.

Suppose that we have a square in the plane $z = 0$ whose opposite corners are at $(-1, -1, 0)$ and $(1, 1, 0)$ and we want to map a two-dimensional texture to this square. The two following equations will do this:

$$s = x/2 + 1/2$$
$$t = y/2 + 1/2.$$

These two equations correspond to using the planes determined by the coefficients $(1/2, 0, 0, 1/2)$ and $(0, 1/2, 0, 1/2)$. We have to enable this facility independently for each texture coordinate:

```
glEnable(GL_TEXTURE_GEN_S);
glEnable(GL_TEXTURE_GEN_T);
```

Figure 8.6 Texture-mapped teapot, using automatic generation of texture coordinates

We use the function `glTexGen*()` to set up the required parameters and to identify the planes.

> ```
> void glTexGen{ifd}(GLenum texcoord, GLenum param, TYPE value);
> void glTexGen{ifd}v(GLenum texcoord, GLenum param, TYPE *plane);
> ```
>
> Sets up automatic texture generation for texture coordinate `texcoord`. The parameter `param` specifies either the mode (GL_TEXTURE_GEN_MODE) or which space (GL_OBJECT_LINEAR, GL_EYE_LINEAR) the plane determined by the array `plane` is specified. If mode is GL_TEXTURE_GEN_MODE, `value` is either GL_OBJECT_LINEAR or GL_EYE_LINEAR.

Thus, for the preceding example, we would use the four function calls

```
GLfloat planes[] = {0.5, 0.0, 0.0, 0.5};
GLfloat planet[] = {0.0, 0.5, 0.0, 0.5};
glTexGeni(GL_S, GL_TEXTURE_GEN_MODE, GL_OBJECT_LINEAR);
glTexGeni(GL_T, GL_TEXTURE_GEN_MODE, GL_OBJECT_LINEAR);
glTexGenfv(GL_S, GL_OBJECT_LINEAR, planes);
glTexGenfv(GL_T, GL_OBJECT_LINEAR, planet);
```

We still would use all the other texture functions to define the required texture parameters, but we would not use `glTexCoord*()`.

If we use GL_OBJECT_LINEAR mode, the texture map is fixed to the surface; if we move the surface, we move the texture with it. Thus, the texture appears painted to the surface. If we use GL_EYE_LINEAR mode, texture coordinates are in eye space, so that when we move the object, the texture coordinates assigned to vertices change. Thus, the texture changes as we move the object.

8.10 Texture Objects

In the default mode of operations, a "present texture" is part of the OpenGL state. This texture is moved to OpenGL's texture memory from processor memory when we execute `glTexImage*()`. If we have only a single texture map, we incur the overhead of the move only once. However, if we have multiple textures in our program, we may have a problem. Suppose that each object has its own texture. Then, just as with material properties, every time we render a different object, we must reload its texture. With any sizable texture dimensions, performance can suffer dramatically.

OpenGL provides an alternative: **texture objects**. The idea is simple. We form an object that consists of a texture and its parameter values. We can then fill texture memory with multiple objects and have OpenGL use a texture determined by the identifier of the object. As long as there is sufficient memory to hold the texture objects, we can avoid reloading texture maps. Memory is not sufficient for all the textures that we need, we can prioritize the texture objects to minimize the amount of data movement from the processor to texture memory.

 In most systems, texure memory is a limited resource, and we want to minimize reloading textures into texture memory.

Just as with display lists, texture identifiers are integers. We can use the function glGenTextures() to find a contiguous set of unused integers.

void glGenTextures(GLsizei n, GLuint *name)

Returns in name the first integer of n consecutive unused integers for texture object identifiers.

The function glIsTexture() allows us to check whether a given ID is already in use.

GLboolean glIsTexture(GLunint name)

Returns GL_TRUE if name is already a texture ID, GL_FALSE if it is not.

A single function, glBindTexture(), both switches between texture objects and forms new texture objects.

void glBindTexture(GLenum target, GLuint name)

Binds name to texture of type target.

If we call glBindTexture() with name and name has not been used before, the subsequent calls to the various texture functions define the texture object with the ID name. If name exists from a previous call to glBindTexture(), that texture object becomes the present texture and is applied to surfaces until the next call to glBindTexture(). If glBindTexture() is called with name set to 0, the normal texture calls apply, and the present texture that is part of the OpenGL state and the present values of the texture parameters apply.

We can get rid of texture objects and free the resource that they consume through glDeleteTextures().

> void glDeleteTextures(GLsizei n, GLunint *namearray)
>
> Deletes n texture objects from namearray, which holds texture-object names.

If texture memory lacks enough room for all our textures, we can set a priority for each texture object:

glTexParameterf(name, priority);

The value of priority is in the range (0.0, 1.0), with 0.0 being the lowest priority. When OpenGL needs room for a texture, the lowest-priority texture is removed from texture memory.

8.11 Texture Maps for Image Manipulation

Often, texture maps are easier to work with than pixels are. Because texture maps are mapped to geometric objects, we can manipulate the geometric object, and OpenGL will "stretch" the texture to fit the projection of the object. For example, suppose that we want to reshape an image. This problem arises when we have two or more images taken with different cameras or from different angles. We then have to stretch one of the images to fit over the other. The traditional approach to this problem was to find matching points in the two images and then to find mathematical functions to map points in one to points in the other. A simpler solution is to let OpenGL do the work with texture maps. We can make texture maps of the two images, map each to a quadrilateral, and then manipulate the corners of the quadrilaterals interactively until we obtain the desired stretching.

Another example of the advantage of using texture maps is that the objects onto which we map our images are subject to the transformations in the OpenGL geometric pipeline. Thus, when we display an image as a texture map and then resize the window, we can use the reshape callback to keep the entire image in the resized window. Here is the PPM display program from Chapter 7, rewritten to use texture maps.

```
#include <stdio.h>
#include <stdlib.h>
#include <GL/glut.h>
```

```
    int n;
    int m;

GLuint *image;

void display()
{

    glClear(GL_COLOR_BUFFER_BIT);
    glBegin(GL_QUADS);
        glTexCoord2f(0.0, 0.0);
        glVertex2i(0, 0);
        glTexCoord2f(0.0, 1.0);
        glVertex2i(0, m - 1);
        glTexCoord2f(1.0, 1.0);
        glVertex2i(n - 1, m - 1);
        glTexCoord2f(1.0, 0.0);
        glVertex2i(n - 1, 0);
    glEnd();
    glFlush();
}


void myreshape(int h, int w)
{
    glMatrixMode(GL_PROJECTION);
    glLoadIdentity();
    gluOrtho2D(0.0, (GLfloat) n, 0.0, (GLfloat) m);
    glMatrixMode(GL_MODELVIEW);
    glLoadIdentity();
    glViewport(0, 0, h, w);
}


int main(int argc, char **argv)
{
    FILE *fd;
    int   k, nm;
    char c;
    int i;
    char b[100];
    float s;
    int red, green, blue;

    printf("enter file name\n");
    scanf("%s", b);
```

```
fd = fopen(b, "r");
fscanf(fd,"%[^\n]", b);
if(b[0]!='P'|| b[1] != '3')
{
    printf("%s is not a PPM file!\n", b);
    exit(0);
}
fscanf(fd, "%c", &c);
while(c == '#')
{
    fscanf(fd, "%[^\n]", b);
    fscanf(fd, "%c", &c);
}
ungetc(c,fd);
fscanf(fd, "%d %d %d", &n, &m, &k);
nm = n*m;
image = malloc(3*sizeof(GLuint)*nm);
s = 255./k;


for(i = 0; i < nm; i++)
{
    fscanf(fd, "%d %d %d", &red, &green, &blue);
    image[3*nm - 3*i - 3] = red;
    image[3*nm - 3*i - 2] = green;
    image[3*nm - 3*i - 1] = blue;
}
glutInit(&argc, argv);
glutInitDisplayMode(GLUT_SINGLE | GLUT_RGB);
glutInitWindowSize(n, m);
glutInitWindowPosition(0, 0);
glutCreateWindow("image");
glutReshapeFunc(myreshape);
glutDisplayFunc(display);
glPixelTransferf(GL_RED_SCALE, s);
glPixelTransferf(GL_GREEN_SCALE, s);
glPixelTransferf(GL_BLUE_SCALE, s);
glPixelStorei(GL_UNPACK_SWAP_BYTES, GL_TRUE);
glPixelStorei(GL_UNPACK_ALIGNMENT, 1);
glEnable(GL_TEXTURE_2D);
glTexImage2D(GL_TEXTURE_2D, 0, 3, n, m, 0, GL_RGB,
    GL_UNSIGNED_INT, image);
glTexParameterf(GL_TEXTURE_2D, GL_TEXTURE_WRAP_S, GL_CLAMP);
glTexParameterf(GL_TEXTURE_2D, GL_TEXTURE_WRAP_T, GL_CLAMP);
glTexParameterf(GL_TEXTURE_2D, GL_TEXTURE_MAG_FILTER,
    GL_NEAREST);
glTexParameterf(GL_TEXTURE_2D, GL_TEXTURE_MIN_FILTER,
    GL_NEAREST);
```

```
glClearColor(0.0, 0.0, 0.0, 1.0);
glColor3f(1.0, 1.0, 1.0);
glutMainLoop();

}
```

Note that as you resize the window, the relative size of the image in the window remains the same.

Curves and Surfaces

Until now, all our OpenGL geometric primitives, such as lines and polygons, have been flat. Even when we worked with OpenGL quadrics, these surfaces were rendered using flat polygons. OpenGL provides curves and surfaces through a mechanism called evaluators, which allows us to generate Bézier curves and surfaces. This mechanism is flexible, as we can generate polynomial curves of an arbitrary degree and convert other types of polygonal curves and surfaces into Bézier curves and surfaces.

9.1 Parametric Curves

In almost all applications in computer graphics, the best choice for curves is based on **parametric polynomial curves**. With such curves, we can represent a curve in two, three, or four dimensions, using a separate equation for each spatial variable, using independent variable, or parameter, u:

$$x = x(u) = a_{x0} + a_{x1}\, u + a_{x2}\, u^2 + \dots + a_{xn}\, u^n$$
$$y = y(u) = a_{y0} + a_{y1}\, u + a_{y2}\, u^2 + \dots + a_{yn}\, u^n$$
$$z = z(u) = a_{z0} + a_{z1}\, u + a_{z2}\, u^2 + \dots + a_{zn}\, u^n$$
$$w = w(u) = a_{w0} + a_{w1}\, u + a_{w2}\, u^2 + \dots + a_{wn}\, u^n$$

For a curve in two dimensions, we use only x and y; in three dimensions, x, y, and z, and for four dimensions, all four of x, y, z, and w. If we use only two or three, the standard defaults for the others ($z = 0$, $w = 1$) are applied.

Parametric curves give a point in homogeneous coordinate space ($x(u)$, $y(u)$, $z(u)$, $w(u)$) for each value of u. Generally, we define a **curve segment**, a finite piece of a curve, by allowing u to range over the values

$$u_{\min} <= u <= u_{\max}$$

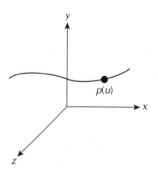

Figure 9.1 Parametric curve

Figure 9.1 shows that the individual curves for the spatial variables are combined to form the three-dimensional curve $p(u) = (x(u), y(u), z(u))$.

For now, we shall consider only curves for which we need specify x, y, and z, fixing $w = 1$. If we want a curve for a particular n, we must define $3(n + 1)$ coefficients. We can do so by providing $3(n + 1)$ independent conditions that we would like the curve to satisfy. Each type of condition that we apply determines a distinct type of curve. For example, we can provide a set of three-dimensional points that the curve must pass through. Such a curve is said to **interpolate** the set of points, as shown in Figure 9.2.

We shall work with cubic polynomials of the following form, with u conventionally varying over the range $(0, 1)$:

$$q(u) = a_0 + a_1\, u + a_2\, u^2 + a_3\, u^3$$

We can obtain other ranges of u by a simple scaling and translation. Cubics are by far the most popular curves with which to work, because they provide a good combination of flexibility and efficiency. Here, q can be any of x, y, z, or w. Thus, we need four independent conditions to determine each set of parameters for a curve. For interpolation, we must provide four points through which the curve must pass. However, in computer graphics, interpolating curves are not the most useful type.

If we work with cubics, four conditions are not enough to model a curve over a significant part of space. Rather than work with higher-order polynomials, we can define many curve segments, each defined by a subset of the conditions that we would like to impose on the whole curve. For example, the two segments in

Figure 9.2 Interpolating curves through p_0, p_1, p_2, p_3.

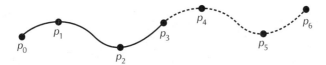

Figure 9.3 Two interpolating curve segments with the join point at p_3

Figure 9.3 are both valid over a small part of space corresponding to its values of u between 0 and 1. Each segment is determined by the data locally. In computer graphics, this type of local control of the shape of a curve is of great importance. However, when we work with multiple curve segments, we must be careful of what happens at the **join points**, the places where adjacent segments meet. Simply ensuring that two segments meet reduces the flexibility in curve design. For the example in Figure 9.3, we see that if we use p_0, p_1, p_2, p_3 as the data for the first curve, we must use p_3 as the first data point in the second curve segment to be sure that we have a continuous curve at the join point.

Once we decide on the conditions that we would like our curves to satisfy, we have three sets of $n + 1$ equations for the $n + 1$ coefficients for x, y, and z. These conditions are generally stated in terms of points in space called **control points** that are supplied by the user, often interactively.

9.2 Parametric Surfaces

Parametric surfaces are defined by functions of two variables.

$$x = x(u, v)$$
$$y = y(u, v)$$
$$z = z(u, v)$$
$$w = w(u, v).$$

Thus, each value of u and v gives one point in three- or four-dimensional space, as in Figure 9.4. Here, $p(u, v) = (x(u, v), y(u, v), z(u, v))$.

In computer graphics, these functions usually are bicubic polynomials, each of the following form, defined for both u and v over the range $(0, 1)$:

$$q(u, v) = a_{00} + a_{10}\, u + a_{01}\, v + a_{11}\, uv + a_{20}\, u^2 + a_{02}\, v^2 + a_{21}\, u^2 v + a_{12}\, uv^2 + a_{22}\, u^2 v^2 + a_{30} u^3 + a_{03}\, v^3 + a_{31}\, u^3 v + a_{13}\, uv^3 + a_{32}\, u^3 v^2 + a_{23}\, u^2 v^3 + a_{33}\, u^3 v^3.$$

Again, q can be any of x, y, z, or w. With 16 coefficients, we need 16 conditions in each variable to determine each **surface patch**. For example, if we want to interpolate a set of control points, each patch would pass through 16 points. Thus, to determine an (x, y, z) surface patch with $w = 1$, we have to determine 48 coefficients.

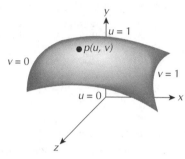

Figure 9.4 Parametric surface patch

9.3 Bézier Curves and Surfaces

In computer graphics and CAD, we are willing to come only close to some of the control points rather than interpolating them if the resulting curve is smoother than the curve that interpolates all the control points. Although we could define "close" in many ways, the most popular choice is the **Bézier curves** and **surfaces**.

Figure 9.5 shows a cubic Bézier polynomial $q(u)$ in which again, q can be x, y, z, or w. This curve is determined by the four control points Q_0, Q_1, Q_2, and Q_3. The cubic Bézier curve interpolates Q_0 and Q_3 and uses the line segments between Q_0 and Q_1 and Q_2 and Q_3 to determine the slope of the curve at the end points. Such curves are very smooth and the curve is confined to lie in the box formed by the control points called the **convex hull**, which also is shown in Figure 9.5. For a sequence of control points, the next curve segment uses Q_3, Q_4, Q_5, and Q_6, thus ensuring continuity at the join point.

Bézier surfaces are defined in a similar manner. For bicubic surfaces, we use 16 control points $\{Q_{ij}\}$ for i and j ranging from 0 to 3. The surface patch interpolates the four corner points, Q_{00}, Q_{03}, Q_{30}, and Q_{33} and fits in the convex hull of the 16 control points. Bézier surfaces are extensions of Bézier curves. For a constant value of u or v, the surface $p(u, v)$ reduces to a Bézier curve in v or u.

When we go to higher-order curves and surfaces, we need to use more control points to determine each curve segment or surface patch. For example, the Bézier

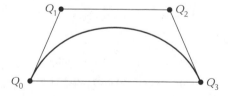

Figure 9.5 Bézier curve and its convex hull

curve of degree 7 uses eight control points. It interpolates the end points and uses the other control point data to approximate various derivatives at the end points. The polynomials that are used in u and v to determine these curves and surfaces are from a family of polynomials known as the **Bernstein polynomials**, which can be implemented very efficiently.

If we strip away the elegant mathematics and look at the results, we can identify the properties of Bézier curves and surfaces that make them so important in computer graphics.

- Bézier curves and surfaces are smooth.
- Bézier curves and surfaces are defined locally by control points.
- Bézier curves and surfaces of any order can be generated as accurately as desired in an efficient manner.
- Any other polynomial curve and surface can be obtained from a Bézier curve or surface.

This last point is important because it makes it simple to obtain other types of curves and surfaces while still using the efficient algorithms for the Bézier curves and surfaces that are in OpenGL. Later, we shall see an example of how we can do this.

9.4   **One-Dimensional OpenGL Evaluators**

OpenGL implements Bézier curves and surfaces through a mechanism known as **evaluators**. These evaluators can compute a user-specified number of points on a Bézier curve or surface of any degree. OpenGL then uses these points on the curve or surface to generate standard OpenGL primitives, such as line segments and polygons, that approximate the curve or surface. Figure 9.6 shows a cubic Bézier curve determined by control points Q_0, Q_1, Q_2, and Q_3 on which five points have been computed exactly by an evaluator. The dashed line shows an approximating polyline (GL_LINE_STRIP) that is determined by these points. Because we can have OpenGL compute as many points as we like on the curve, we can achieve as much accuracy as we need for our application.

For a curve, we use a one-dimensional evaluator that we set up by glMap1*().

```
void glMap1{fd}(GLenum entity, TYPE u0, TYPE u1, GLint stride,
        GLint order, TYPE* data)
```

Sets up a one-dimensional evaluator for entity over the range (u0, u1), using a Bernstein polynomial of degree order − 1. There are stride variables of TYPE (GLfloat or GLdouble) between successive data points in the array data.

Figure 9.6 Line segment approximation to the Bézier curve determined by Q_0, Q_1, Q_2, and Q_3

We can use this evaluator for a variety of entities. If we want a curve, we set `entity` to `GL_MAP1_VERTEX_3`. Every time we use the evaluator, through functions that replace calls to `glVertex*()`, such as `glEvalcoord1*()` and `glMapGrid1*()`, an (x, y, z) point is evaluated. We can also form four-dimensional points (`GL_MAP1_VERTEX_4`), normals (`GL_MAP1_NORMAL`), colors (`GL_MAP1_COLOR_4`), and texture coordinates. Each type of entity for which we use an evaluator must be enabled with a call such as

```
glEnable(GL_MAP1_VERTEX_3);
```

We can choose the order of the Bézier curve we would like to use. The order of a curve is one greater than the degree of the polynomial and is equal to the number of points it takes to determine the curve. We can use any range of the parameter u in our curves because the range of values (u_0, u_1) can be scaled to $(0, 1)$ by the substitution

$$u' = (u - u_0)/(u_1 - u_0).$$

Once one or more evaluators have been enabled, we can form approximations to Bézier curves. The simplest method is to replace each call to `glVertex*()` with a call to `glEvalcoord1*()`. Rather than using a point in two, three, or four dimensions, as does `glVertex*()`, `glEvalCoord1*()` passes a value of u to all enabled evaluators. The evaluators then produce a point, a normal, a color, or a texture coordinate, depending on which evaluators are enabled. For example, suppose that we want to set up and enable an evaluator for vertices using u over the range $(0, 1)$ and want 21 points on a line strip that approximates the curve. We can use the code

```
glBegin(GL_LINE_STRIP);
    for(i = 0; i <= 20; i++) glEvalCoord1f(i / 20.0);
glEnd();
```

```
void glEvalCoord1{fd}(TYPE u)
void glEvalCoord1{fd}v(TYPE *u)
```

Forces the evaluation of all enabled one-dimensional maps for the value u.

Suppose that we had defined the evaluator over another range, as in

```
glMap1f(GL_MAP1_VERTEX_3, u0, u1, 3, 4, data)
```

We could have 21 points over this range by

```
glBegin(GL_LINE_STRIP);
    for(i = 0; i <= 20; i++)
        glEvalCoord1f(u0 + i *(u1 - u0)/ 20.0);
glEnd();
```

We also could have enabled a color evaluator by the code

```
glMap1f(GL_MAP1_COLOR_4, u0, u1, 3, 4, colors);
glEnable(GL_MAP1_COLOR_4);
```

The array colors[] should have four RGBA colors in it. As the preceding loop is executed, we would generate not only a line segment for each call to glEvalCoord1f() but also a new color for each vertex by using a Bézier curve determined by the colors in the array. Hence, if smooth shading were enabled (GL_SMOOTH), we would see a smooth color change over the line strip, starting with the first color in the array and ending with the last color. Note that we would come close to the second and third colors but not pass through them.

The advantage of using glEvalCoord1*() is that we can use any values of u, not just equally spaced values as in our example. However, if we want to use 21 values of u, then we must make 21 function calls, using glEvalCoord1*(). OpenGL provides an alternative for equally spaced values of u. First, we use the function glMapGrid1*() to set up an equally spaced set of values of u. Then we use glEvalMesh1()to apply the evaluators over the grid with a single function execution. Thus, for 21 points from $u0$ to $u1$ we can use the following to set up the grid:

```
glMap1f(GL_MAP1_VERTEX_3, u0, u1, 3, 4, data);
glEnable(GL_MAP1_VERTEX_3);
glMapGrid1f(21, u0, u1);
```

We can then draw a line strip by

```
glEvalMesh1(GL_LINE, 0, 20);
```

```
void glMapGrid1{fd}(GLint n, TYPE u0, TYPE u1);
```

Sets up an equally spaced grid of n points between u0 and u1.

```
void glEvalMesh1(GLenum mode, GLint first, GLint last)
```

Renders in mode (GL_LINE, GL_POINT) all enabled evaluators from the first to last values of u defined by glMapGrid().

9.5 Two-Dimensional Evaluators

Two-dimensional evaluators allow us to evaluate two-dimensional Bernstein polynomials and to form Bézier surfaces. The mechanism is a direct extension of what we did for one-dimensional curves. However, we have more options in how we can display these surfaces. Surfaces are defined by two-parameter polynomials $p(u,v)$, where for a fixed u or v, we have a parametric polynomial in the other variable. Thus, the mechanisms for working with surfaces are very similar to the ones we introduced for curves. We define the evaluator by glMap2*() and then use it with glEvalCoord2*().

```
void glMap2{fd}(GLenum entity, TYPE u0, TYPE u1, GLint
    ustride, GLint uorder, TYPE v0, TYPE v1, GLint vstride,
    GLint vorder, TYPE data)
```

Defines a two-dimensional evaluator for entity, using Bézier polynomials in u and v. The control points are stored in the array data.

```
void glEvalCoord2{fd}(TYPE u, TYPE v)
void glEvalCoord2{fd}v(TYPE *uv)
```

Forces the evaluation of all enabled two-dimensional evaluators for the specified values of u and v.

For regular spacing, we can use the functions glMapGrid2*() and glEvalMesh2() to reduce the number of function calls.

```
void glMapGrid2{fd}(GLint n, TYPE u0, TYPE u1, GLint m, TYPE
    v0, TYPE v1)
```

Sets up a two-dimensional grid with n evenly spaced steps between u0 and u1 in u and with m steps between v0 and v1 in v.

```
void glEvalMesh2( GLenum mode, GLint ufirst, GLint ulast, GLint
    vfirst, GLint vlast)
```

Renders in mode (GL_LINE, GL_POINT, or GL_FILL) all enabled evaluators from the ufirst to ulast values of u and vfirst to vlast in v as defined by glMapGrid2*().

9.6   An Interactive Example

The following example allows the user to enter data points from the terminal and draws cubic Bézier curves defined in the plane by each successive group of points. The program allows you to clear the screen and to restart or add additional points via the keyboard.

```
#include <GL/glut.h>
#define MAX_CPTS 25

GLfloat cpts[MAX_CPTS][3];
int ncpts = 0;

static int width = 500, height = 500;

void drawCurves()
{
    int i;

    for(i = 0; i < ncpts - 3; i += 3)
    {
        glMap1f(GL_MAP1_VERTEX_3, 0.0, 1.0, 3, 4, cpts[i]);
        glMapGrid1f(30, 0.0, 1.0);
        glEvalMesh1(GL_LINE, 0, 30);
    }
    glFlush();
}

static void display()
{
    int i;
    glClear(GL_COLOR_BUFFER_BIT);


    glBegin(GL_POINTS);
    for(i = 0; i < ncpts; i++)
        glVertex3fv(cpts[i]);
```

```
    glEnd();

    glFlush();
}


static void mouse(int button, int state, int x, int y)
{
    float wx, wy;

    if(button != GLUT_LEFT_BUTTON || state != GLUT_DOWN)
        return;

    wx = (2.0 * x) / (float)(width - 1) - 1.0;
    wy = (2.0 * (height - 1 - y)) / (float)(height - 1) - 1.0;

    if(ncpts == MAX_CPTS) return;

    cpts[ncpts][0] = wx;
    cpts[ncpts][1] = wy;
    cpts[ncpts][2] = 0.0;
    ncpts++;

    glColor3f(0.0, 0.0, 0.0);
    glPointSize(5.0);
    glBegin(GL_POINTS);
    glVertex3f(wx, wy, 0.0);
    glEnd();
    glFlush();
}


void keyboard(unsigned char key, int x, int y)
{
    switch (key)
    {
        case 'q': case 'Q':
            exit();
            break;
        case 'c': case 'C':
            ncpts = 0;
            glutPostRedisplay();
            break;
        case 'e': case 'E':
            glutPostRedisplay();
            break;
        case 'b': case 'B':
            drawCurves();
        break;
    }
}
```

```
void reshape(int w, int h)
{
    width = w;
    height = h;
    glMatrixMode(GL_PROJECTION);
    glLoadIdentity();
    glOrtho(-1.0, 1.0, -1.0, 1.0, -1.0, 1.0);
    glMatrixMode(GL_MODELVIEW);
    glViewport(0, 0, w, h);
}


int main(int argc, char **argv)
{

    glutInit(&argc, argv);
    glutInitDisplayMode(GLUT_RGB);
    glutInitWindowSize(width, height);
    glutCreateWindow("Bézier Curve");
    glutDisplayFunc(display);
    glutMouseFunc(mouse);
    glutKeyboardFunc(keyboard);
    glutReshapeFunc(reshape);
    glClearColor(1.0, 1.0, 1.0, 1.0);
    glColor3f(0.0, 0.0, 0.0);
    glPointSize(5.0);
    glEnable(GL_MAP1_VERTEX_3);
    glutMainLoop();
}
```

This program uses the first four control points to define the first curve segment. The program then takes groups of three successive control points and combines them with the final control point of the just-drawn segment to define the next segment. This strategy ensures that the resulting set of curve segments is continuous. However, there is no guarantee of any more smoothness at the join points.

9.7 Other Types of Curves

A Bézier curve is a polynomial that is defined by a set of control points and a set of conditions that we impose on the curve. If we use the same control points and a different set of conditions, we obtain another type of curve. For example, if we require that the curve pass through the control points, we obtain an interpolating curve. If we want such a curve, we do not have to give up on OpenGL and generate other types of curves with our own code. We just have to look at things a little differently.

Suppose that we have a cubic Bézier polynomial. If we pick four points on this curve, they define an interpolating cubic polynomial that must be the same polynomial with which we started. In other words, a cubic polynomial is both a Bézier curve and an interpolating curve for different sets of control points. If we want a cubic interpolating polynomial and have the four control points that define it, we can convert these four points to four other control points—in fact, two are the same in this case—that define an identical Bézier polynomial. The advantage of this strategy is that we can use OpenGL evaluators on these new control points to generate the desired curve efficiently. For each type of curve that we want, we can apply a matrix to its control points to create the desired Bézier control points. For the cubic interpolating curve, the matrix is

$$
M = \begin{bmatrix}
1 & 0 & 0 & 0 \\
-\frac{5}{6} & 3 & -\frac{3}{2} & \frac{1}{3} \\
\frac{1}{3} & -\frac{3}{2} & 3 & -\frac{5}{6} \\
0 & 0 & 0 & 1
\end{bmatrix}.
$$

We form a $4 \times n$ array of the control points, where n is the number of dimensions (two, three, or four) and multiply M on the right by this array, forming a new $4 \times n$ array of the new control points.

9.7.1 B-Splines

Bézier curves and surfaces are members of a family of curves and surfaces called **splines**. Each type of spline is defined by a slightly different set of conditions involving the control points and the type of continuity that we want to enforce at the join points. The most popular type of spline is the cubic B-spline, which has continuity of the first and second derivatives at the join points. To obtain this degree of smoothness, a new B-spline curve segment is defined for each additional control point. Thus, if control points Q_0, Q_1, Q_2, and Q_3 define the first segment, Q_1, Q_2, Q_3, and Q_4 define the second. Each curve segment is rendered only between the two middle control points.

The following matrix converts a set of control points for a cubic B-spline to a set of control points for a cubic Bézier curve that is identical:

$$
M = \begin{bmatrix}
\frac{1}{6} & \frac{2}{3} & \frac{1}{6} & 0 \\
0 & \frac{2}{3} & \frac{1}{3} & \frac{1}{3} \\
0 & \frac{1}{3} & \frac{2}{3} & 0 \\
0 & \frac{1}{6} & \frac{2}{3} & \frac{1}{6}
\end{bmatrix}.
$$

The following code contains the major modifications to our previous example to draw the three types of curves from the same control points. The desired type of curve could be entered interactively. Figure 9.7 shows the three types of curves from the same set of control points.

```c
typedef enum
{
    BEZIER,
    INTERPOLATED,
    BSPLINE
} curveType;

void vmult(float m[4][4], float v[4][3], float r[4][3])
{
    int i, j, k;

    for (i = 0; i < 4; i++)
    for (j = 0; j < 3; j++)
    for (k = 0, r[i][j] = 0.0; k < 4; k++)
    r[i][j] += m[i][k] * v[k][j];
}

/* Interpolating to Bézier matrix */

static float minterp[4][4] =
{
    {1.0, 0.0, 0.0, 0.0},
    {-5.0/6.0, 3.0, -3.0/2.0, 1.0/3.0},
    {1.0/3.0, -3.0/2.0, 3.0, -5.0/6.0},
    {0.0, 0.0, 0.0, 1.0},
};

/* B-spline to Bézier matrix */

static float mbspline[4][4] =
{
    {1.0/6.0, 4.0/6.0, 1.0/6.0, 0.0},
    {0.0, 4.0/6.0, 2.0/6.0, 0.0},
    {0.0, 2.0/6.0, 4.0/6.0, 0.0},
    {0.0, 1.0/6.0, 4.0/6.0, 1.0/6.0},
};

/* identity matrix for Bézier polynomial */

static float midentity[4][4] =
{
    {1.0, 0.0, 0.0, 0.0},
    {0.0, 1.0, 0.0, 0.0},
```

```
        {0.0, 0.0, 1.0, 0.0},
        {0.0, 0.0, 0.0, 1.0}
};


/* Calculate the matrix used to transform the control points */

void computeMatrix(curveType type, float m[4][4])
{
    int i, j;

    switch (type)
    {
        case BEZIER:
        /* Identity matrix */
            for (i = 0; i < 4; i++)
            for (j = 0; j < 4; j++)
                m[i][j] = midentity[i][j];
        break;
        case INTERPOLATED:
            for (i = 0; i < 4; i++)
            for (j = 0; j < 4; j++)
                m[i][j] = minterp[i][j];
        break;
        case BSPLINE:
            for (i = 0; i < 4; i++)
            for (j = 0; j < 4; j++)
                m[i][j] = mbspline[i][j];
        break;
    }
}

/* Draw the indicated curves using the current control points. */

static void drawCurves(curveType type)
{
    int i, j;
    int step;
    GLfloat newcpts[4][3];

    float m[4][4];

/* Set the control point computation matrix and the step size. */

    computeMatrix(type, m);

    if(type == BSPLINE) step = 1;
    else step = 3;
```

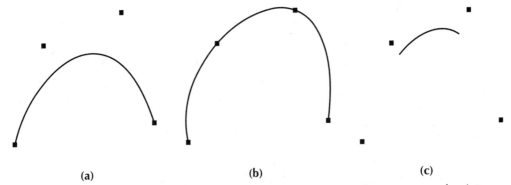

(a)   **(b)**   **(c)**

Figure 9.7 (a) Bézier curve; (b) Interpolating curve; (c) B-spline curve for same control points

```
glColor3fv(colors[type]);

/* Draw the curves */

i = 0;
while (i + 3 < ncpts)
{
        /* Calculate the appropriate control points */

        vmult(m, &cpts[i], newcpts);

        /* Draw the curve using OpenGL evaluators */

        glMap1f(GL_MAP1_VERTEX_3, 0.0, 1.0, 3, 4, &newcpts[0][0]);
        glMapGrid1f(30, 0.0, 1.0);
        glEvalMesh1(GL_LINE, 0, 30);

        /* Advance to the next segment */

        i += step;
}
glFlush();
}
```

9.7.2 NURBS

Nonuniform rational B-spline (**NURBS**) curves and surfaces are a very flexible
family of curves and surfaces that are supported through the GLU library. A
NURBS curve is based on using four-dimensional parametric polynomials $(x(u)$,
$y(u)$, $z(u)$, $w(u))$, where each component can be obtained by OpenGL evaluators.
The desired three-dimensional points are obtained by dividing the first three terms
by $w(u)$, forming a vertex $(x(u)/w(u), y(u)/w(u), z(u)/w(u))$ for each value of u.

9.8 The Utah Teapot

The best-known object in computer graphics is the Utah teapot, created more than 30 years ago to test rendering algorithms. The teapot is composed of 32 cubic Bézier surface patches defined by 306 distinct control points. The data set is widely available and usually is given as 32 lines, each of 16 integers in the range 1–300. Each integer is a pointer to one of the 306 (x, y, z) values. The teapot can be displayed easily, using two-dimensional evaluators. We shall develop a simple program that will draw the teapot with line segments.

We can make the code clearer and shorter if we put the data in two files: `vertices.h` and `patches.h`. The first file, simply a long line that gives the locations of the vertices, begins with the code

```
GLfloat vertices[306][3]={{1.4, 0.0, 2.4},
```

Likewise, the second file defines the patches with one line of code that begins

```
int indices[32][4][4]={{1, 2, 3, 4, 5, 6, 7, 8, 9, 10, 11, 12, 13,
    14, 15, 16},
```

The numbering in this data set goes back to the days when indices began with 1 rather than 0. Thus, the first index, `indices[0][0][0]`, which has the value 1, refers to `vertices[0]`. The rest of the code is fairly straightforward. In the `main()` function, we traverse the data structure and put all the data in one array: `data[32][4][4][3]`. The function `myinit()` sets up a two-dimensional grid with 20 points over the range (0.0, 1.0) in each direction. The data are such that the teapot is oriented along the z-axis, so we start the display callback by rotating it so the top and bottom are perpendicular to the y-axis. We then do two more simple rotations to create an isometric view.

The next issue is how to set up the evaluators. In this example, we use the same equally spaced grid for each patch. This choice is not ideal because the patches are of different sizes and curvature, but it is sufficient for this simple example. When we render with line segments and `glEvalCoord2*()`, we want to create a grid of line segments. We set up an evaluator with the function

```
glMap2f(GL_MAP2_VERTEX_3, 0, 1, 3, 4, 0, 1, 12, 4,
    &data[k][0][0][0]);
```

Note that the stride is different in u and v. In u, successive control points are three floats apart in the data array because the data are stored by rows. However, in v we want to access successive points by columns, and thus the next point is separated from the present point by 12 floats.

We want a series of line segments that correspond to curves with a fixed u and changing v and another set that corresponds to curves with a fixed v and variable *u.* We can get a smooth uncluttered image if we draw a few polylines but evaluate many points on each polyline. We can do this by using two loops in the display function; the first draws curves of constant *v* and the second draws curves of constant *u.* For each patch, we draw five curves in *u* and five in *v.* Each curve is approximated by using the evaluator 21 times. Here is the entire program, followed by its output (see Figure 9.8).

```c
#include <stdlib.h>
#include <GL/glut.h>

GLfloat data[32][4][4][3];

/* 306 vertices */

#include "vertices.h"

/* 32 patches */

#include "patches.h"

void display(void)
{
    int i, j, k;

    glClear(GL_COLOR_BUFFER_BIT);
    glColor3f(1.0, 1.0, 1.0);

    glLoadIdentity();
    glTranslatef(0.0, 0.0, -10.0);
    glRotatef(-35.26, 1.0, 0.0, 0.0);
    glRotatef(-45.0, 0.0, 1.0, 0.0);


/* data aligned along z-axis, rotate to align with y-axis */

    glRotatef(-90.0, 1.0,0.0, 0.0);
    for(k = 0; k < 32; k++)
    {
        glMap2f(GL_MAP2_VERTEX_3, 0, 1, 3, 4,
            0, 1, 12, 4, &data[k][0][0][0]);
        for (j = 0; j <= 4; j++)
        {
            glBegin(GL_LINE_STRIP);
            for(i = 0; i <= 20; i++)
                glEvalCoord2f((GLfloat)i/20.0, (GLfloat)j/4.0);
            glEnd();
            glBegin(GL_LINE_STRIP);
```

```
                    for(i = 0; i <= 20; i++)
                        glEvalCoord2f((GLfloat)j/4.0, (GLfloat)i/20.0);
                    glEnd();
                }
        }
        glFlush();
}
void myReshape(int w, int h)
{
        glViewport(0, 0, w, h);
        glMatrixMode(GL_PROJECTION);
        glLoadIdentity();
        if(w <= h)
            glOrtho(-4.0, 4.0, -4.0 * (GLfloat) h / (GLfloat) w, 4.0 *
                    (GLfloat) h / (GLfloat) w, -20.0, 20.0);
        else
            glOrtho(-4.0 * (GLfloat) w / (GLfloat) h, 4.0 * (GLfloat) w /
                    (GLfloat) h, -4.0, 4.0, -20.0, 20.0);
        glMatrixMode(GL_MODELVIEW);
}


void myinit()
{
        glEnable(GL_MAP2_VERTEX_3);
        glClearColor(1.0, 1.0, 1.0, 1.0);
}


main(int argc, char *argv[])
{
        int i, j, k, m, n;
        for(i = 0; i < 32; i++) for (j = 0; j < 4; j++)
            for(k = 0; k < 4; k++) for (n = 0; n < 3; n++)
            {
/* put teapot data into single array for use by OpenGL */

                m = indices[i][j][k];
                for(n = 0; n < 3; n++) data[i][j][k][n] =
                        vertices[m - 1][n];
            }
        glutInit(&argc, argv);
        glutInitDisplayMode(GLUT_SINGLE | GLUT_RGB);
        glutInitWindowSize(500, 500);
        glutCreateWindow("teapot");
        myinit();
        glutReshapeFunc(myReshape);
        glutDisplayFunc(display);

        glutMainLoop();
}
```

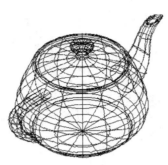

Figure 9.8 Teapot rendered using one-dimensional grids in *u* and *v*

Since we are using a regular grid, we can take another approach to avoid all the function calls, by using `glMapGrid2*()` and `glEvalMesh2()`. Thus, we can define the grid as part of the initialization by

```
glMapGrid2f(4, 0.0, 1.0, 4, 0.0, 1.0);
```

We can evaluate it by the following in the display callback. The resulting image is in Figure 9.9.

```
glEvalMesh2(GL_LINE, 0, 4, 0, 4);
```

This image is not as informative as the results of the previous example because here, we are using a much rougher spacing in both variables, whereas in the previous example, we used a fine resolution on each polyline that we drew. If we were to use a higher number of curves in each direction, we would get a smoother but denser image. For example with eight rather than four intervals in *u* and *v* we get the image in Figure 9.10.

If we want to display the teapot with line segments, the use of `glEvalCoord*()` is probably better in spite of the extra function calls. However, the use of `glEvalMesh2()` should be much better if we want polygons (`GL_POLYGON`) rather than line segments (`GL_LINE`). However, how we do shading is a problem.

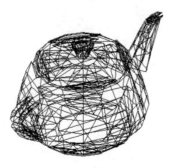

Figure 9.9 Teapot rendered using two-dimensional grid

Figure 9.10 Denser rendering of teapot with two-dimensional grid

9.9 Normals and Shading

When we want shading, we need to define normals. As we saw in Chapter 6, in OpenGL normals are usually defined in the application program, using the function `glNormal*()`. If we want the smoothest shading, we should define a new normal before each vertex. The equivalent for surfaces would be to define a normal before each call to `glEvalCoord*()`. Although we could do this in principle, in reality, we would have to compute a normal for all the vertices that were defined implicitly by the evaluators. Such a calculation would involve knowing the mathematics of parametric surfaces, something we cannot expect application programmers to possess. The situation is even worse for regular grids, where rather than make multiple calls to `glEvalCoord*()` within a loop, we make a single function call to `glEvalMesh2()`, which leaves us no place in the program to define normals.

OpenGL handles this problem by computing the normals automatically for the surfaces. To generate these normals, we need only enable autonormalization by

```
glEnable(GL_AUTO_NORMAL);
```

Thus, to generate a shaded teapot, we can start with the code we used for the teapot, using `glMapGrid2f()` and `glEvalMesh2()`. For example, if we want each patch to be approximated with 64 polygons, we use

```
glMapGrid2f(8, 0.0, 1.0, 8, 0.0, 1.0);
glEvalMesh2(GL_FILL, 0, 8, 0, 8);
```

Within `main()`, we can enable autonormalization and define our lights and materials. For example, the following light and material properties produce the image in Figure 9.11.

```
GLfloat ambient[] = {0.2, 0.2, 0.2, 1.0};
GLfloat position[] = {0.0, 0.0, 2.0, 1.0};
```

Figure 9.11 Rendering the teapot using autonormals

```
GLfloat mat_diffuse[] = {0.6, 0.6, 0.6, 1.0};
GLfloat mat_specular[] = {1.0, 1.0, 1.0, 1.0};
GLfloat mat_shininess[] = {50.0};

glEnable(GL_LIGHTING);
glEnable(GL_LIGHT0);

glLightfv(GL_LIGHT0, GL_AMBIENT, ambient);
glLightfv(GL_LIGHT0, GL_POSITION, position);

glMaterialfv(GL_FRONT, GL_DIFFUSE, mat_diffuse);
glMaterialfv(GL_FRONT, GL_SPECULAR, mat_specular);
glMaterialfv(GL_FRONT, GL_SHININESS, mat_shininess);
```

If we use only 16 polygons per patch, we get the slightly rougher image in Figure 9.12. Note that the shading of each patch is still very smooth, but we can notice the silhouette edge around the outside because we have not used enough polygons for each patch.

Figure 9.12 Rendering the teapot with fewer polygons than in Figure 9.11

Chapter 10

Putting It Together
and Moving On

In this last chapter, we survey some of the OpenGL features not covered earlier. However, we start with a last example. This example shows most of the OpenGL features that we have discussed in previous chapters and will give you the opportunity to experiment with these features, as most can be turned on and off interactively.

10.1 A Demo Program

The following program demonstrates many of the OpenGL features discussed in the first nine chapters. This demonstration program has been very useful in OpenGL tutorials that we have given in a variety of venues. The program allows the user to experiment with many of OpenGL's options for displaying a rotating cube. Options are selected, using either the mouse or the keyboard. These options include

- **Lines/polygons:** You can switch between using polygons and lines.
- **Flat/smooth:** You can switch between shading modes.
- **Lighting:** You can use various materials and light sources, or you can use constant colors for the polygons.
- **Texture:** You can turn on a checkerboard texture with or without mipmapping.
- **Fog:** You can add fog to the scene that uses OpenGL blending.
- **Hidden surface removal:** You can turn it on or off.
- **Line smoothing:** You can antialias lines in line-drawing mode.
- **Motion:** You can move either the cube or the light source.
- **Ortho/perspective:** You can switch between these viewing modes.

Figure 10.1 Trackball

10.1.1 A Virtual Trackball

The only new feature of this program is the virtual trackball, a device that has some of the characteristics of a mouse. A typical trackball is pictured in Figure 10.1 One of the advantages of an ideal frictionless trackball is that a user can start it spinning, giving it a constant velocity that could be used to change a position or an orientation in the program at a constant rate. If the user's hand simply moves the trackball, the rotation of the trackball is reflected in a change of position in the program.

The program creates a virtual trackball from the physical mouse by projecting the position of the mouse upward to the virtual hemisphere, as in Figure 10.2. As the mouse moves, the program tracks the change in position on the hemisphere. Two positions on the hemisphere determine both an axis of rotation and an angle to rotate about this axis, as shown in Figure 10.3. These two positions can also be used to determine a velocity of rotation that can be used within the idle callback. Rotation can be terminated with a single mouse click and no motion. Note that to obtain the desired behavior, we need to use both the mouse and motion callbacks.

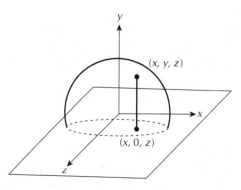

Figure 10.2 Projecting position on plane to hemisphere

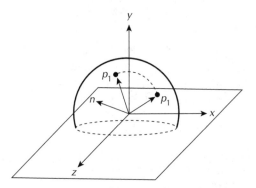

Figure 10.3 Two points and origin determining a rotation

10.1.2 Demo Code

```
/* Rotating cube demo*/

/* Prints out instructions */

/*Both normals and colors are assigned to the vertices */
/*Cube is centered at origin so (unnormalized) normals
are the same as the vertex values */

#include <stdlib.h>
#include <math.h>
#include <GL/glut.h>
#include <GL/glu.h>


#define bool int
#define false 0
#define true 1

/*
** Global settings controlled by keyboard input.
*/
bool texEnabled        = false;
bool mipmapEnabled     = false;
bool fastTexture       = true;
bool fogEnabled        = false;
bool depthEnabled      = true;
bool lineAAEnabled     = false;
bool lightingEnabled   = false;
bool smoothEnabled     = false;
bool drawLines         = true;
bool idleSpin          = true;
bool perspectiveXform  = false;
```

```
/*
** Global settings.
*/

float       near = 3.0;        /* near clipping plane in eye coords */
float       far = 7.0;         /* far clipping plane in eye coords */
float       viewxform_z = -5.0;

int         winWidth, winHeight;

float       angle = 0.0, axis[3], trans[3];
bool        trackballEnabled = true;
bool        trackballMove = false;
bool        trackingMouse = false;
bool        redrawContinue = false;

GLfloat lightXform[4][4] = {
    {1.0, 0.0, 0.0, 0.0},
    {0.0, 1.0, 0.0, 0.0},
    {0.0, 0.0, 1.0, 0.0},
    {0.0, 0.0, 0.0, 1.0}
};
GLfloat objectXform[4][4] = {
    {1.0, 0.0, 0.0, 0.0},
    {0.0, 1.0, 0.0, 0.0},
    {0.0, 0.0, 1.0, 0.0},
    {0.0, 0.0, 0.0, 1.0}
};
GLfloat *trackballXform = (GLfloat*)objectXform;

void display(void);
void spinCube(void);
void setMenuEntries(bool);

/*-------------------------------------------------------------*/
/*
** Materials setup.
*/
typedef struct materialStruct {
    GLfloat ambient[4];
    GLfloat diffuse[4];
    GLfloat specular[4];
    GLfloat shininess;
} materialStruct;

materialStruct brassMaterials = {
    {0.33F, 0.22F, 0.03F, 1.0F},
    {0.78F, 0.57F, 0.11F, 1.0F},
    {0.99F, 0.91F, 0.81F, 1.0F},
    27.8F
```

```
};
materialStruct redPlasticMaterials = {
    {0.3F, 0.0F, 0.0F, 1.0F},
    {0.6F, 0.0F, 0.0F, 1.0F},
    {0.8F, 0.6F, 0.6F, 1.0F},
    32.0F
};
materialStruct colorCubeMaterials = {
    {1.0F, 1.0F, 1.0F, 1.0F},
    {1.0F, 1.0F, 1.0F, 1.0F},
    {1.0F, 1.0F, 1.0F, 1.0F},
    {100.0F}
};

materialStruct *currentMaterials = &redPlasticMaterials;

void materials(materialStruct *materials)
{
  /* define material properties for front face of all polygons */
    glMaterialfv(GL_FRONT, GL_AMBIENT, materials->ambient);
    glMaterialfv(GL_FRONT, GL_DIFFUSE, materials->diffuse);
    glMaterialfv(GL_FRONT, GL_SPECULAR, materials->specular);
    glMaterialf(GL_FRONT, GL_SHININESS, materials->shininess);
}

/*-------------------------------------------------------------*/
/*
** Lighting setup.
*/
typedef struct lightingStruct {
    GLfloat ambient[4];
    GLfloat diffuse[4];
    GLfloat specular[4];
} lightingStruct;

lightingStruct whiteLighting = {
    {0.0F, 0.0F, 0.0F, 1.0F},
    {1.0F, 1.0F, 1.0F, 1.0F},
    {1.0F, 1.0F, 1.0F, 1.0F}
};
lightingStruct colorCubeLighting = {
    {0.2F, 0.0F, 0.0F, 1.0F},
    {0.0F, 1.0F, 0.0F, 1.0F},
    {0.0F, 0.0F, 1.0F, 1.0F}
};

lightingStruct *currentLighting = &whiteLighting;

void lighting(lightingStruct *lightSettings)
{
```

```
/* set up light 0 ambient, diffuse, specular, and spotlight */

    glLightfv(GL_LIGHT0, GL_AMBIENT, lightSettings->ambient);
    glLightfv(GL_LIGHT0, GL_DIFFUSE, lightSettings->diffuse);
    glLightfv(GL_LIGHT0, GL_SPECULAR, lightSettings->specular);

    glLightf(GL_LIGHT0, GL_SPOT_EXPONENT, 0.0F);
    glLightf(GL_LIGHT0, GL_SPOT_CUTOFF, 180.0F);
    glLightf(GL_LIGHT0, GL_CONSTANT_ATTENUATION, 1.0F);
    glLightf(GL_LIGHT0, GL_LINEAR_ATTENUATION, 0.0F);
    glLightf(GL_LIGHT0, GL_QUADRATIC_ATTENUATION, 0.0F);

    glLightModeli(GL_LIGHT_MODEL_LOCAL_VIEWER, GL_TRUE);
}

/*----------------------------------------------------------------*/
/*
** Light position setup.
*/
void setLightPos()
{
    GLfloat light0_pos[4] = {0.90F, 0.90F, 2.25F, 0.00F};
    GLfloat light0_spotDir[3] = {0.0F, 0.0F, -1.0F};

    glLightfv(GL_LIGHT0, GL_POSITION, light0_pos);
    glLightfv(GL_LIGHT0, GL_SPOT_DIRECTION, light0_spotDir);
}

/*----------------------------------------------------------------*/
/*
** Initial texture settings.
*/
void texture()
{
    GLubyte image[64][64][3];
    int i, j, r, c;
    for(i = 0; i < 64; i++)
    {
        for(j=0;j<64;j++)
        {
    c = (((( i & 0 x 8) == 0) ^ ((j & 0 x 8)) == 0))*255;
    image[i][j][0] = (GLubyte) c;
    image[i][j][1] = (GLubyte) c;
    image[i][j][2] = (GLubyte) c;
        }
    }
    glPixelStorei(GL_UNPACK_ALIGNMENT,1);
    glTexImage2D(GL_TEXTURE_2D, 0, 3, 64, 64, 0, GL_RGB,
        GL_UNSIGNED_BYTE, image);
```

```
            glTexParameterf(GL_TEXTURE_2D, GL_TEXTURE_WRAP_S, GL_CLAMP);
            glTexParameterf(GL_TEXTURE_2D, GL_TEXTURE_WRAP_T, GL_CLAMP);
            glTexParameterf(GL_TEXTURE_2D, GL_TEXTURE_MAG_FILTER,
                GL_NEAREST);
            glTexParameterf(GL_TEXTURE_2D, GL_TEXTURE_MIN_FILTER,
                GL_NEAREST);
            gluBuild2DMipmaps(GL_TEXTURE_2D, 3, 64, 64, GL_RGB,
                GL_UNSIGNED_BYTE, image);
        }


        /*
        ** Set initial state.
        */
        void initSettings(void)
        {
            texture();
            glLineWidth(3.0);
            setMenuEntries(true);
        }


        /*-------------------------------------------------------------*/
        /*
        ** Set state according to user interaction.
        */
        void userSettings(void)
        {
            lighting(currentLighting);
            materials(currentMaterials);

            if(lightingEnabled)
            {
                glEnable(GL_LIGHTING);
                glEnable(GL_LIGHT0);
            }
            else
            {
                glDisable(GL_LIGHTING);
                glDisable(GL_LIGHT0);
            }

            if(smoothEnabled)
                glShadeModel(GL_SMOOTH);
            else
                glShadeModel(GL_FLAT);

            if(idleSpin)
                glutIdleFunc(spinCube);
            else
                glutIdleFunc(NULL);
```

```
if(texEnabled)
    glEnable(GL_TEXTURE_2D);
else
    glDisable(GL_TEXTURE_2D);
if(fastTexture)
    glHint(GL_PERSPECTIVE_CORRECTION_HINT, GL_FASTEST);
else
    glHint(GL_PERSPECTIVE_CORRECTION_HINT, GL_NICEST);
if(mipmapEnabled)
    glTexParameterf(GL_TEXTURE_2D,
    GL_TEXTURE_MIN_FILTER,GL_NEAREST_MIPMAP_NEAREST);
else
    glTexParameterf(GL_TEXTURE_2D,
        GL_TEXTURE_MIN_FILTER,GL_NEAREST);

if(fogEnabled)
{
    float fogColor[] = {0.7, 0.6, 0.6, 1.0};

    glClearColor(fogColor[0], fogColor[1], fogColor[2],
        fogColor[3]);
    glEnable(GL_FOG);
    glFogi(GL_FOG_MODE, GL_LINEAR);
    glFogf(GL_FOG_DENSITY, 1.0);
    glFogf(GL_FOG_START, near);
    glFogf(GL_FOG_END, far);
    glFogfv(GL_FOG_COLOR, fogColor);
}
else
{
    glDisable(GL_FOG);
    glClearColor(0.0,0.0,0.0,1.0);
}

if(lineAAEnabled)
    glEnable(GL_BLEND);
else
    glDisable(GL_BLEND);

if(lineAAEnabled)
{
    glEnable(GL_LINE_SMOOTH);
    glBlendFunc(GL_SRC_ALPHA, GL_ONE_MINUS_SRC_ALPHA);
}
else
    glDisable(GL_LINE_SMOOTH);

if(depthEnabled)
    glEnable(GL_DEPTH_TEST);
```

```
    else
        glDisable(GL_DEPTH_TEST);

    glMatrixMode(GL_PROJECTION);
    glLoadIdentity();

    if(perspectiveXform)
    {
        glFrustum(-1.25, 1.25, -1.25, 1.25, near, far);
        viewxform_z = -5.0;
    }
    else
    {
        glOrtho(-2.0, 2.0, -2.0, 2.0, near, far);
        viewxform_z = -5.0;
    }
    glMatrixMode(GL_MODELVIEW);
}

/*-------------------------------------------------------------*/
/*
** Draw the cube.
*/
GLfloat vertices[][3] = {{-1.0, -1.0, -1.0},
    {1.0, -1.0, -1.0}, {1.0, 1.0, -1.0}, {-1.0, 1.0, -1.0},
    {-1.0, -1.0, 1.0}, {1.0, -1.0, 1.0}, {1.0, 1.0, 1.0},
    {-1.0, 1.0, 1.0}};

GLfloat normals[][3] = {{-1.0, -1.0, -1.0}, {1.0, -1.0, -1.0},
    {1.0, 1.0, -1.0}, {-1.0, 1.0, -1.0},
    {-1.0, -1.0, 1.0}, {1.0, -1.0, 1.0},
    {1.0, 1.0, 1.0}, {-1.0, 1.0, 1.0}};

GLfloat fnormals[][3] = {{0.0, 0.0,-1.0},
    {0.0, 1.0, 0.0}, {-1.0, 0.0, 0.0},
    {1.0, 0.0, 0.0}, {0.0, 0.0, 1.0}, {0.0,-1.0, 0.0}};

GLfloat colors[][3]={{0.0,0.0,0.0},{1.0,0.0,0.0},
    {1.0, 1.0, 0.0}, {0.0, 1.0, 0.0},
    {0.0, 0.0, 1.0}, {1.0, 0.0, 1.0},
    {1.0, 1.0, 1.0}, {0.0, 1.0, 1.0}};

void polygon(int a, int b, int c, int d, int face)
{

    /* draw a polygon via list of vertices */

    if(drawLines)
    {
```

```
            glColor3f(1.0, 1.0, 1.0);
            glBegin(GL_LINE_LOOP);
                glVertex3fv(vertices[a]);
                glVertex3fv(vertices[b]);
                glVertex3fv(vertices[c]);
                glVertex3fv(vertices[d]);
            glEnd();
    }
    else
    {
            glNormal3fv(fnormals[face]);
            glBegin(GL_POLYGON);
                glColor3fv(colors[a]);
                glTexCoord2f(0.0, 0.0);
                glVertex3fv(vertices[a]);
                glColor3fv(colors[b]);
                glTexCoord2f(0.0, 1.0);
                glVertex3fv(vertices[b]);
                glColor3fv(colors[c]);
                glTexCoord2f(1.0, 1.0);
                glVertex3fv(vertices[c]);
                glColor3fv(colors[d]);
                glTexCoord2f(1.0, 0.0);
                glVertex3fv(vertices[d]);
            glEnd();
    }
}

void colorcube(void)
{

    /* map vertices to faces */

    polygon(1, 0, 3, 2, 0);
    polygon(3, 7, 6, 2, 1);
    polygon(7, 3, 0, 4, 2);
    polygon(2, 6, 5, 1, 3);
    polygon(4, 5, 6, 7, 4);
    polygon(5, 4, 0, 1, 5);
}

/*--------------------------------------------------------------*/
/*
** These functions implement a simple trackball-like motion control.
*/

float lastPos[3] = {0.0F, 0.0F, 0.0F};
int curx, cury;
int startX, startY;
```

```
void
trackball_ptov(int x, int y, int width, int height, float v[3])
{
    float d, a;

/* project x, y onto a hemisphere centered within width, height */
    v[0] = (2.0F*x - width) / width;
    v[1] = (height - 2.0F*y) / height;
    d = (float) sqrt(v[0]*v[0] + v[1]*v[1]);
    v[2] = (float) cos((M_PI/2.0F) * ((d < 1.0F) ? d : 1.0F));
    a = 1.0F / (float) sqrt(v[0]*v[0] + v[1]*v[1] + v[2]*v[2]);
    v[0] *= a;
    v[1] *= a;
    v[2] *= a;
}


void
mouseMotion(int x, int y)
{
    float curPos[3], dx, dy, dz;

    trackball_ptov(x, y, winWidth, winHeight, curPos);

    dx = curPos[0] - lastPos[0];
    dy = curPos[1] - lastPos[1];
    dz = curPos[2] - lastPos[2];

    if(dx || dy || dz)
    {
        angle = 90.0F * sqrt(dx*dx + dy*dy + dz*dz);

        axis[0] = lastPos[1]*curPos[2] - lastPos[2]*curPos[1];
        axis[1] = lastPos[2]*curPos[0] - lastPos[0]*curPos[2];
        axis[2] = lastPos[0]*curPos[1] - lastPos[1]*curPos[0];

        lastPos[0] = curPos[0];
        lastPos[1] = curPos[1];
        lastPos[2] = curPos[2];
    }

    glutPostRedisplay();
}

void
startMotion(long time, int button, int x, int y)
{
    if(!trackballEnabled) return;
```

```
        trackingMouse = true;
        redrawContinue = false;
        startX = x; startY = y;
        curx = x; cury = y;
        trackball_ptov(x, y, winWidth, winHeight, lastPos);
        trackballMove = true;
}

void
stopMotion(long time, int button, int x, int y)
{
        if(!trackballEnabled) return;

        trackingMouse = false;

        if(startX != x || startY != y)
            redrawContinue = true;
        else
        {
            angle = 0.0F;
            redrawContinue = false;
            trackballMove = false;
        }
}


/*-----------------------------------------------------------------*/

void display(void)
{
    glClear(GL_COLOR_BUFFER_BIT|GL_DEPTH_BUFFER_BIT);

    /* view transform */
    glLoadIdentity();
    glTranslatef(0.0,0.0,viewxform_z);

    if(trackballMove)
    {
        glPushMatrix();
        glLoadIdentity();
        glRotatef(angle, axis[0], axis[1], axis[2]);
        glMultMatrixf((GLfloat *) trackballXform);
        glGetFloatv(GL_MODELVIEW_MATRIX, trackballXform);
        glPopMatrix();
    }
    glPushMatrix();
    glMultMatrixf((GLfloat*)lightXform);
    setLightPos();
    glPopMatrix();
    glPushMatrix();
```

```
        glMultMatrixf((GLfloat *) objectXform);
        colorcube();
        glPopMatrix();
        glutSwapBuffers();
}

/*-------------------------------*/

void mouseButton(int button, int state, int x, int y)
{
    switch (button)
    {
        case GLUT_LEFT_BUTTON:
            trackballXform = (GLfloat*)objectXform;
            break;
        case GLUT_MIDDLE_BUTTON:
            trackballXform = (GLfloat*)lightXform;
            break;
    }
    switch(state)
    {
        case GLUT_DOWN:
            startMotion(0,1, x,y);
            break;
        case GLUT_UP:
            stopMotion(0,1, x,y);
            break;
    }
}

void myReshape(int w, int h)
{
    glViewport(0, 0, w, h);
    winWidth = w;
    winHeight = h;
}

void spinCube()
{
    if(redrawContinue) glutPostRedisplay();
}


void userEventAction(int key) {
    switch(key) {
    case '0':                        /* wireframe/polygon  */
      drawLines = !drawLines;
      break;
```

```
case '1':
  smoothEnabled = !smoothEnabled;
  break;
case '2':                    /* lighting */
  lightingEnabled = !lightingEnabled;
  break;
case '3':                    /* texture */
  texEnabled = !texEnabled;
  break;
case '4':                    /* fog */
  fogEnabled = !fogEnabled;
  break;
case '5':                    /* HSR */
  depthEnabled = !depthEnabled;
  break;
case '6':                    /* line aa */
  lineAAEnabled = !lineAAEnabled;
  break;
case '7':                    /* perspective texture */
  fastTexture = !fastTexture;
  break;
case 'b':
  currentMaterials = &brassMaterials;
  break;
case 'c':
  currentMaterials = &colorCubeMaterials;
  break;
case 'C':
  currentLighting = &colorCubeLighting;
  break;
case 'i':
  idleSpin = !idleSpin;
  break;
case 'm':                    /* mipmapped texture */
  mipmapEnabled = !mipmapEnabled;
  break;
case 'p':                    /* perspective/ortho */
  perspectiveXform = !perspectiveXform;
  break;
case 'r':
  currentMaterials = &redPlasticMaterials;
  break;
case 'w':
  currentLighting = &whiteLighting;
  break;
case 27:
  exit(0);
default:
  break;
```

```
        }
        userSettings();
        glutPostRedisplay();
}

void keyboard(unsigned char key, int x, int y)
{
        userEventAction(key);
}

/*---------------------------------------------------------------*/

typedef struct menuEntryStruct {
        char *label;
        char key;
} menuEntryStruct;

static menuEntryStruct mainMenu[] = {
        "lines/polygons",      '0',
        "flat/smooth",         '1',
        "lighting",            '2',
        "texture",             '3',
        "fog",                 '4',
        "HSR",                 '5',
        "line smooth",         '6',
        "motion",              'i',
        "ortho/perspective",   'p',
        "quit",                27,
};
int mainMenuEntries = sizeof(mainMenu)/sizeof(menuEntryStruct);

void selectMain(int choice)
{
        userEventAction(mainMenu[choice].key);
}

static menuEntryStruct materialsMenu[] = {
        "brass",               'b',
        "white",               'c',
        "red plastic",         'r',
};
int materialsMenuEntries =
        sizeof(materialsMenu)/sizeof(menuEntryStruct);

void selectMaterials(int choice)
{
        userEventAction(materialsMenu[choice].key);
}
```

```
static menuEntryStruct lightingMenu[] =
{
    "white",            'w',
    "color",            'C',
};
int lightingMenuEntries =
    sizeof(lightingMenu)/sizeof(menuEntryStruct);

void selectLighting(int choice)
{
    userEventAction(lightingMenu[choice].key);
}

void setMenuEntries(bool init)
{
    int i, sub1, sub2;

    if (init)
    {
        sub1 = glutCreateMenu(selectMaterials);
        for (i = 0; i < materialsMenuEntries; i++)
        glutAddMenuEntry(materialsMenu[i].label, i);
        sub2 = glutCreateMenu(selectLighting);
        for (i = 0; i < lightingMenuEntries; i++)
            glutAddMenuEntry(lightingMenu[i].label, i);
            glutCreateMenu(selectMain);
        for (i = 0; i < mainMenuEntries; i++)
            glutAddMenuEntry(mainMenu[i].label, i);
            glutAddSubMenu("materials", sub1);
            glutAddSubMenu("lighting", sub2);
            glutAttachMenu(GLUT_RIGHT_BUTTON);
    }
}

/*-------------------------------------------------------------*/

void
main(int argc, char **argv)
{
    glutInit(&argc, argv);

    glutInitDisplayMode(GLUT_DOUBLE | GLUT_RGB | GLUT_DEPTH);
    glutInitWindowSize(500, 500);
    glutCreateWindow("colorcube");
    glutReshapeFunc(myReshape);
    glutDisplayFunc(display);
    glutIdleFunc(spinCube);
    glutMouseFunc(mouseButton);
    glutMotionFunc(mouseMotion);
```

```
        glutKeyboardFunc(keyboard);
        initSettings();
        userSettings();
        glutMainLoop();
}
```

10.2 Other OpenGL Features

Although we have not covered all OpenGL functions, we have covered most of them. Our major omissions are in covering some of the extra buffers available in OpenGL—which we will introduce in the next section—and in some of the more detailed functionality available through some of the extensions and GLU. Probably the most important are the use of the OpenGL tessellator and the use of NURBs. Both of these facilities are supported through the GLU library.

With the tessellator, we can get around the restriction that OpenGL guarantees correctness only for convex polygons. The code in the tessellator will handle general polygons, even ones that are not simple. Unfortunately, many options and parameters must be specified to tell the tessellator how we wish polygons to be handled. In addition to specifying options that determine how the polygon is to be displayed we also have to give the tessellator explicit instructions on how to handle complex cases such as in Figure 10.4. Because of this complexity, we will not discuss tessellation further.

NURBS curves and surfaces provide far more flexibility than do the Bézier curves and surface and therefore are very popular in the CAD and animation communities. However, as with tessellators, the extra flexibility comes at the price of requiring the user to define many parameters and options. In addition, use of NURBS requires more understanding of their mathematical underpinnings than we can present here.

Figure 10.4 Complex polygon that must be tessellated before rendering

10.3 Buffers

OpenGL supports a few other buffers, although not all of them need be available on all implementations. These are the **accumulation** and **stencil buffers**. In addition, there may be extra color buffers, or **auxiliary buffers**. All these buffers are initialized and cleared in the same manner as the color and depth buffers. Each has its own identifier (GL_ACCUM, GL_STENCIL, GL_AUX1, GL_AUX2) and can be opened and cleared as the other buffers, as in the code

```
glutInitDisplayMode(GL_RGB | GL_DOUBLE | GL_STENCIL | GL_ACCUM);
```

```
glClear(GL_COLOR_BUFFER_BIT | GL_CLEAR_DEPTH_BUFFER_BIT |
    GL_ACCUM_BUFFER_BIT | GL_STENCIL_BUFFER_BIT);
```

The auxiliary buffers behave as do the front and back buffers. Hence, we can use them with the same functions we used for reading and writing in Chapter 7. Some potential uses of these buffers are for **multipass rendering**, whereby the same objects are rendering more than once. One typical application is for producing images for an immersive environment. Here, we want to create images for the front, back, sides, and even the ceiling and floor of a physical room that has light projectors for each surface. We can write an OpenGL program that can produce these images, using six virtual cameras and rendering into six color buffers.

10.3.1 The Accumulation Buffer

If you start working with images using OpenGL, you will eventually come up against the limited resolution of color buffers. Consider the following compositing problem. Suppose that we want to merge a set of images into a single image. The obvious approach is to use the blending functions from Chapter 7. Suppose that we are working with a typical implementation that has 8 bits for each of red, green, and blue in its physical color buffers. If we simply add corresponding RGB values for the images, we will probably exceed the 1.0 maximum for the color components. If we scale the color values to prevent exceeding this maximum, we reduce the resolution of each color because although OpenGL uses floating point values in its calculations, the components are stored physically with the limited resolution of 8 bits per component.

One solution to this type of problem is to create a buffer, the accumulation buffer, that has more bits per color component. We can add the contents of a color buffer into the accumulation buffer, using a scale factor. Once we have accumulated all the images, we can read out a scaled version of the accumulation buffer back into a color buffer, thus maintaining the available color resolution and not overflowing a color buffer. We need only one function, glAccum(), to use the accumulation buffer, if one is available.

```
void glAccum(GLenum operation, GLfloat value)
```

Defines the `operation` performed with the accumulation buffer (GL_ACCUM, GL_LOAD, GL_RETURN, GL_ADD, GL_MULT) and the associated constant (`value`).

The operation GL_ADD allows us to add images in with the specified constant multiplier. The operation GL_RETURN returns the scaled contents of the accumulation buffer to the present drawing buffer.

The accumulation buffer provides some new and interesting capabilities for multipass rendering. For example, suppose that we render the same scene multiple times, each with the camera moved, or **jittered** slightly, and accumulate these images in the accumulation buffer. Each of the images will have slightly different aliasing artifacts that will be averaged out in the accumulation buffer. Thus, we have performed antialiasing on the whole scene rather than on a line-by-line or polygon-by-polygon basis.

10.3.2 The Stencil Buffer

Stencils are masks that we can use to determine where to draw. A typical use of the stencil buffer is to create windows of arbitrary shape within the rectangular drawing area of the viewport. For example, we can create a round porthole by forming a stencil buffer, starting with all 1s and putting 0s in a circular area. Then, as we draw in the color buffer, each pixel we form by rasterization is tested against the stencil buffer to see whether it should be drawn in the color buffer. We can create more complex behaviors by using the stencil buffer because we can modify its contents, depending on the value of the pixel generated by the rasterizer.

10.3.3 Fragment Tests

Although we have referred to the pixels that are produced by the renderer, the renderer in OpenGL produces **fragments**, which can be smaller than a pixel. For example, if only part of a pixel on the screen is occupied by a particular polygon, the renderer can produce a fragment whose size is proportional to the amount of the screen pixel that is covered by the polygon.

Pixels that are produced by the renderer go through a sequence of tests—scissor, alpha, stencil, depth—and operations—blending, dithering, logical—on their way to the color buffer. We have seen most of these tests and operations in previous chapters. For example, the depth test involves comparing the depth of the fragment with a depth in the depth buffer. Blending and logical operations determine how a visible pixel is combined with what is already in the color buffer.

Usually, these tests and operations are performed routinely as part of the standard rendering process. However, we can also program these tests directly to accept or to reject pixels. For example, with the **scissor test**, we can define a rectangular area in which all fragments are accepted and all fragment outside of it are rejected. Such operations and tests are of particular importance in interactive applications.

10.4 Writing Portable, Efficient, Robust Code

We would all like to write programs that can be ported to other systems and run without modification, regardless of the differences in hardware. We would also like our programs to run efficiently on all systems. And, of course, we would like our programs to be readable and easy to modify. It would be nice if every OpenGL program possessed all these features.

Although OpenGL programs tend to be clear and fairly portable, there can be problems. One is that once we start using advanced features, such as the accumulation and stencil buffers, we often lose portability, since these features are not supported on all implementations. Although we could check in our programs for the existence of the features, it is not clear what a program should do—other than exit—if the desired facilities are not present.

Differences in the properties of the display are easier to handle. We can use the inquiry functions, such as glIntegerv(), to obtain the properties of a particular display and to adjust within the application.

Efficiency is a more difficult issue. First, with few exceptions, the underlying algorithms are hidden from the user. We do not know—and usually do not need to know—how an OpenGL implementation fills polygons or interpolates textures. Second, different implementations have been optimized using different criteria. Hence, even if we buy a board with excellent triangle rendering speeds, the board might not have the same relative performance for texture mapping. This situation is especially noticeable with boards for PCs, most of which have been optimized for the operations required in games.

Finally, as the capabilities of graphics hardware continue to improve at a rapid pace, the limiting factor in many applications is not the time required for graphics operations but rather the time taken to move data. Fortunately, OpenGL provides sufficient functionality and is close enough to the hardware that it should be an important graphics API for years to come.

Index

Function Index

GL Functions

GLU Functions

GLUT Functions